Tending the Light

Tending the Light
Essays on Montessori Education

By John R. Snyder

North American Montessori Teachers' Association
13693 Butternut Road
Burton, OH 44021
Tel 440-834-4011
Fax 440-834-4016
staff@montessori-namta.org
www.montessori-namta.org

Published by North American Montessori Teachers' Association, with the support of the AMI Elementary Alumni Association, AMI/USA, the Montessori Administrators Association, and Gerard Leonard.

ISBN: 978-0-692-35158-1

In memory of Dennis Schapiro, who for seven years gave me gentle encouragement and an open forum in which to write about Montessori education, without which many of these pieces would never have seen the light;

And to Donna Bryant Goertz, mentor, friend, inspiration, without whose deep understanding of children and commitment to serving the whole child I would have had much less to write about.

Contents

||||||||||||||||||||||||||||||||||||||||||||||

Foreword

In this book we find evidence that John Snyder is a Montessorian par excellence. Not only did he guide a community of elementary children, ages nine through twelve, for a decade as an enlightened generalist, he also lived out that role fully in his life beyond the campus. John wrote poetry, gazed through the telescope upon the celestial realms, led a church choir, studied philosophy and theoretical computer science, and acted as consultant to corporate management. And all of this informed his work with children and with educators in real time and in person as well as through the written word.

Here John describes in powerful, deep, and lovely language the philosophy, theory, and practice of his Montessori years. John has developed his work with children and with their parents, with guides and with support staff, and with mentors, consultants, and administrators both at Austin Montessori School and beyond. Through his collected writings—writings for this school, as well as for conferences and professional publications—not only Montessorians but all who care about the lives of children can find a source of information, inspiration, and guidance.

A man of wicked wit and brilliant mind, John first entered my life as assistant in the community of children I guided at Austin Montessori School. Don Goertz, Executive Director of Austin Montessori School and my husband, had brought him to me as the father of an entering student and as a potential AMI trainee and future classroom guide for our school. Could John, age forty-three, so large of physical stature and resonant of voice, become small and quiet enough to serve as assistant to my work? He could. Could he tame his mind and bend his language to the service of this humble work of observing and supporting? He did.

Explorer of heart and mind, feeling and spirit, John has gathered up for us and set down in this book lively and moving stories of real children, exact and detailed descriptions of practices, and sensate philosophies for living a life of joyful service and continuing transformation. The great man made himself small to enter into the wide universe of a child without disturbing its balance. John added himself in to their movement much as Calder might add the final and brilliant piece to a mobile, always necessary and complementary, never dominant or intrusive.

And all that John did with the children, all of that philosophy, psychology, art, music, poetry, science, gardening, cooking, camping, astronomy, language, mathematics, and refinement of relationships—all of that mattered to me as the founder of the school in which John worked. During his years in the classroom community with the children and later as Elementary Coordinator and Assistant to the Director, John provided a strong moral compass, clear-thinking leadership, and compassionate partnership for Don and me.

I commend to you this book and the wisdom found herein. May it inspire you to a deeper understanding of yourself, your children, and—if you are a guide—your joyful life of service to the child.

Donna Bryant Goertz
Founder, Austin Montessori School

A Note from the Publisher

||||||||||||||||||||||||||||||||||||||||||||||||||||||||||||||||||||||||||||||||||||||||||||||||||||||||||||||||||||||||||||||||||||||||||||||

John Snyder is a divergent thinker who expresses himself and his Montessori origins as a compassionate storyteller confronting myriad second-plane (elementary) challenges: student homework, to use or not to use computers, reading out loud, the idea of contribution to one's community, the child and the universe, the child in nature, and the Human Tendencies made relevant to every teacher and parent. What separates John from an ordinary experienced trained teacher sharing advice is his foray into the imagination. *Tending the Light* begins its spiral upward to the symbolic firmament with an essay of the same title, drawn with finality to a higher purpose, to keep burning within the child the "light which is called intelligence."

This recognition of the intangible and transcendent reality of child development is the essence of John's singular understanding of the role of the teacher.

> To any who might accuse us of resisting accountability to standards, we must reply that our accountability is necessarily to a much higher, much more challenging standard: that of the astonishing potential of the developing human mind, before which we stand daily in near-religious awe. Full realization of this unbounded and unpredictable potential is what we give up when we settle for higher numbers on exams and more uniform performance across a lockstep curriculum.

Tending the Light transports us to a place where every day is Earth Day, where the service ethic is pervasive, and where the teacher is a companion to the student in a spiritual journey in which the quiet inner vision of the self is supported and made visible through activity. John communicates the philosophical principles on which he bases educational decisions to parents, bypassing insider Montessori terms yet conveying the essentials using contemporary authors and research.

He works with parents as he works with their children, with complete trust and in the most positive spiritual light. John does not preach—he describes what he sees, a shared life of the mind and spirit for the teacher and the student through the Montessori experience. "Light in body and spirit" are the conditions around which John weaves Thich Nhat Hanh's desiderata, and the reader arrives at the "interiority" or hidden powers, referring to invisible inner formation in the context of the Montessori prepared environment.

John describes the "Great Work" trajectory of collaborating with others, doing big projects, and subsequent development of generous understanding in contemporary terms as social-emotional skills. A personal aspiration to make a contribution to the school community and later to life on earth is the true Montessori outcome. The educational intent is moral and organic, never about subject matter for its own sake, but rather for the sake of maintaining a healthy, natural, continuous evolution of the biosphere and the human condition—knowledge is a means of equilibrium and well-being. The elementary is connected to adolescence many times throughout the book, as it finds meaning and direction preparing for the Third Plane's orientation to a greater reality, a keener community, widening exploration of the real – and it is understood that the prepared environment for the adolescent must carefully build capacity for increasingly independent learning and doing, approaching a real readiness to serve society.

John's craft employs metaphors and complexity—the club metaphor, the AMPs acronym, the grid of forgettable and unforgettable learning, the importance of flow, learning from peers in a purposeful community that balances freedom and responsibility, capturing the meanings and diverse forms of creativity by studying the history of creative works through time. Somewhere between the formality of the disciplines and the history of past and present, young people emerge with sentiments of gratitude and artistic self-expression. John tells all Montessorians: Allow formation within an elementary prepared environment to touch higher and higher values of love, peace, creativity, and independent exploration. Inquiry is aided by the principle of the key lesson. The teacher has the courage to clear new pathways and develop new keys to meet the challenge of the present and future, leading the child to more precise self-construction based on principles that grow from the student's own experiences.

Although much of the book is practical, John has a gift for language that defies stereotypes. *Tending the Light* lives up to its own expectations because John reveals a grand vision of what defines the spiritual and creative dimension of the developing human. John sees human tendencies as verbs, accessible for evaluation purposes. He calls for a prepared environment and prepared adults that can nurture growing humans with a full range of temperaments and behavior, blossoming first as nine-to-twelve-year-olds and later on as adolescents. The mood of the book is sensitive to the child's need for guidance; the outcomes of elementary classrooms are assessed through observation of a rising spiritual order which pertains to work, behavior, and self-disciplined obedience.

John will be the first in his generation to bring out a different way to understand Montessori as she says in her own words. *"In addition to the work of observing material reality, there is a creative work which lifts man up from earth and transports him into a higher world which every soul may attain, within its individual limits"* (*AMM*, chapter 9). John believes in the deep creative possibilities of the developing human, attainable with "four gifts"—the human mind, the human hands, the human capacity for love, and language. I believe that John brings the modern collective unconscious to *Tending the Light*—his sources are contemporary and yet his classical tribute is predominately spiritual, summarized by Sofia Cavalletti's ode to wonder, written almost forty years ago:

> *Wonder is a dynamic value; nevertheless it does not drive us to activism, but draws us into activity, to an activity we do as persons immersed in the contemplation of something that exceeds us. Maybe the particularity of wonder is that we find activity and contemplation inseparably blended within it. Education to wonder is correlative with an education that helps us go more deeply into reality.*[1]

David Kahn
Executive Director, North American
Montessori Teachers' Association
(NAMTA)

---

[1]Cavalletti, Sofia. *The Religious Potential of the Child*. Paulist Press: Paramus, New Jersey, 1973 (138–39).

Preface

||||||||||||||||||||||||||||||||||||||||||||||

It is immensely gratifying, very humbling, and a little miraculous to me that this book, so long in my imagination, has, with the help of so many friends and colleagues, finally come into being. Although I wrote steadily and widely during my career as a Montessori guide and administrator, I always thought of collecting and publishing these writings as a project for my retirement years. And so it is, although I never intended to retire so young.

In the spring of 2011, during my second year as a school administrator, I was diagnosed with ALS (Lou Gehrig's Disease), a progressive disease that gradually disconnects all of the muscles of the body from the control centers in the brain. With the help and understanding of my school community and equipment provided by the state of Texas, I was able to keep working until the summer of 2013.

When my Montessori friends learned that I was interested in publishing a book, a number of them stepped forward with offers of help. Leaders of AMI-affiliated societies in the US, including David Kahn and Jacquie Maughan of the North American Montessori Teachers' Association, Chris Trostel and John Hooper of the AMI Elementary Alumni Association, Bonnie Beste and Adam Lewis of AMI/USA, and Sue Pritzker of the Montessori Administrators Association worked with their respective boards and networks to fund the production of the book.

David Kahn graciously offered his time and expertise, and his highly experienced colleague Amy Losasso was kind enough to design the interior and manage production. To my delight, we were able to add Aurora Bell, a former student of mine now working in the publishing industry, for editorial support. To these three, I offer heartfelt gratitude for their collegiality, expertise, and significant contributions to the improvement of the manuscript. Thanks also to Jamie Rue and Donna Bryant Goertz for reading the manuscript and offering helpful comments. My spouse Kathleen Snyder lived through many years when I was too often at school and not at home, and she has been a constant source of support for this book project.

I think Maria Montessori would be thrilled, as I am, with the technological advances that have allowed me to compile and edit the book: Dragon Dictate dictation software that transcribes my spoken words and recognizes my editing commands, and a TrackerPro head mouse that tracks my head movements to provide the functionality of a mouse or trackpad.

In his sermons and books, Dr. Martin Luther King Jr., popularized the term "beloved community" as the open-ended expression of enlightened goodwill in a society that takes care of all its members. The Montessori community in North America and around the world, especially the staff of Austin Montessori School and the members of AMI-EAA, has truly been and continues to be my beloved community. The debts, great and small, that I owe my community are beyond reckoning. I am particularly grateful to my trainers Elizabeth Hall, Janet McDonnell, Dr. Kay Baker, and Greg MacDonald for sharing their profound understanding of Montessori education and setting a very high bar for my practice. The opinions expressed here, including the mistaken ones, are strictly my own.

John R. Snyder
ordinarypersonslife.com

Tending the Light

Introduction

||||||||||||||||||||||||||||||||||||||||||||||||||||||||||||||||||||||||||

If you are a Montessori guide (teacher) or assistant, an administrator of a Montessori school or program, a parent looking for deeper insights into Montessori education, or anyone interested in discussions of Montessori best practices, this book is written for you. The essays collected here were written over a span of sixteen years, beginning in 1998, the year I began my professional career as a Montessori educator at Austin Montessori School in Austin, Texas. Many of the essays were written for that school's newsletter or for my regular column in the quarterly *Public School Montessorian*.

I have always tried to take my essayist's pen into areas where I perceived a need. A number of the essays were prompted by questions I received directly from parents, administrators, or teachers. Others were born out of reflection on my own practice—always an area of great need—observations in classrooms around the country, or discussions with colleagues. The result is, I hope, a body of work that will continue to meet a need wherever Montessori education is found. I offer this book to the Montessori community in the belief that there is value in sharing what has been learned in one Montessori life, however flawed and incomplete.

The book has three parts. Part one is a collection of essays on topics of broad or philosophical interest. Part two, the heart of the book, brings together essays on the art and craft of guiding a Montessori elementary community. This was my life and work for many years, the crucible of my understanding and appreciation of Maria Montessori's insights into the developing heart and mind of the six- to twelve-year-old. Because school and home must forge a strong partnership in order for Montessori education to produce its best results, my work as a guide made me a partner to about sixty parents every year. Part three of the book comprises a few of the things I wrote specifically for parents or for other guides to share with parents.

As noted, quite a number of the pieces were originally written for a smaller, more homogeneous, well-known audience. Often my audience and I could presuppose a shared understanding of Montessori fundamentals. Here it is perhaps useful to spell some of that out.

Based on observation of children of all ages over several decades and at least three continents, Maria Montessori came to organize her work according to a four-stage developmental plan. In English the stages are referred to as "Planes of Development." The First Plane spans ages birth to six. Because development in this Plane creates the foundation and context for all subsequent development, Dr. Montessori considered this plane to be of paramount importance. Her deepest thinking about this age is found in the book *The Absorbent Mind* (*AM*).

While the First Plane is characterized by uncritical "absorption" of what the child finds in their environment and by a focus on individual development, the Second Plane, ages six to twelve, is characterized by new powers of reasoning, an orientation to ideas and the imagination, and a focus on building a relationship to a community of peers. Montessori's book on the elementary was originally published in English as *Spontaneous Activity in Education*, but is now called *The Advanced Montessori Method* (*AMM*), volumes one and two. Other primary texts for the elementary include *From Childhood to Adolescence* (*FCA*) and *To Educate the Human Potential* (*TEHP*).

The years of adolescence, or Third Plane, see another burst of cognitive and social development and a focus on finding meaning and value through contribution to an adolescent community that participates in the local economy and culture. Having come to a deeper understanding of oneself, one's gifts, and the needs of the world, young adults of the Fourth Plane, ages eighteen to twenty-four, begin to establish th emselves in society and to prepare more intensively for a life of contributory work.

The primary tenet of Montessori education is that each plane has specific developmental tasks that can best be supported by careful preparation of an educational environment both at school and at home. The environment at each Plane differs significantly from those of the other Planes because it reflects the psychosocial characteristics and needs of children at that particular age. And, of course, each Plane prepares the child for the developmental challenges of the subsequent Plane.

The essays in this book assume this understanding of child development and the strategy of preparing an environment tailored to each Plane. The Montessori classroom community is constituted of children whose ages span at least three years guided by an intensively trained adult, possibly with the aid of an assistant. They also assume that the Montessori classroom will provide the full complement of Montessori pedagogical materials for children of that Plane and little else, so as to leave as much time as possible for the child's own explorations. The schedule of the school day will include two extended periods of uninterrupted work time, one or both of which is at least three hours long. At the elementary level, most lessons will be given to small groups of three to five children who will then be left to choose what to work on and for how long. The children are not given assignments and are not graded, rated, or ranked. In the elementary, peer-to-peer learning and collaboration are not only encouraged but seen as an essential part of the child's development and the glue that holds together the community. With these fundamentals in place, one can begin to build a practice faithful to Maria Montessori's vision.

The title of the book, *Tending the Light*, is an allusion to my favorite Montessori quote about the elementary, a statement I have come to think of as Montessori in a nutshell: "Our care of the child should be governed, not by the desire 'to make him learn things' but by the endeavor always to keep burning within him that light which is called the intelligence" (*AMM*, vol. 1). I have come to believe, as Montessori did, that that light, properly tended, will increasingly illuminate the darkness of the world. As she wrote, "Directing our action toward mankind means, first and foremost, doing so with regard to the child. The child, that 'forgotten citizen,' must be appreciated in accordance with his true value. His rights as a human being who shapes all of mankind must become sacred, and the secret laws of his normal psychic development must light the way for civilisation" (*Education and Peace*). It is this light that I always hoped and believed I was tending, a work that I invite you, whatever your connection to children, to explore in the following pages. ❖

Part One

Thinking about Montessori

On Comparing Apples and Oranges: A Perspective on Montessori and Conventional Education

||||||||||||||||||||||||||||||||||||||||||||||||||||||||||||||||||||||||||||||||||||||||||||||||||||||||

An earlier version of this article, dated June 2006, was my first regular column for the quarterly Public School Montessorian. *Over the next seven years, I wrote almost thirty articles for editor and publisher Dennis Schapiro, work that forms the core of this collection. A revised version was published in 2010 on MariaMontessori.com, the blog of the Montessori Administrator's Association.*

Montessori teachers and school administrators often hear versions of the following questions from parents who are wondering how well their children in Montessori elementary programs are being academically prepared for middle school or high school: *How does the Montessori curriculum compare to traditional curricula? Are Montessori elementary programs usually academically "accelerated" in relation to their traditional counterparts? How do Montessori graduates compare to other students?*

It is difficult, and I think unhelpful, to make blanket statements on these questions, one way or the other. To be sure, there are some recent scientific studies, as well as a hundred years of anecdotal evidence from around the world, that attest to the academic efficacy of the Montessori approach. Dr. Montessori herself famously claimed that graduates of her elementary schools would know as much as the average Italian high school student of her day. But all this should not mislead us into thinking conventionally about what is really a very unconventional approach to education.

Montessori's work was not aimed at creating accelerated learning, better grades, or precocious children. Her desire was to support the development of the whole child, the whole human being—not to isolate certain cognitive powers of the human being and to build an educational system based solely on these. Her method of support had mostly to do with removing what she saw as impediments to human development that are common features of conventional educational systems (both in her time and in ours). These included traditional understandings of the role of the adult in the classroom.

Dr. Montessori supported the children's development by creating some brilliant educational materials designed to dovetail perfectly with the cognitive and psychological characteristics that she observed in children at various stages of development. Always pragmatic, she would try her ideas out in a number of classrooms, keeping the materials that children loved and used and removing the rest. In some cases, she found that materials made for a certain age were of more interest to children of a different age; she would duly note this and make adjustments.

The history of education is littered with the ruins of many, many educational reform movements—all of them seeking to find a better way for children to learn or a better way to shape future society. We were able to celebrate the centennial of the Montessori "method" in 2007, even as the worldwide Montessori movement was beginning to achieve unprecedented momentum, because Montessori's ideas were based on a lifetime of careful observation of children in real educational settings and not on what seemed right to some educational philosopher or political appointee with this or that academic or political axe to grind.

I was reminded of the importance of this real-world foundation of Montessori at a 2010 lecture by Professor Dan Willingham of the University of Virginia, a leading researcher into the cognitive science behind learning (and a Montessori parent). Professor Willingham pointed out the qualitative difference between what he as a scientist can observe in an artificial laboratory setting and what Montessori guides can observe daily in the dynamic real world of the prepared environment. Said Willingham, "The Montessori method is way beyond what cognitive science knows. We are slowly catching up."

So, speaking to the questions with which we began, we do see many children who go farther faster in Montessori than they would have been allowed to do in a school with a lockstep curriculum—even a curriculum for the "gifted and talented." We see some who do not. The important difference is that even the ones who do "average" academic work—and even those who struggle to do any academic work at all—come out of the process with their psyches, spirits, and moral values intact; with positive attitudes toward any future educational endeavors; and with a feeling of "ownership" that comes only from being supported to educate oneself.

I was recently at a Montessori elementary teachers' conference in Ohio. During a heated conversation about how much more new academic material Montessori elementary teachers should cover with the children, Laurie Ewert-Krocker, one of the key architects of the prestigious adolescent program at Hershey Montessori School near Cleveland, Ohio, stood up to say, "I need to tell you, it's not about how much material you cover. It's about how *unimpeded* these children have been in their development. If you [elementary guides] will keep sending us *whole children*, we'll take care of turning them into great artists, scientists, and so forth."

Although they would not think to put it into the same words as Ms. Ewert-Krocker, high schools love Montessori graduates. I have been told by teachers at a number of high schools that our former Montessori students are the only ones that will speak up in class or show an active interest in learning. They are never the ones to ask, "Will this be on the exam?" They have "ownership" of their own educations. They are responsible, organized, and helpful. They know how to work with others and how to mediate conflict—two key leadership skills.

A former Austin Montessori student who was attending a well-respected private high school was told by an instructor that he could skip class because he was ahead of the other students and did not need a review session. The boy hesitated for a moment and then asked, "Why would I want to do that?"

What the teacher did not know is that "rewards" such as getting to skip class would make no sense to most adolescents nurtured in the Montessori tradition. They would not have been comparing themselves to the rest of the class; they would not expect to be extrinsically rewarded for something excellent that they saw themselves as doing for themselves, not for a teacher; and missing out on possible learning would likely be seen as a punishment, not a reward.

By means of contrast, I can also think of former students who waited until adolescence to learn to read fluently, to do independent research, to make friends with math or writing, or to find enough inner peace to sustain lasting friendships. When they really needed to do those things, they did them—and that, too, is part of being a former Montessori student.

My point is that all these children—those who are on the developmental "fast track" and those who were not—were equally well served by their Montessori experience because they each got exactly what they needed at that time to do their very different work of self-construction. To a Montessorian, success in education is not about how many Montessori graduates are ready for "advanced placement" (although many are), or about how many go on to world-class universities (although a disproportionate number do), but about serving real children as they need to be served.

Sometimes the question is not so much about children's performance as it is about the relative difficulty and sophistication of the curricula in Montessori and traditional public schools. Funny word, "curriculum." It comes from the Latin *currere*, meaning "to run," as does its close cousin "course" (in both its noun and verb forms). The metaphor is that of a racecourse laid out ahead of time for all the runners to follow—and may the best man win. If we speak of "curriculum" *with its common meaning*, we are already far, far away from the approach that Dr. Montessori worked out for her schools—one about which she never failed to claim, *not I, but the children showed me*. If this racecourse metaphor is what we mean by "curriculum," then we would have to say that Montessori education has no "curriculum" at all in the traditional sense. It has no predefined path through knowledge that all children will follow, no mandatory checklists of lessons, no set of lessons tied to the child's calendar age (or "grade"), no academic forced marches of any kind.

Because we may find it difficult to imagine how learning can be structured without a traditional curriculum, to hear that Montessori has none can be alarming. We are all heirs to several thousand years of educational thinking that begins by asking the questions, "What is to be known?" and "What is the structure of that knowledge? How does this fact or skill depend on others?" The natural end product of such questioning is a curriculum—a logically coherent, stepwise plan for leading a student through a culture's particular answer to "What is to be known?"

Having established the curriculum, the conventional educator may turn to "pragmatic" questions of method, instructional technique, educational setting, measurement, and so forth. Conclusions about these pragmatic issues may (or may not!) be informed by studies of the cognitive, emotional, and social characteristics of the children for whom the curriculum was designed. Curriculum design, then, is one thing; curriculum "implementation" another. In this common approach, "the children" are an abstraction to be modeled, not a living part of the process.

Maria Montessori's big insight, the difference that made all the difference, was to start *not with questions about knowledge,* but with the "question of the child." This "question of the child" was something that she came back to again and again throughout her long career. In effect, she turned the conventional approach on its head by asking, *What sort of being is this who learns? How does this being naturally exercise its powers of learning? How may we best serve the work of this being?* Only when she thought she had (through observation and experimentation) some insight into these questions was she ready to ask the questions of *what* and *when*—the sort of questions that are traditionally answered by curricula.

If Montessori education does not have a traditional, linear "curriculum," what does it have? A vast, interconnected ecology of human knowledge, precisely and economically represented, both in its content and in its interconnectedness, in the Montessori materials and the enticing, inspiring key lessons and stories that go along with them—what Dr. Montessori eventually came to call Cosmic Education. In an environment that concretely mirrors the structure of knowledge, children are led by these lessons and materials to explore the interconnections for themselves, both individually and in groups, guided by the teacher who constantly observes them and serves their optimal development. Skills develop naturally and deeply, according to the child's specific blueprint for development.

While there is no unique, linear path through the field of knowledge, children who are given the full six or seven years of the elementary for their guided explorations forge their own paths through all of the disciplines. They get to all of the topics that would be in a traditional linear curriculum, but there is a qualitative difference in how they "own" their learning. Nothing has been crammed or forced and immediately forgotten. There is no throwaway learning in the Montessori classroom. Instead, the child has a personal relationship with what they have learned; the knowledge is *theirs*. The result of such unimpeded learning is a young adolescent—a *whole* person, in Ewert-Krocker's terms—who has acquired the skills, knowledge, and self-confidence necessary for their work in the next stage of life.

So let us, like Dr. Montessori, start with the "question of the child" instead of the "question of knowledge" and not worry too much about comparing the Montessori holistic approach to standard curricula. Better to ask "Will my child have all that he or she needs to develop to full potential in this classroom?" Chances are, if the child's natural drive to learn is stimulated by an educational environment that is always leading children out of the classroom and into exploration of the whole world *and* supported by a home environment that protects the authentic nature of the child from harmful influences, we will get to experience for ourselves Montessori's own surprise and joy at just how far beyond our "expert" expectations the child can go. ❖

Whole Child, Whole World: Learning Outside the Elementary Classroom

Written in 2007, this article draws heavily on my Washington Montessori Institute training, as well as my experiences assisting Donna Bryant Goertz and leading my own Upper Elementary community.

The classroom materials, lessons, and methods of presentation in the Montessori elementary are designed to support the characteristics of what Maria Montessori called the Second Plane of Development—that time in the child's life when their intellectual and spiritual growth occurs largely in and through the community of their peers. Because the elementary child's way of thinking is qualitatively changing from uncritical absorption to critical reasoning and the child is moving from mostly individual work to mostly collaborative work, the guide's ways of supporting the child's self-education must also change.

For example, books become increasingly important throughout the Second Plane, since the child's reading ability is growing. Sensorial materials, while still a vital part of the environment for all six years of the elementary, are presented with the understanding that they are preparations for "doing it all in your own head"—no longer ends in themselves, but ladders that can be abandoned once one has climbed up. Above all, the children who have been so protected during their first plane years are now ready to explore the world outside the classroom. This free flow of experience, information, and inspiration between the classroom and the outside world is perhaps the single most telling difference between the elementary and the Children's House.

Going Out

Just as the young child in the Children's House is provided with real implements and given real responsibilities in the care of the environment and care of the self, the child of the Second Plane must be given real situations in which to exercise will and judgment with responsibility. Moreover, in order for the child to have a sufficiently rich experience of the world to serve as the foundation for the more abstract thinking of adolescence, it is important for much of the child's learning to take place outside the classroom. This dual development of responsibility and experience is accomplished by "Going Out"; that is, through well-prepared forays into the world in search of knowledge and experiences not available through classroom study alone. These exploratory trips differ from traditional field trips insofar as they are initiated, planned, and executed by the children, not the teacher, and they arise organically from the interest and work of the child, not from a plan of instruction made by adults.

A Going Out for a young elementary child might be as simple (from the adult perspective) as a trip to the public library to look for books not available at school. An older child who is more capable and ready to take on more responsibility might organize a trip to a university to interview a zoologist or a poet, a trip to a local business to see how neon signs are made, or a trip to an apiary to learn about beekeeping. For children in urban schools, Going Out can also mean planning to spend some extended time in nature, where studies of plants, animals, weather, and geology come alive, motivating the more abstract work of the classroom both before and after the trip.

In *From Childhood to Adolescence*, Montessori writes:

> There is no description, no image in any book that is capable of replacing the sight of real trees and all the life to be found around them in a real forest. Something emanates from those trees which speaks to the soul, something no book, no museum is capable of giving. The wood reveals that it is not only the trees that exist, but a whole, interrelated collection of lives. And this earth, this climate, this cosmic power are necessary for the development of these lives. The myriads of lives around the trees, the majesty, the variety are things one must hunt for, and which no one can bring into the school.

It is difficult to overstate the importance Montessori attached to such Goings Out by the elementary child. Indeed, she called them "the key to culture" (*FCA*). Whereas the Children's House provides a kind of protective "cocoon" in which the child can develop safely and without distraction, the Montessori elementary's "Cosmic Education" claims the world for the classroom. Montessori writes, "When the child goes out, it is the world itself that offers itself to him. Let us take the child out to show him real things instead of making objects which represent ideas and closing them in cupboards" (*FCA*). If she were writing today, she might well add, *Let us take the child out to show him real things instead of creating software that represents ideas and putting it on classroom computers or iPads.*

There is a story that comes from Mario Montessori's work training teachers in London—a story that all Montessori guides would do well to keep in mind. As the story goes, a young teacher approached him to say that, contrary to what she had been led to believe in training, her students had no interest in botany, and there was nothing she could do to influence them to use the botany materials. Mr. Montessori told her to meet him the next morning at the entrance to the Royal Botanic Gardens at Kew—site of the world's largest living plant collection—and to bring the children. As the children entered the plaza of this grand and beautiful garden with its fountains, its huge diversity of plant life from all around the world, and its carefully tended beds, they ran to see the flowers, calling out with excitement to each other as each new discovery was made. Mario approached the young teacher to say, "But I thought you said the children had no interest in botany!"

Whenever our students' interest lags in any area, we too can ask ourselves if they are not perhaps telling us in the only way they can that they need help experiencing this area as part of real life, not merely as something adults think they should learn.

Going Out and the Human Tendencies

In her advocacy of learning outside the classroom, Dr. Montessori was careful to distinguish her ideas from two prevailing misconceptions of the day. On one hand she addressed herself passionately to traditional educators for whom learning was the byproduct of the teacher's activity in the classroom and for whom trips into the outside world could only be a waste of time and a distraction for the children. On the other hand were reformers who wanted to see school children outside getting fresh air and engaging in healthy exercise for reasons of "personal hygiene." To Montessori's way of thinking, both camps failed to see that effective education and a thriving childhood depended not on the plans and arrangements of teachers but on the children's deep intrinsic interest in the world. From that vantage point, it was easy for her to see that the only way to fully engage this aspect of the child was to open the doors of the classroom and let them go out into the world to explore.

Montessori knew that the result of such freedom would be children who positively expressed what she called the "Human Tendencies." Indeed, in a well-planned Going Out, children can find expression of almost every universal human tendency: *exploring* linked to intrinsic interest; *ordering,* in the planning and execution of the things that will need to be done before and during the trip; *imagining,* in the conception of the Going Out and the hypothetical thinking involved in the planning phases; *orienting oneself* in a strange place or situation, leading to a greater sense of orientation within the cultural milieu; *controlling oneself* in a very stimulating and perhaps daunting situation; *working* and *moving* during the trip itself; *abstracting,* in the gathering of data and the subsequent synthesis and follow-up work in class; *repeating,* by reliving the experience through presentations to the teacher or class; *perfecting,* in the care with which the planning and execution are done and, upon return, the reflection about what could have been done differently to make the trip even more successful; and *communicating* and *belonging,* in every aspect of the group's planning and execution.

Whole World, Whole Child

There is yet one more aspect of Montessori's deep understanding of the child-in-the-world that must be mentioned. It goes beyond pragmatic observations about "what works," important as those may be for practicing Montessorians. It is this: The world is a unity, and the child is a part of that oneness. Montessori saved her most passionate invective for educators and psychologists of her day who had programs and curricula for educating this or that isolated aspect of the child—moral education, practical education, social education, physical education, religious education, intellectual education, et cetera. She called such educators "vivisectionists" of the child's psyche, and saw their efforts as not only doomed to failure but positively harmful to the normal development of the child as a whole being (*TEHP*).

For her, this being that is the child could only be whole in its natural setting, and, for human beings, that setting was the whole world, both natural and "supra-natural" (i.e., cultural and technological). The education offered the child must reflect in its own unity that unity which is the child. According to Montessori:

> A child enclosed within limits, however vast, remains incapable of realizing his full value and will not succeed in adapting himself to the world. For him to progress rapidly, his practical and social lives must be intimately blended with his cultural environment. [...] *Knowledge and social experience must be acquired at one and the same time.* (*FCA*, emphasis added)

She went on to say that a child always cooped up in a classroom, developing only their intellectual side at the expense of developing their independence and ability to navigate their culture and community, was analogous to a disabled individual only one of whose legs had grown and developed.

It is in Going Out that knowledge, carefully acquired and practiced in the classroom, and social experience to be found only in interaction with the surrounding culture come together to give the child an experience truly liberating and elevating. For this reason, Montessori wanted every elementary guide to understand of Going Out that "the goal is not an immediate one—not the [trip itself]—but rather to make the spiritual being […] capable of finding his way by himself." And, in more than one sense, is this not the ultimate goal of Montessori education as a whole? ❖

Imagination:
The Child's Key to the Universe

||||||||||||||||||||||||||||||||||||||||||||||||||||||||||||||||||||||||||||||||||||||||||||||||||||||||||||||||||||||||||||||||||||||||||||||||||||||||||||||||||||||

This article, published in 2007, grew out of a writing assignment for my elementary training course.

As a classically educated scholar, Dr. Montessori thought it important to understand, both theoretically and practically, how human beings come to have true knowledge of the world. The answer she developed is incarnate in her plans for education of the first-, second-, and third-plane child. Because she began with the Aristotelian belief that "nothing is in the intellect that was not first in the senses," the challenge for her was to understand how such basic sense impressions became the loftiest of human knowledge, knowledge from which issue the artistic, scientific, and social achievements of humankind. She came to see *imagination* as the link between these lower and higher forms of knowledge. Over the years she sought to express her insights in various ways, finally employing some ideas from the contemporaneous psychology of the unconscious.

In Montessori's view, knowledge must be based on exact perceptions of objects and states of affairs in the real world. She saw the First Plane of Development as the time in a child's life when they are actively absorbing these kinds of sense impressions and factual knowledge. She therefore cautions against presenting the young child with fantastic stories and the like, in a mistaken attempt to strengthen imagination. As the child matures into the Second Plane, sensorial impressions are no longer enough. Now the younger child's tendency for order in the physical environment turns inward toward the ordering of *ideas*; Montessori even speaks of this as being a "sensitive period for imagination." The conceptual relationships between things and the generalized properties of things become at least as important, and then more important, than sensorial impressions of those things.

Imagination and abstraction are the processes by which the second-plane child (and the adult) orders the disconnected impressions and facts of the world. Such ordering requires that the individual hold present in the mind, through *imagination*, things that are not in fact present physically. When this can be done, the mind can begin to see patterns in experience, the process of *abstraction*, and to visualize the possible or potential existence of something that one has not directly experienced or which may, in fact, never have existed.

In *From Childhood to Adolescence*, Montessori writes:

> The world is acquired psychologically by means of the imagination. Reality is studied in detail, then the whole is imagined. The detail is able to grow in the imagination, and so total knowledge is attained. The act of studying things is, in a way, meditation on detail. This is to say that the qualities of a fragment of nature are deeply impressed upon an individual.

Montessori employed the psychological notion of "engrams," an idea scientifically accepted in her day, to explain her view of the interactions of sense impressions and higher processes of the mind. Engrams are "traces" left in the subconscious mind by experiences in the physical world. Engrams were understood to be not just passive traces but active agents constantly combining and recombining to construct the content of the subconscious. What we call "intuition" and "inspiration" Montessori understood as the coming to consciousness of the subconscious work of engrams.

The hypothetical thinking that arises so strongly in the Second Plane is closely related to imagination. It is the kind of thinking we employ in art, science, and other creative endeavors. In *The Advanced Montessori Method*, Montessori distinguishes between the "creative imagination of science" and the "artistic imagination" (*AMM* vol. 1). *Scientific imagination* depends on the epistemological objects of science, that is, things that science has "admitted" to the universe as real and existing. Ideally, the scientific imagination allows human beings to understand and manipulate their environments to improve their quality of life. Scientific imagination in tandem with action leads to innovation.

In Montessori's view the *artistic imagination* was more exalted insofar as it was not restricted by logical reasoning. She believed that the artistic imagination did not directly change the external world in the same sense as did the scientific imagination; instead, through synthesis of past experience, it brought something new into the world. The creations of an artist or composer are built up from the artist's life experiences. As the artistic imagination operates, the first action is recombination, or synthesis, of images (although such recombination may be unconscious and present to the mind as pure intuition). Physical creation is the second action. Montessori took the position that the artistic creation is created for the sake of creation itself, not as a way of directly changing the environment. In both the artistic and scientific cases, she saw it as very important that imagination gives birth to something new in the world, something that would benefit others as well as oneself. As she wrote, "Imagination does not become great until man, given the courage and strength, uses it to create. If this does not occur, the imagination addresses itself only to a spirit wandering in emptiness" (*FCA*).

Supporting the Development of Imagination

In the Children's House

Montessori saw the child's self-construction as the supreme act of creativity. She spoke of the time from birth to age three, with its amazing leaps forward in motor and linguistic abilities, as the "period of creative excellence." In the 3–6 class we give the possibility of continued development of the major acquisitions of the infant: coordinated movement, communication, and independence.

In the Children's House, our task is to give the child facts from which they make images. We give the child experiences that create images of size, dimension, weight, color, temperature, texture, and the like. We also give the child practice carrying those images in the mind (memory games). The language work in the Children's House is also essential to this further development because the facts of human culture and life have a linguistic basis. All the interesting ways that people have lived can be expressed through language, hence the careful definitions of terms and explorations of language that accompany so much of the work in the Children's House.

In the Children's House, the child is protected from exposure to fantasy and unreality since they have not yet learned how to distinguish between what is real and what is unreal. To expose the young child to unreality is to confuse them and make their task of self-construction more difficult. Imagination is weakened, not strengthened, by such premature exposure.

As we saw, creativity depends on the development of new ideas through use of the imagination. It also depends on knowledge of tools and skills with which to express these ideas and on order, to provide form and structure for the creation. Without ideas in the imagination, there is nothing to express. Without tools and the skill to use them, there are no means of expression. Without order, creative expression tends to be incomprehensible to others. In the Children's House, therefore, the child begins to prepare their imagination (ideas), hand (for tool use), and organizational abilities (for order).

In the Elementary (Cosmic Education)

The work of the Children's House is primarily the work of the hand and the memory, and while this continues to be somewhat the case in the elementary years, there is the addition of a new and formidable power of intellect. Montessori called the Second Plane the period of the "reasoning mind," and the educational approach to this Plane is designed to engage the child's imagination and intellect like nothing the child has heretofore encountered. Montessori writes in *To Educate the Human Potential:*

> The secret of good teaching is to regard the child's intelligence as a fertile field in which seeds may be sown, to grow under the heat of flaming imagination. Our aim therefore is not merely to make the child understand, and still less to force him to memorize, but so to touch his imagination as to enthuse him to his inmost core.

Imagination, then, is the key to the psyche of the second-plane child, and Cosmic Education employs that key to unlock the child's innate love of learning. If the child's intelligence is the soil, and imagination the light and heat, it is this innate love of learning through one's own activity that waters the seeds of interest constantly being sown by the teacher so that they grow into beautiful and sturdy trees of knowledge.

As Montessorians, we actively engage the elementary child's imagination and support its development in a number of ways:

- through the constant use of storytelling,

- through humor,

- through art,

- through the use of impressionistic materials such as the impressionistic geography, history, and biology charts,

- through the presentation of materials and activities that lead gradually to abstraction,

- through preparing the child to go out into the world outside the classroom,

- by allowing the children to develop according to their own timetables,

- and by encouraging the children to find their own answers, think for themselves, and share their thinking with others.

Montessori speaks often of "sowing seeds" of knowledge. She understood that it was impossible for us to bring the whole world into the classroom and that it was impossible for any child to experience everything. Imagination is once again the key here. It is not necessary for us to present everything; we need only present with great precision some key details and carefully chosen examples. In this, Montessori stressed the importance of choosing the right keys to unlock a given area of knowledge and the precision and exactness with which we present them to the imagination of the child:

> [The] imagination has need of support. It needs to be built, organized. Only then may man attain a new level. He is penetrating the infinite. A study outline here presents itself: *to bring the whole by means of the presentation of detail.* (*FCA*)

Montessori observed that once the child's imagination was engaged and their interest aroused, the child was driven to understand the whole phenomenon exactly and completely. This is far better than our trying to impose "high standards" on the child. She writes:

> The child's imagination is vague, imprecise, without limits. But from the moment he finds himself in contact with the external world *he requires precision.* The requirement is such that the adult would be unable to impose it. Its full potential lies within the child. When a child's interest is aroused on the basis of reality, the desire to know more on the subject is born at the same time. At such a moment exact definitions may be presented. (*FCA*)

The Second Plane is also the time of great moral development. Children are preoccupied with questions of good and bad, right and wrong. They want to understand the motivations behind people's actions. Why did that person do that? Why did that person react the way she did when I did what I did? How do I behave in this group? In order to answer this type of question, the child must be able to imaginatively take the place of the other: empathy is an imaginative act. The child must be able to think hypothetically about social and moral scenarios and reason about right and wrong. When moral problems arise, the child must be able to imagine possible solutions.

In the elementary, we provide the freedoms that lead to a great deal of social interaction, which in turn brings to the foreground these social and moral questions. While we encourage the children to work out their own problems, we also give them guidance, both in the form of explicit coaching in conflict resolution and in the form of modeling moral behaviors ourselves.

When the children have educated themselves, inspired by imagination, by the enthusiasm of collaborative learning, and the discoveries they themselves have made in the world by going out of the classroom, they will be prepared to undertake the tasks of the Third Plane, adolescence. They will be ready to discover who they are in the wider world and how they may use their powers of imagination for the good of the planet. ❖

Tending the Light of Intelligence

||||||||||||||||||||||||||||||||||||||||||||||||||||||||||||||||||||||||||||||||||||||||||||||||||||||||||||||||||||||||||||||||||||||||||||||||||||||||||||||||||

This article from 2007 develops the earlier discussion on imagination with particular emphasis on the reasoning mind of the second-plane child and how the Montessori elementary is designed to meet their needs.

Dr. Montessori famously wrote in *To Educate the Human Potential*:

> The secret of good teaching is to regard the child's intelligence as a fertile field in which seeds may be sown, to grow under the heat of flaming imagination. Our aim therefore is not merely to make the child understand, and still less to force him to memorize, but so to touch his imagination as to enthuse him to his inmost core.

There is a related exhortation in the chapter on "Intelligence" in *The Advanced Montessori Method*, volume 1, which I think of as "Montessori elementary in a nutshell":

> Our care of the child should be governed, not by the desire "to make him learn things," but by the endeavor always to keep burning within him that light which is called the intelligence.

In this, Montessori has herself sown a seed which we as classroom teachers can, if we work carefully and reflectively, nurture into a strong and flexible practice that can serve children of all cultures, temperaments, predispositions, backgrounds, and abilities. Montessori gently but firmly turns our attention away from the aims and concerns of traditional education to the key concern of Cosmic Education: supporting the natural development of the reasoning mind in all its aspects.

It is for *this* purpose that we appeal to the child's imagination to inspire her to work. It is for *this* purpose that we painstakingly prepare a physical and social environment in which the elementary child can self-educate. It is for *this* purpose that we give the lessons, build the Going Out program, and communicate high expectations for the children's learning.

In the Children's House, the teachers must constantly ask themselves, "What *tasks* am I doing for the children that they could be doing for themselves?" While this question is still a good one at the elementary level, the more important question for the elementary teacher is "What *thinking* am I doing for the children that they could be doing for themselves?"

The Second Plane is the time of great development in thinking and great passion for exploring and understanding the world and, indeed, the cosmos. It is the springtime of the intellect in which all the many seeds planted in the Children's House begin to bloom most beautifully. One sees the intertwined growth of what the Greeks called "practical reason" and "theoretical (intellectual) reason." Whereas the younger child often repeats tasks for the sheer joy of doing them, the second-plane child often seems to be thinking just for the sheer joy of thinking.

A story from Albert Einstein's childhood is most instructive. Five-year-old Einstein was shown a magnetic compass by his father. This mysterious device with the needle that was moved by some invisible force made "a deep and lasting impression" on young Albert ("Profile"). Albert's father and the family's friends noted Albert's fascination with such things and continued to offer him similar experiences. At the age of 10, a family friend introduced Albert to Kant's philosophy and to Euclid's *Elements*. Euclid became such a touchstone for his young mind that he came to call it "the holy little geometry book" ("Young Einstein"). Einstein also loved to tinker around in his father's shop, building things and carrying out his own investigations.

Montessorians can easily recognize these sorts of experience as cognate with the work in the Montessori elementary. The salient point is that by the time Einstein came in contact with the very rigid German education establishment, he was already well-acquainted with the true life of the mind and with the development of his own particular mind in all its particular beauty and idiosyncrasy.

Albert, the young adolescent, was famously unhappy with and unsuccessful in the rigid confines of traditional schooling, complaining that it killed the students' creativity and natural passion for learning. Einstein's experience was exactly what Montessori observed as she contrasted her own experiments in the classroom with the traditional methods of her day. One might well speculate that had Einstein's developing mind been straitjacketed by traditional education from a very early age, the world might not now remember him as the great scientist and humanitarian that he actually became.

As Montessorians into whose care thousands of potentially world-class minds are annually given, we do well to evaluate everything we do by asking whether or not it supports the children's love of learning and development of independent thinking.

We also do well to remember—along with Montessori, developmental psychologist Howard Gardner, and others—that human intelligence is a multi-faceted thing. One mind may be liberated by the mysteries of magnetism and geometry, another by the mysteries of animal and plant life, another by the challenges of music or drama, another by the infinite depths of language or the compelling questions of human behavior and culture. This is a key insight behind Montessori's development of Cosmic Education for the second-plane child and her exhortations to bring the whole universe to the elementary-age child.

Montessori Aids Thinking

So how do we keep the light of intelligence "burning within [the child]?" By consistently making intelligent, informed choices about lesson content, the structure of the physical environment, and the modes of interaction between guide and child and between child and child.

As to content, we must, as Montessori said, sow as many seeds as possible in the time we are given, and draw these seeds from all areas of human knowledge and experience. This responsibility and the breadth and depth of human knowledge dictate that we do not have time to indulge adult fantasies about pre-designed, grade-leveled curricula, nor do we have time to expect every child to pursue, much less master, every lesson given.

Much like the adults in Einstein's young life, we cannot predict what encounters with the world will produce "deep and lasting impressions" in each child. We must have unshakeable faith that every child will respond deeply to something, and we must keep sowing more and more seeds, remembering, as AMI elementary trainer Dr. Kay Baker reminds us, that Montessori's directive was to *sow* the seeds, not to *plow* the field and *plant* the seeds.

The goals of sowing the maximum number of seeds and fueling the "light of intelligence" and the goals of delivering a standard curriculum and assessing the children's performance on it lead to very different decisions about how to spend our time and energy in the classroom. This is, in fact, the single greatest source of conflict between the Montessori paradigm and the "accountability to standards" paradigm.

If we Montessorians sacrifice—whether to school district directives, parent pressure, or our own fears—this way of working with the children and this orientation toward our role as guides, we give up any chance of producing the miraculous results that Montessori saw in her own classrooms.

To any who might accuse us of resisting accountability to standards, we must reply that our accountability is necessarily to a much higher, much more challenging standard: that of the astonishing potential of the developing human mind, before which we stand daily in near-religious awe. Full realization of this unbounded and unpredictable potential is what we give up when we settle for higher numbers on exams and more uniform performance across a lockstep curriculum.

How we choose our goals also affects how we view and present the Montessori materials. If our goal is to support the maturation of innate intelligence, broadly construed, we will offer the materials as means of self-education and, above all, of child-directed *exploration*. Exploration requires uninterrupted work time and the freedom to "fail" or discover dead ends as well as more fruitful outcomes. If our goal is to achieve high scores on standardized tests or "universal coverage" vis-à-vis a standard curriculum, we will tend to use the materials as "manipulatives" in a traditional teacher-oriented system of direct instruction and thinly-disguised drill.

Paradoxically, a century of Montessori classroom experience shows that the only way to achieve the results that attracted the world's interest to the work of Dr. Montessori is to protect the children's freedom to choose and to work at their own pace and to resist our ever-present impulses to control, to direct, to over-teach—all ways of doing for the children what is properly the children's own thinking.

Truly collaborative learning is a hallmark of the Montessori way of aiding the natural development of intelligence and independence. Like most Montessori freedoms, freedom to collaboratively learn runs against the grain of the current emphasis on standards-based individual performance and assessment. However, our experience as Montessori educators is that the best way for elementary-age children to learn is for self-selected, mixed-age, interest-driven groups to learn together, under the guidance of an adult trained in the art of inspiring, empowering, and then stepping back to observe.

Clues that this is the case crop up in all sorts of places. For example, in 2007 a major Norwegian study of intelligence and birth order recently attracted attention in the mainstream press.[1] Researchers studied almost a half-million Norwegians, including about 62,000 pairs of brothers to see if they could detect a link between performance on standard IQ tests and birth order. There has long been evidence, albeit inconclusive, that oldest children do better on intelligence tests than their younger siblings, and there has been much "nature vs. nurture" speculation as to possible causes.

The Norwegian study found that, on average, older brothers do indeed slightly outperform their younger brothers. Attempting to determine whether the difference was due to biological or environmental factors, the researchers then examined the test scores of brothers who had become the eldest child in the family after the death of a first-born brother. They were surprised to find that these young men's scores were, on average, the same as those who were biologically eldest. In other words, these boys had, after the death of their sibling, come from behind to achieve parity with the whole population of first-born brothers.

[1]See Benedict Carey, "Research Finds Firstborns Gain the Higher I.Q.," in the New York *Times,* June 22, 2007.

Stanford social psychologist Robert Zajonc suggests that the cause of these observed improvements in IQ scores could be the beneficial effects of becoming the mentor and tutor for younger children in the family. In other words, the act of teaching or coaching one's younger siblings could, in the words of the *Times*, "benefit the teacher more than the student." Montessori elementary teachers who daily observe the interactions between older and younger students in the mixed-age classroom will have no trouble understanding the effect to which Zajonc is pointing.

In his book *Mind in Society*, Lev Vygotsky famously theorized that children learn best when they are challenged to perform just beyond their best individual effort and then helped to success by a more knowledgeable partner. Hierarchy-minded American educators have typically interpreted this to mean "helped by the teacher" and reduced the idea to that of traditional instruction through "scaffolding," but Vygotsky himself left open other possibilities.

In the Montessori elementary we see the salutary effects of peer-aided learning. We see the children often stretching each other far beyond where we as adults might have assumed children could cognitively go. They need not be "Einsteins" to reap the benefits of such collaboration. ❖

A Closer Look

||||||||||||||||||||||||||||||||||||||||||||||||||||||||||||||||||||||||||||||||||||

This article dates from my years as Elementary Level Coordinator at Austin Montessori School. It was written for parent readers of the school's newsletter. It later appeared on MariaMontessori.com. The little daily miracles and triumphs that go on in the Montessori elementary are often opaque to those who have not had the opportunity to learn how to see with trained Montessori eyes. In this piece, I try to convey how much is in the background of even a simple situation.

I look up from my desk work to see two Early Elementary children—a boy and a girl—entering my office. They enter quietly, but their body language speaks of a certain excitement; one of them is clutching a book.

"We would like to read two poems, if you are available," one of them says. I come from behind my desk to sit and listen. One of the poems is about dolphins; the other is about insects. The children read aloud, taking turns with the verses. Clearly, they have made a plan and practiced how they will work together as readers.

After the readings, I ask the children how they had come to choose those particular poems. As it happens, each child chose a poem they really liked and the other one agreed to help them recite it.

In this very simple scenario, there is so much that is deeply, positively "Montessori elementary." Here are a few of things I see. The children are working from joy, not from coercion or a sense of duty. Working together they have attempted more and accomplished more than they would have done working alone. Because they have been shown what it means to be fully prepared and how to practice, they have been able to prepare themselves. Because they are prepared, they have the self-confidence to risk offering the poems to me, a friendly but somewhat formidable adult.

Although the children are friendly with each other, their relationship in this case is based on their working together—on their shared love of poems. The boy, in particular, has not had to overcome cultural messages about poetry being a "girl thing," because he is growing up in a closely aligned school and family culture that does not carry those messages (just as it does not carry messages about math and geometry being "boy things"). There has been some give and take in the relationship—each child following and leading at different times during the process.

As second-plane children, they are driven to explore language and its various powers, and they are being supported in that by being given positive avenues for exploration and opportunities at just the right level of difficulty to be challenging but not daunting. And, because they are working from personal choice, these explorations still *feel* like explorations to them, not like things they are being dragged into. When they are older they will not have discomfort around poetry to deconstruct, disentangling feelings that are actually about poetry from feelings that are actually vestiges of fear, anger, humiliation, or boredom associated with the way educators heavy-handedly staged their early experiences of poetry.

As the children take their leave and I return to my work, I feel blessed for the ten-thousandth time to have been alive at just this time in just this place and to have had the opportunity to see the child through Montessori's eyes. ❖

Where Every Day Is Earth Day

Another piece for the parent readers of Austin Montessori School's newsletter.

For the world, Earth Day comes and goes, but at Montessori schools here and around the world every day is an "Earth day." When one takes one's cues from the interests and needs of children, it has to be that way, for children have a need for experience of the natural world second only to their needs for food, water, and family attachment.

The beauty, grandeur, power, spontaneity, and complexity of the natural world speak directly to the elementary child's whole being—to the keen, still-developing *senses*, to the attachment to things via *feelings*, and to the *intellectual passion* to comprehend the lives of other living beings and their many mysterious relationships. Rachel Carson, whose pioneering work in defense of nature helped set the stage for the first Earth Day, insightfully wrote, "I sincerely believe that for the child [...] it is not half so important to *know* as to *feel*. If facts are the seeds that later produce knowledge and wisdom, then the emotions and the impressions of the senses are the fertile soil in which the seeds must grow."

Although I'm sure she did not intend to, in those two sentences, Carson perfectly captured the reason Montessori schools are committed to making every day Earth day for the children. Children learn not just with their heads but with their whole bodies, and facts presented to them without a foundation in felt experience do not even "stick," much less flower into anything approaching understanding or the passion to learn more.

In a very important lecture on the formation of the elementary curriculum, Dr. Montessori expressed a similar sentiment:

> There is no description, no image in any book that is capable of replacing the sight of real trees, and all the life to be found around them in a real forest. Something emanates from those trees which speaks to the soul, something no book, no museum is capable of giving. The forest reveals that it is not only the trees that exist, but a whole, interrelated collection of lives. And this earth, this climate, this cosmic power are necessary for the development of these lives. The myriads of lives around the trees, the majesty, the variety are things one must hunt for, and which no one can bring into the school. How often is the soul of man—especially that of the child—deprived because [school] does not put him in contact with nature. (*FCA*)

Her solution was to throw open the windows and doors of the elementary classroom and let the children go experience nature with their whole being. This is the foundational insight that shows up very practically in our provision of outdoor work environments, school gardens, wooded playgrounds, Upper Elementary and Adolescent Community camping trips, swimming in natural waters, nature hikes, and other excursions. It is a large part of what is behind our strong advice about keeping the time-killing, anti-developmental distractions of TV and video games out of children's lives and giving them, instead, encouragement and opportunity to be active outdoors in as many different ways as possible.

If we as adults protect or renew our own connection with nature in order to offer that gift to our children, we truly will be laying the foundation for their happiness, for, as Rachel Carson also wrote, "Those who contemplate the beauty of the earth find reserves of strength that will endure as long as life lasts" (*FCA*). ❖

Is Montessori Education Inherently Service Oriented?

||||||||||||||||||||||||||||||||||||||||||||||||||||||||||||||||||||||||||||||||||||||||||||||||||||||||||||||||||||||||||||||||||||||||||||||||||||||

This essay is my response to a very important question posed to me by a friend and colleague: Is the purpose of Montessori education the development of adults fully equipped to live happy and fulfilling lives according to their own personal definitions of happiness and fulfillment, or is there a bias toward developing adults who seek happiness and fulfillment through service, broadly construed, to the world?

> The world has largely forgotten that in the beginning of the century Maria Montessori's vision of education became the foundation of a movement created to uphold the rights of the child, to protect the child, to serve the child so that it will grow to fulfill its potential *for the betterment of humanity.* (Renilde Montessori, emphasis added)

Maria Montessori, throughout her life, repeatedly had the experience of people trying to slot her work into some pre-existing philosophical, political, ideological category. She frequently vented her frustration about this in her various lectures and writings, having come to believe that what she was advocating stood outside anything that she saw existing constituencies doing.

In her youth, she was a socialist and feminist organizer, but through her work with children and through her own life experience of two world wars, a civil war, personal experience with Mussolini in Italy and colonialism in India, and repeated betrayals on the part of this or that political or ideological ally, she came to believe that hope for humanity was not to be found in political, economic, or religious ideologies or programs, but in coming to a deeper understanding of the innate—and she believed, largely untapped—powers of the human spirit to create culture, solve problems, and cultivate virtue. Naturally, she did not believe this was possible without an understanding of optimal child development, since she saw the adult human as the work of the child that the adult had been.

She believed she had made some important inroads into such an understanding, but even at the end of her life she still described it as a project hardly begun. In her inaugural lecture of the Montessori Training Course in 1948, she writes:

> When we start thinking of all the great energies that we find around us, of this great human intelligence that expresses itself in the discoveries and the creations that keep on being made, we wonder where they come from. Where have they come from if not from the child, from the newborn man, who creates and constructs man? If this is so, why is it that this mysterious child does not attract the attention of the scientists and of all men? The study of the child itself has been very modest in comparison to the studies in other fields.

To be more specific, I think Montessori was largely successful in holding together a number of things that tend to get split apart in other ideological contexts:

First, there is no doubt that she highly prized self-sufficiency and independence. She practiced both and fought for them in her own life, but, I think, her real dedication to them came from her work with children. If too much is done for the child, if the child is too protected from the challenges and complications of their life, then they have no opportunity to connect with that in themself which has the power to overcome difficulty. The over-served child cannot develop a positive self-image. They either come to believe that they are entitled to be served in perpetuity, or they learn helplessness, or both. The deep-seated anxiety, resentment, and confusion that results manifest in adolescence and adulthood as a wide variety of self-harming and antisocial behaviors. As adult citizens they are easily manipulated by other individuals, peer groups, or institutions. Having no spiritual and intellectual core of their own, they attach themselves easily to ideologies and institutions that provide predigested answers and "absolute truths"—anything that can provide an exoskeleton to give structure and support to the weakened psyche. Prevented from developing their innate capacity for self-discipline, they require external control—a scenario that plays itself out every day in traditional education, not to mention society as a whole.

Our libertarian and anarchist friends love this side of her thinking and work, seeing in it the freedom they value—freedom to "march to a different drummer," freedom to pursue their own goals. But that is only half the story. Others are attracted to the strong emphasis on "peaceful community," but want us to "enforce the peace" in the classroom by authoritarian means—the only way they know from their own upbringing and education. In this way, Montessori education has often served as a sort of Rorschach test, whereby different groups see what they want to see in it and overlook or dismiss the rest. This is made easier because, in my opinion, Montessori did not present a complete and coherent theory of social change. She had certain themes that she constantly returned to, but in the end they do not add up to a complete social theory. (I cannot fault her for that, since her life was primarily devoted to revolutionizing education, not theorizing about society.)

Freedom to Montessori was always "freedom with responsibility." That is, responsibility both to oneself in holding high personal standards and doing the sometimes difficult work of self-reflection and character building, and responsibility for the uplift of one's community. It is in this sense that I think one would have to say she had a "service orientation." Her dictum about working with children that "every unnecessary help is a hindrance" reflects this balance in her thinking insofar as it calls for restraint on the part of the helper as an act of respect and help in itself, but recognizes that not all help is unnecessary.

I think she saw the individual and society as inseparable, two sides of a coin—as the individuals go, so goes society, and vice versa. And I see nothing in her thought that would suggest that development of the individual and the exercise of individual freedom are ends in themselves. She always comes back to the idea that individuals find their highest meaning in service to the community, in dedication to the uplift of humanity. I think this was so central to her way of thinking that she sometimes just took it for granted and did not say a lot about it. To Montessori, a human being developing and perfecting itself simply for its own pleasure and personal gain would have, by definition, been a case of developmental deviation.

These Montessori values are deeply embedded in the way we work with children of all ages, although they are much more in the foreground at the elementary and adolescent levels, since these are the developmental periods in which the children are naturally working on understanding what it means to be a part of a high-functioning, compassionate community and what they as individuals bring to that table. Starting in the elementary, the focus is always on the big picture: how human civilization as we find it came to be through the collective efforts of creative, hard-working individuals and communities striving to overcome obstacles, find better solutions, and be better people—all of this arising out of the earlier and ongoing development of life on earth, and of earth itself, all the way back to the beginning of time.

So we tell many stories about the "cosmic task" of this or that species, culture, community, or individual—by which we mean what unique contribution was made to the upward development of the whole. At the adolescent level, there is much talk about "valorization," in reference to the crucial developmental process whereby the individual finds value and meaning by contributing to the community and by receiving from the community appreciation and recognition of that contribution. This reciprocal process of valorization is seen as crucial because it is precisely that which solves the problem, both for the individual and the community, of the "alienation" of the individual in its community that received so much attention from nineteenth and twentieth century philosophers and social commentators. It is the keystone in Montessori's thinking about development of "the new Man," building as it does on the individual self-construction of the First Plane and the dual explorations of individual and community in the Second Plane.

The polity and culture of the elementary classroom provides an open field in which to explore these issues. The relationship of individual to community is present as a subtext in virtually every interaction that happens in the elementary classroom, including those that on first appearance would seem to be purely academic.

It is part of how we give lessons, how the children formulate and execute collaborative projects, how the community decides its code of behavior, how interpersonal conflict is handled through peer mediation and coaching, how the community makes decisions and chooses whole-class projects, and so on. Moreover, as a global exercise in freedom and responsibility, the community must be allowed to experience the full range of human emotion and behavior (for that is a huge part of the work of children in the Second Plane, without which they will not be prepared for the developmental challenges of adolescence) and must be accountable for coming to terms with it all and struggling through situations to find enlightened solutions— solutions that somehow balance the needs of the individuals and the needs of the community as a whole, solutions that respect the dignity of both.[1] ❖

---

[1] I would highly recommend to anyone who wants to understand the values side of Montessori to keep a copy of Montessori's *Education and Peace* close by and visit it often.

Part Two
The Montessori Elementary— Theory into Practice

A Letter to Teachers at the Beginning of a New School Year

Originally written to be read aloud at Austin Montessori School's first staff meeting of the 2013–14 school year, the first year after my early retirement.

I have had the opportunity over the last fifteen years to see many Montessori schools, some in person and many refracted through dialogue with the people who work there. It takes time, good fortune, and much hard work to build a Montessori school that is pedagogically sound, financially sound, provides the necessary support to families, and is a great place to work. And, since a school is not a thing but a dynamic living organism, even schools that manage to bring all these things together cannot sit on their laurels.

Where can we find energy for our work? Can we rely on traditional workplace motivations such as career advancement, financial profit, or professional recognition? Are we driven to be better by our personal perfectionism, competition with peers, or a sense that others are watching and ready to judge? My experience in both the business world and the Montessori world is that these motivators are not enough and may even be in some ways inimical to the deepening and perfecting of our work with children and families.

Instead, I would encourage you to work together to help each other establish, both individually and as a community, strong connections to the two spiritual energies that I believe are the origin and foundation of authentic Montessori practice: joy and love.

What these two things are, how they relate, and how we can cultivate them individually and collectively in our Montessori practice is a long conversation that you can hold over the course of this year. Here, I would only like to offer a few sketches of what they mean to me.

I have found a number of reliable sources of joy in our practice. First, there is the joy of being with the children in a way that we know serves their deepest developmental needs. Dr. Montessori's books and lectures are full of her own expressions of this joy. I think, for example, of her writing "to aid life, leaving it free... is the basic task of the educator" (*TMM*) and "we teachers can only help the work going on, as servants wait upon a master" (*AM*). This joy is a sympathetic joy, something that arises when we see the joy of the children. It presupposes that our practice is strongly founded and sustained by observation—otherwise we miss much of what we and the children have to be joyful about.

Another source of joy is knowing that we are spending our time and our precious life energies in truly meaningful work. It's not easy work, and it often challenges us to the core, but it is good work, something that really matters in the world and for the future. It is hard to overestimate the importance of this and to appreciate fully how fortunate we are to have found this rare jewel that is meaningful work.

Dr. Montessori wrote, "Joy, feeling one's own value, being appreciated and loved by others, feeling useful and capable of production are all factors of enormous value for the human soul." (*FCA*) She was pointing to yet another source of joy, the joy that comes from being a valued member of a community. Montessori work can only be done in community; this is true both in principle and in practice. When our personal energies flag, it is the community around us that must carry us, support us, re-energize us. What can you do to create a community like that at your school?

I will leave you with one more thought. Dr. Montessori said that the first thing the elementary guide must do, the preparation out of which everything else in the work flows, is to fall in love with the universe. She modeled that love so well for us, and we can model it for the children. Workers in flow are workers in love. (Although she was writing about the elementary, I think this is true at all levels. Perhaps for those working with the younger children the link to the universe is more clearly visible through the developing children themselves, but that's a story for another day.)

A guide whose love of the universe in its infinite manifestations is strong can be lacking in all manner of pedagogical technique and nuance, yet the children around them will also be on fire with interest and enthusiasm for exploration and learning. Likewise, the impeccable technician, even one who has met the challenge of completely mastering the complex relational structure of the albums, "if they have not love, they are as a sounding brass and a tinkling cymbal" (to borrow the words of St. Paul to the Corinthians). The children around them may learn to be well-behaved performers, adapted to the perfectionistic standards of the adults, but the transformative self-construction that we Montessorians seek will be nowhere in sight, and a connection to joy will be lost for both the children and the adults.

Thank you for listening. Best wishes for your new year.

John ❖

Seeing Ourselves as Others See Us

O wad some Power the giftie gie us
To see oursels as ithers see us!
It wad frae mony a blunder free us,
An' foolish notion.
—Robert Burns, from "To a Louse"

Robert Burns's famous lines were penned to puncture inflated egos, but they can work the other way, too. While others often do see our faults and pretenses more clearly than we do, they may also see the brilliance and worth of what we take for granted. Two visitors to our school have recently reminded me of this.

The first visitor was a young woman who had recently completed her certification to teach in public schools. She had heard about "the Montessori method" in her college studies but wanted to see it in action. I arranged a day for her to observe at both elementary levels and then meet with me to discuss her observations. After her observations, I asked her what she thought. She replied, "Sometimes all you can say is 'wow!'"

One thing that particularly stood out for this young teacher, who had completed her practice teaching at one of Austin's most highly respected public elementary schools, was what she described as "the calm energy—the children's sense of peacefulness—how they're not rushed from one thing to another." She said that during her practice teaching she had observed the constant low-level background stress created by the rigid scheduling and frequent interruptions of traditional schooling. She wanted to know how to become a Montessori teacher.

The second visit was from a former Austin Montessori School student, a young man who had spent only three years in our school about twenty years before, all of them in Donna Bryant Goertz's Early Elementary class. He had gone on to public school in fourth grade, graduated from the Austin Independent School District's liberal arts and sciences magnet high school, received a degree from a prestigious Midwestern liberal arts college, and was now living in Japan, where he was teaching English as a Second Language and completing a master's degree at Columbia University.

He wanted to know what it would take to become a Montessori elementary teacher. This would have been no great surprise to me had he grown up in Montessori, but his time in our school had been brief. I asked him what it was about his experience here that had him thinking about Montessori training. He said, "I don't have many specific memories. I remember some of the other children and a few things we did. Mostly, I just still have the feeling. I remember that I felt important, valued and respected. I remember that I was given responsibility and that I really liked that. I've always carried that with me. Now that I'm teaching in traditional schools, I can see that if the children were given freedom and responsibility and allowed to explore, they would go so much farther than we are able to take them."

To see oursels as ithers see us can be downright inspiring! ❖

The Bridge of Trust: Working Successfully with Parents and Colleagues

||||||||||||||||||||||||||||||||||||||||||||||||||||||||||||||||||||||||||||||||||||||||||||||||||||||||||||||

This sequence of five topics is drawn from a daylong lecture prepared for students in Dr. Jean Miller's elementary training course at the Montessori Institute of North Texas. The idea for the lecture was born in conversation with Dr. Miller about practical aspects of Montessori teaching that go beyond the theory and praxis that make up the core material of elementary training. I was privileged to present this material to three cohorts of Dr. Miller's students. Subsequently, I have shared it with many teachers and administrators, and it has been by far my most popular work. Clearly, it addresses issues that often challenge working Montessorians.

BUILDING THE BRIDGE OF TRUST

Good Montessori elementary training is tough. There is so much to learn about the philosophy, the materials, the art of presentation, the preparation of the environment, how to work from observation. Certainly those things are at the core of what distinguishes a Montessori guide from a good conventional teacher—what is taught, how it is presented, and what supports are in place for the success of the enterprise.

Yet, all this is only about a third of what makes or breaks a new Montessori guide. There are two other vital aspects—parent relations and work habits—and it is actually in these two areas that we most often find guides getting into trouble and leaving the profession.

By parent relations, I mean everything that goes into the guide's relationship to the parents whose children are in their care or whose children will be in their care when they are of age. This encompasses formal communications such as parent education, parent conferences, children's progress reports, accident reports, memos about class activities, formal thank yous, as well as informal communications such as chatting at school events, daily hellos and goodbyes, informal thank yous, routine phone calls, and so on.

By work habits, I mean everything that goes into being a successful worker (or professional, if you prefer that word). This encompasses working effectively with the school administration and one's teaching and non-teaching colleagues; time management; self-evaluation and receiving the evaluations of others; pursuing continuing education; professional grace and courtesy in communications (for example) and in personal presentation.

It is vital to see the Montessori teaching profession as comprising all three of these overlapping but distinct professional arts and not just as the work done in the prepared environment with the children. That way lies disaster, frustration, and potentially even the abandonment of the profession.

Cultivating good parent relations and work habits is every bit as important as knowing the Great Stories forward and backward and a good deal more important than, say, knowing the square root materials down to their last juicy detail. Yet, too many new guides see these non-curricular areas as "add-ons" or opportunities to take shortcuts whenever possible. Too bad for the children in their classes—these guides will always work under a cloud of suspicion and anxiety, missing much of the joy of the work.

Since these two areas are so important to our practice and our happiness as Montessori guides, I would like to explore them in some depth, starting with a concept that is deeply connected both to good parent relations and work habits: *trust*.

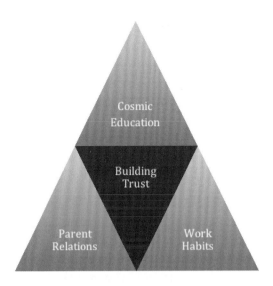

Why Is Trust So Important?

Trust is important in any profession or job, but much more so in professions in which one takes on tasks that represent real risks to the client. Surgeons. Lawyers. Airline pilots. Police. Therapists and clergy (because of privacy issues). Those who work for non-profit charities (because of financial risks and responsibilities). Teachers.

Constantly working to build trust is important because, in our work with children, it is inevitable that there will be difficult times when that trust is tested. At no time are perfectly reasonable people so irrational as when something is wrong with their children or when they perceive that their child is in some sort of danger. Feelings that arise at these times are deeply rooted in the biological imperatives of parenting. It was true of me as the parent of a growing boy, and I have seen it to be true of scores of parents in my community. Often, a strong history of trustworthy interactions is all that pulls the guide and the parents through.

People in "high-risk" professions therefore need to go overboard to send signals of safety, competence, prudence, discretion, and reliability to those who depend on them. Entering one of these professions entails giving up certain personal prerogatives and cultivating certain personal disciplines. Moreover, because schools are collective endeavors, the actions of one person on staff can have serious consequences for the whole enterprise—in a way that would not be true for employees of most business corporations. Schools, especially independent schools, definitely feel the effects of the "weakest link" phenomenon. I have seen enough damage done to individuals and schools to be willing to say that if one is not prepared to rethink one's life through the lens of what builds trust, one should find a different line of work.

From the guide's perspective, working in the high-risk, high-stakes teaching profession without the trust of the parents and one's colleagues is a truly miserable experience. Everything you do is questionable and questioned. Everyone is poised to put the worst possible spin on your actions and decisions. Everyday mistakes are blown out of proportion and seen as certain proof of your unworthiness, incompetence, or venality. Evidence of competence and trustworthiness will tend to be discounted or overlooked once it begins to cause cognitive dissonance in those who have formed a negative opinion of you.

Cognitive dissonance is the foundational concept in social psychology that people will act to reduce the internal conflict they feel when simultaneously holding two contradictory ideas. One way we reduce cognitive dissonance is to filter out evidence for the idea we don't want to keep holding. This can work for or against you as a guide, depending on whether you are giving others more evidence of your trustworthiness or the opposite.

Children pick up even the unspoken discomfort of their parents (and your discomfort around their parents) and may then begin to become difficult for you to work with, leading to even more anxiety in you and in the parents. This is the beginning of a negative spiral that not infrequently leads to the loss of a family for the school. When one family leaves, other families may be shaken. It's not uncommon to see the exodus of several families during the first year or two of a new guide's practice—I speak from personal experience.

One does not have to be perfect, and most parents will give a new guide the benefit of the doubt, but first impressions do count for a lot, even with parents and staff who think they are above all biases and see everything objectively.

It is important to always keep in mind that parents whose children are with new guides are necessarily in conflict. On one hand, it is in their best interest to offer trust and support to the new guide, because that is what the new guide needs from them in order to succeed. On the other hand, it is in their best interest to view the new guide with a modicum of suspicion, because a great deal hangs in the balance—the safety and well-being of their precious child. (Remember the biological imperative?) So, these parents tend to be hyper-vigilant, watching carefully for any evidence that would let them off the fence, that would let them settle into one or the other of their mixed emotions and resolve their cognitive dissonance.

The Bridge of Trust

I like to think about (and to talk to the children about) the *bridge of trust*. Between any two people there can be a bridge of trust. The bridge is either strengthened or weakened by every interaction you have with the other person. The earliest interactions lay the foundations for the bridge. If the bridge is new ("still under construction"), even a small negative interaction can damage it or break it down altogether so that it can no longer bear the weight of the relationship. By contrast, a very strong bridge can withstand many little bumps and bruises and tremors without significantly weakening. It takes time and focused effort to build a very strong bridge.

Success in teaching is very largely a matter of bridge building and bridge tending. If you can take this perspective—that you are voluntarily entering into a profession that requires the highest standards of personal presentation and conduct and continuous improvement—your chances of success and a long career will be greatly enhanced. And it will be a lot more fun in the long run.

Two Dimensions of Trust

There are two dimensions of trust, and it can be very helpful to keep these in mind when thinking about your relationships. The two dimensions are *trust in intent* and *trust in competence*. That is, we intend certain things, and then we act to produce what we intend. Often even our best efforts are not enough to produce what we intend—this is the all-important gap between our vision and our practice. We may feel at times that this gap is a bottomless abyss, ready to swallow us up if we come too close to it, but, in fact, it is better seen as the open space in which we live and practice. The tension between vision and practice is the source of great energy for life, the motive force that propels us forward into growth and development.

Of the two dimensions of trust, trusting someone's intent is the deeper kind of trust and the one that most directly affects our feelings of safety. Parents absolutely must trust a teacher's intent—both for their children and for themselves as parents—before they can feel safe and supportive. On the other side of the coin, for must of us, it is far more wounding to have others lack confidence in our intent than it is for them to lack confidence in our competence or ability to do the job. Competence is something that can be developed through practice and education, but lack of trust in our intent feels like a questioning of our moral sense, of our personal integrity, of who we really are at our core. We intuitively understand this when we have to express our own misgivings about how someone has handled a particular task: "I know you meant well, but..."

I bring this up in part because, as guides, we do run into people who are quite unskilled at telling the difference between the two kinds of trust, very unskilled at looking at their own thinking and feelings and knowing what is actually the source of their discomfort with us or our performance. There are people who, perhaps because of the specific kinds of wound they have received from important people in their lives, will over-generalize your little incompetencies and turn them into criticisms of your intent, of you as a person. Forget to remind them of the date of their parent conference and suddenly you are the distant father who neglected to come to their high school graduation. Forget that you promised them last year that they could help chaperone the fall camping trip, and suddenly you are a monster single-mindedly bent on forcing them out of the school and compromising their child's social standing in the community.

Through patient, skillful communication one can sometimes bring such people to see the difference between one's intent and one's ability to consistently produce what one intends. Even when that is not possible, just knowing about the two dimensions of trust and how easy it is for some people to mix them up can give one a little more space in which to work with one's own strong reactions to being accused and criticized.

Bridge Tending

I bring up the two dimensions of trust for another reason, as well. They are critical to our understanding of our own work with the children—especially our daily work of bridge tending with each of them.

There is a very important sense in which children are in the world to make mistakes. Their job is to fail and to fail as often and as quickly as they can, because it is through this kind of trial and error that learning comes. Dr. Montessori understood this very well, and she famously said in *The Absorbent Mind* that we must all "cultivate a friendly feeling towards error, to treat it as a companion inseparable from our lives, as something having a purpose, which it truly has." We go to great pains in Montessori to remove the usual negative consequences of error precisely because we know that error is key to learning and we want the children to feel free to try and fail, try again and fail again, try again and do a little better...all the way to mastery.

Being around all this trial—and especially all this error—is really difficult for many of us. It takes a lot of patience and a very clear head. *It requires being able to completely trust and honor the child's intent through long periods of not being able to trust the child's competence.* We need to hold that vision of the child *for* the child, because the child needs us to be able to help them back to it when they begin to doubt themselves. We patiently give the child chance after chance after chance because we know that holding onto the vision will eventually produce results—and because it is not ours to decide when the learning process should end, only ours to serve the process and keep it going.

When we have personal agendas for the children, when we identify ourselves with the children's results, when we have strict timetables for the children's development, we are on very dangerous ground: dangerous to ourselves as guides who are then susceptible to burnout and dangerous to the children who are developing in the performance-oriented, self-alienating environment we have established.

Transitive Trust

As valuable as the "trust as a bridge" metaphor may be, we should be careful not to infer that trust is a static, rigid structure. On the contrary, it is an organic, dynamic, evolving relation with stages and phases and many changes of weather. Over the years that a child could be in your class, the trust between you and the family will change not only in quantity but also in quality.

In most cases, the first kind of trust the family extends to you as a guide new to their family and children is what I call *transitive*, to borrow a term from mathematics and grammar, indicating a property that moves from one object to the other.

Transitive trust is trust that you inherit by virtue of your association with already trusted people or institutions. The parents trust the school; the school trusts you enough to give you responsibility for a class; therefore you must be trustworthy. New parents hear from trusted parents of older children that you are a good sort, so you are given transitive trust—the benefit of the doubt.

Transitive trust is a good place to start, but it is only a start. Soon enough the scaffolding of transitive trust holding up the new bridge will be removed as the parents begin to have direct experience of you as a person and as a guide for their children. While the scaffolding is in place is the time to put special effort into bridge-tending, keeping in mind the parents' need to trust both our intent and goodwill and our ability to effectively guide their children.

SPEAKING TO PARENTS ABOUT THEIR CHILDREN

Any discussion of trust must eventually come around to *communication*. The root meaning of *communication* is *to share*, and good communication allows us to do just that. Not only to exchange ideas, but to share them—to come to a common understanding and perspective from which we can act in concert.

Communication with parents and colleagues is a vast topic, but there are a few areas I would like briefly to spotlight in this and future essays. Beyond that it is good and even necessary for us to make communication in all its facets a personal lifetime study, tapping into as many different resources for our own development as possible.

There are many, many books on general and specific aspects of communication and much good advice. For example, the Nonviolent Communication work of Marshall Rosenberg is one well-developed approach. There is also much to be learned from the work of Albert Ellis, William Glasser, Haim Ginott, and Rudolf Dreikurs (whose work was popularized by Adele Faber and Elaine Mazlish's *How to Talk so Kids Will Listen*). I advise teachers to read widely in this literature, looking for an approach that speaks to them. There are many paths, but one destination.

Any approach to communication worth its salt will require a good deal of introspection and personal change, not merely the memorization of pat phrases or "techniques" to employ in this or that situation (although those things may have their place within the system). And most authors would agree that the most important part of learning to communicate well is learning to listen well.

Speaking to Parents about Children

No matter how we come to view communication, one of the most important and sometimes difficult situations we as teachers encounter is the parent conference. These little slices of time we have with parents are of the utmost importance in our project of building bridges of trust. Even the easiest, most cordial conferences call for our most serious attention, both in preparation and in execution. We must know what it is we need to communicate, and we must balance that need with skillful listening to what the parents need to communicate to us. The subject of conversation—these children that are the reason for our being in conference—is of deep interest to both parties, and how we speak to parents about their children is very important. Much hangs in the balance.

For one thing, as Montessori guides, we have a particular perspective on childhood that is very different from conventional views and, sadly, often very different from the views that parents have of their own children. Our Montessori view can be summed up in several affirmations (some of which are taken from the work of Sandy Blackard, a brilliant parent educator in Austin, Texas).[1]

---

[1]Blackard's work is available at languageoflistening.com.

- All behaviors—even dysfunctional ones—are ultimately driven by healthy needs. Recognizing the need allows us to see and ally ourselves with the good in children, regardless of their behavior.

- Everything children do and say (including what they do not do and do not say) is a communication. Children are driven to communicate until they feel heard and understood.

- Children are in the world to learn and to challenge themselves to move beyond their current capacities. That is their nature. Children intuitively know how to set the right level of challenge for themselves and will do so if we will let them.

- We can only work with the communications we have from the children, from what Dr. Montessori called "the periphery." We are not privy to the child's innermost thoughts, feelings, and needs or to what it is like to be them. We work only with the periphery, not with the core. Even our understanding of the periphery is always provisional and open to modification based on further evidence from observation.

This is the view that we must hold for ourselves, for the children, and for their parents. All of our communications about the child, whether "good news" or "bad news," must be framed in these terms. Parents can easily lose hope in themselves and their children, and we can help them by speaking even of challenging issues in terms that inspire hope and confidence.[2]

For example, we can say, "Donald is more often using his words instead of force to express frustration," instead of "Donald still sometimes pushes other children when he's angry." Both may be true, but one inspires hope and the other invites frustration or defensiveness and overreaction.

We can say, "I am looking for the best way to gain and keep Lena's trust," instead of "Lena tries to hide things from me." Or "Candace

---

[2]In this, as in most things Montessori, I am indebted to my mentor Donna Bryant Goertz.

looks for praise less often and seems more connected to her own inner satisfaction," instead of "Candace relies more on adult praise than is healthy for a child her age."

"I am working with Delma to enlarge her awareness of the needs and feelings of others, and I am working with Delma's classmates to help them see how Delma is growing in this way" is more effective than, "I am working on it, but the other children often see Delma as harsh and selfish."

Or we can skillfully and graciously stand our Montessori ground even as we give the parents good reason to come stand with us: "Nan has been concentrating on math. I am supporting her to extend and deepen this interest because I see that this is the way she has chosen to develop a long concentration span, strong self-motivation, and a cheerful perseverance. When these qualities are solidly established in her character, I will work with her to transfer them to writing and other subjects."

This way of framing communication about the child has nothing to do with soft-pedaling, sugarcoating, or New-Age happyspeak. It is a reflection of our confidence in the ultimate goodness and strength of human nature and of our confidence in the child to find her own way, with a little help from her friends. It is a concrete expression of who we understand ourselves to be vis-à-vis the child, namely, as "aids to life" or those who are privileged to stand by and watch the work of a master (the child constructing herself), offering only as much help as the child needs and can accept. It is not an act of cowardice or evasion, but an act of deeply humanistic courage to believe in the power of the human being to perfect itself and to transcend its current imperfect circumstances through its own efforts. It is also a gift of hope and support to parents who may otherwise be overwhelmed by their children's difficulties.

Yes We Can—Together!

Parents are under much pressure to "understand" their children. A parent who doesn't understand their child? What kind of parent is that? *Not a very good one,* says society. But we know that children are enigmatic, complicated, confusing—and they consciously or unconsciously know how to hide from us, to push our buttons so that we can no longer see them clearly. It can be a great relief to parents when someone who is so often with their child demonstrates some understanding of the child and gives the parents a way of thinking about and supporting them. On the other hand, when a parent feels that their child is not being understood, all of their own personal feelings of not being understood (all the way back to infancy) erupt into consciousness.

As Donna Bryant Goertz has written:

> Individual parent conferences are such a rich opportunity for building a relationship that I like to hold a conference very early in the year with each parent of a new child. I reserve an hour and a half for each new parent. This is a time to let a parent feel the full force of my delight in having her child in my class. Parents need to know their child is a wanted and treasured community member. Before I approach any hard work with a parent or with a child I like to have initiated a trust based on the parent's introduction to our living and learning culture, my knowledge and skill as a guide, and to my fondness of the child. Every parent deserves to hear in one piece the issues we plan to address, the positive characteristics of the child upon which we plan to build, and the shining goal toward which we aim. I want the parent to see clearly that I consider every child to have issues, and that these issues are the stuff of life that provide the child with necessary opportunities for struggle and growth.

We can be comfortable not having all the answers about a particular child. (We never will, of course, not even in principle.) We can allow the child to be the mystery they are and to model that for the parents—but only if it is done in the context of this deep faith in the powers of the child to find their own way in their own time.

Helping parents frame the bumps in their children's developmental paths in such positive, insightful ways is a true gift to them and to their children. Moreover, it creates another link in the bridge of trust between us and them, inviting them to stand with us to see the dynamically developing child that we see and to enjoy the beautiful view. From that place of common understanding and appreciation, we can work together in creative ways to find solutions that work both at school and at home.

WHEN AND WHAT TO COMMUNICATE WITH PARENTS

I have found in all areas of life that any communication is nearly always better than no communication, but there is such a thing as too much communication between parents and guides. We have been talking about the bridge of trust between guide and parents, and this is where the bridge needs to be strong enough to hold the load without constant patching. For one thing, parents do not need to know every little thing that goes on with their child at school in order for them to do their job as parents—just as you do not need to know every little thing that goes on at home in order to do your job as a guide. That level of monitoring creates anxiety in the parents and also in the child. It sets parents up to be "helicopter parents" who continue to hover around their adolescent and adult children long after they should have retired to the sidelines to enjoy from there the view of whatever their adolescent or young adult is making of their life.

In a well-functioning Montessori elementary, there are many ups and downs during the day, many opportunities for conflict and conflict resolution, many spontaneously arising situations and experiences that allow children to stretch themselves and to venture outside of their comfort zones. As the adults, our job is to give children the tools they need to handle these things themselves and to refrain from rushing in to give "help" to those who are decidedly not helpless. It is not always clear when to give help and when to keep observing, but experience tells me that it is often best to wait just a little longer than our reactivity would otherwise dictate.

Preparing the Social-Emotional Environment

We prepare the physical environment with scientifically validated materials that support the development of all the various facets of the human intellect. But what are the materials for the social-emotional "curriculum"? They are the children themselves and their interactions in the prepared environment. We prepare the social-emotional environment by modeling the values of respect, kindness, flexibility, optimism, good humor, and others that we know the children need to develop; by providing the means for them to practice the skills that underlie emotional intelligence (including the considerable time this practice takes away from "academic" subjects); by gentle coaching; by active listening; by showing the children that we believe them to be capable of growing and learning in the social-emotional arena and by honoring such growth as an important part of their work at school; and by providing the children with many stories of people who have walked this path of human and spiritual development and transcended themselves and their situations to become exemplars of what it means to be fully human.

In short, we offer the children the skills, the freedom and the time they need to develop socially and emotionally. Psychologists, brain scientists, and other researchers who have studied Montessori education tell us that Montessori is exemplary in supporting the development of "executive functions" and high-level thinking skills. And part of what makes our approach work is that we do not constantly involve the parents in all of the day-to-day social-emotional drama. When a parent is told about a challenge their child encountered that day, they will naturally feel that there is something they need to do as a parent to "fix" the situation. Otherwise, why would you be telling them? Usually, there's nothing at all for them to do, and their attempts to invent something to do may constitute an impediment to the child's own work of social-emotional development. Not fair to the parent; not good for the child.

So what *does* one tell parents about the social-emotional ups and downs of the classroom? I think it comes down to two things: patterns and extreme incidents.

Communicating About Patterns

Parents need to be informed of patterns of behavior that you see. A pattern comprises a <u>series of similar events or observations over time</u>. If we are observing as we were taught to observe in our training, patterns of all sorts will naturally emerge, and parents deeply need this information in order to do their work of parenting. There will be patterns for individual children, patterns for certain groups of children, and patterns for the whole community. (There will also be patterns in our own behavior, but that is another story.)

Parents need to know about their child's patterns, both positive and negative. They need to know about the positive patterns because that is what strengthens the bridge of trust between them and their child. They need to know about the negative patterns because there is usually something underneath the surface that is giving rise to the pattern—something that the child has not yet discovered how to shift on their own.

You also need to tell parents about patterns of behavior in order to compare your perspectives and observations with theirs. Just as they need to know about the patterns you are seeing, you need to know about patterns they see at home. If you are all seeing the same patterns, there is something important the child needs for all of you to know. If you are seeing different patterns at home and school, that too is a clue about the origin and meaning of the various patterns. You and the parents are on the same team to discover what is going on, as best you can, and to offer appropriate support to each other and to the child. If you together cannot understand the pattern, it may be time to add others to the team (such as counselors, occupational therapists, or neuropsychologists).

Focusing on the child's patterns also helps the parents (and you) not become too focused on specific incidents. If there is a pattern going on, specific incidents usually find their meaning only in terms of the pattern, and obsessing about the details of this or that incident leads to not being able to see the forest for the trees. The regular periodic parent conferences you probably already have scheduled with the parents are often good times to bring up patterns.

Communicating about Incidents

Parents also need to be informed of incidents that are so upsetting to the child that the child will likely want to process them with the parents after school. Parents need to know enough about the situation not to be caught off guard, in order to know how to listen to and support the child emotionally. As previously discussed, we can support parents by speaking even of challenging issues in terms that inspire hope and confidence, letting them know the issues along with some suggestions for how to support their child at home. "I want to let you know that Sally is working hard today to figure out how to respond when someone keeps hiding her lunchbox. Should she retaliate? Should she tell me and let me sort it out for her? Should she bring her friends into the solution? Should she just ignore the behavior? Should she use humor?

She's looking for ideas and she may need for you to spend more time with her than usual just listening as she brainstorms and considers the possibilities. I'm confident that she and I will discover a good way for a person like her to handle such a situation, but she may need to feel some moral support in the meantime. This is a big, important work for Sally, and I'm really excited by the way she's taking it on."

If you present an upsetting problem to a parent like this, it provides support in several ways: it gives the parent a "heads up," and it gives them a specific role to play—they are not caught off guard and they do not have to scramble to figure out what they as good parents are supposed to do. It also lets them know that you are aware of the problem and are actively working on it.

It is a good idea to let parents know at the beginning of your relationship that this is how you will work with them. You will not be giving daily reports, but you will be very diligent about reporting patterns that you and they need to address together, and you will give them a timely "heads up" about any specific incidents that you think their child may need to process with them after school. Likewise, let them know that you welcome communication from them about things that they are hearing from their children.

Perhaps, nothing is more important to the ultimate success of your work with the children than the cultivation of clear, open, reliable communication with their parents. The extra time and effort you put into this part of your professional practice will be richly rewarded.

UNDERSTAND YOUR RELATIONSHIP TO TIME

Tell me how you personally relate to time, and I can tell you what are likely to be some of your greatest challenges in the classroom. How you relate to time is a huge issue both for your parent community and for your coworkers. It is also a huge issue for your students and provides many opportunities for conflict, if you let it. My wife, a marriage counselor, says that having differing relationships to time is one of the most difficult issues for her client couples to understand and overcome.

Basically, the problem is that one group of personality types (I'll call them "Type J" after one of the categories in the Jungian Myers-

Briggs model of personality) sees time as very organized. For them it is a salient, determinative, foreground feature of everything they do. The other group of personality types—let's call it Type P—sees time as an open-ended field in which to experience life as it happens. To Type J, time is a limited resource to be managed; to Type P, time, like space, is unbounded and free.

These two relationships to time had names to the ancient Greeks (who thought of everything!). To a Type J, time means *chronos*—clock time. To a Type P, time means *kairos*—the organic unfolding of a process or event in its "right" or "appropriate" time.

Understanding Your "Time Type"

Because we are working with children on a long arc of development, each traveling at their own speed, we need both to understand our own relationship to time and to learn to see time through the lens of the other personality types.

The Type P's are naturally comfortable with this kind of extended process, but they may need to develop the ability to tell the difference between the child who needs time for development and the child who is stalled developmentally and needs some help from the outside to structure reality and get back on track. The P's may need help finding the right balance between providing space for process and providing the kind of consistent, predictable structure that allows children to feel safe enough to really explore their world. The irony is that while P's may think they are giving children all the freedom in the world, the children are not able to be authentically free because things are too unpredictable and open-ended.

The Type J's working in Montessori—myself among them—are always at risk of becoming the Project Manager of the children's long-term project of self-construction. They will naturally know how to "make the trains run on time" in the classroom, but they may need to develop the ability to "chill out" and let natural processes run their course. Sure, the clock says that it is time to come in from the playground, but does what is going on developmentally on the playground say that it is time to come in or time to stay out a bit longer? Yes, the plan was to tell the first Great Story on Tuesday, but when Tuesday comes, is it really kairos, the right moment for the telling? To the unreflective J, spontaneity can come to be "the enemy"—and do I need to remind you that the English translation of Dr. Montessori's book about the elementary is called *Spontaneous Activity in Education*? Much food for thought there.

Regardless of one's personality type, informed observation and self-knowledge are the ways out of every difficulty with time and timing, as they are with every sort of difficulty in one's practice.

Working with the Other Type

Nobody in our very chronos-driven culture reaches adulthood without having some pretty bad experiences with differing views of time. The P's, in particular, will likely have been made to feel defective, immature, incompetent, inconsiderate, self-indulgent, or worse.

The J's will have had their natural inclination presented to them as a mark of their moral superiority, and their tendency to view the P's as lacking something will likely have been positively reinforced to the point that they have some difficulty seeing any value at all in the kairos-oriented view of time. Often, they will think the P's just need to grow up and get with the program.

For this reason, the P's often come to identify chronos as social oppression, a variety of control-related neurosis, and something to be actively and consciously resisted or avoided. One sees guides who, on principle, refuse to wear a wristwatch or carry a timepiece. Or one sees guides who are so obsessed with managing and measuring time that they have no time to stop and smell the roses—to really be present in the moment.

To the P's, I would say that regardless of how unfair it may seem, if you are living in America (and most of the Western world), you are living in a J, chronos time culture. You need to make your peace with that and not expect the culture to meet you halfway on this issue. You are actually the bearer of a great gift to your J colleagues—the gift of relaxed spontaneity and sensitivity to process—but they will very likely need some help from you to see the gift you bear. You can do that by going out of your way to reach out to them in terms they can understand, just as you would do with a child you were trying to reach.

This means developing ways of time management that work for you and allow you to keep appointments and commitments in a timely way. In the chronos world, an appointment is a social contract defined by time. If the appointment is at 10:00 for one hour, the chronos world expects it to start at 10:00 and end at 11:00, regardless of any other considerations. The J's may intellectually understand that when the time rolls around, 10:00 and 11:00 might not actually be the best start and stop times, but they will see it as part of the rules of the game to work within the agreed upon boundaries, no matter what.

To put it bluntly, when a P turns up 10 or 15 minutes late for a meeting with a J or with a group that includes some J's, the J is quite possibly thinking, *This person is a flake. If they can't keep a simple agreement like this, why should I trust them with anything important? It's really insulting to me for them to be late. I only have a short amount of time for this meeting and there are important things for us to do here. Seems like maybe they don't really care. How passive aggressive! Why don't they just come out and say what they think about me or our project? It's so selfish of them to make us all wait, wasting our time. They must think they're the center of the universe.*

Synchronizing with others is an indispensable part of collaboration, and that means making friends with chronos. In some situations, being late really does have negative consequences for others.

To the J's, I would say become aware that your view of time is personal and cultural, not a reflection of the mind of God. Chronos is only half of the story about time. Being a Type J does not give you permission to be critical of other people. On the contrary, it is important to begin to see how uncomfortable it must be for the P's to live in a culture that is so clock-oriented, so oblivious to process. Consider how much more energy and focus it took for them to arrive on time to the meeting than it did you.

You can begin to get a sense of this by imagining how uncomfortable you would feel working in a culture that had no clock time, no solid sense of beginning-middle-end, no social contract about time or keeping appointments. This sort of kairos relationship to time is, in fact, the one that human beings have had for most of our tenure on the planet. Clock time is a historically recent phenomenon, and one that really didn't gain the upper hand until the last 150 years or so (driven largely by the rise of railroads).

Do not give up on calendars and clock time, but do look for ways to accommodate your P children, colleagues, and parents within those limits. For example, if someone is predictably late to a meeting, do not sit around fuming about it—think of it as an opportunity to take a break, take a walk, go smell the roses, or enjoy your breathing for a few minutes. Let *nothing* happen for a few minutes and learn to see that as okay. Watch your own reactions from a little distance and learn to be curious about them: *Why is this such a big deal for me? Hmm.*

Colleagues can learn this kind of generosity toward each other, but it is more difficult working with parents whom you see relatively infrequently and often never get to know very deeply. In those situations, it's best to adapt to *their* style as much as possible. It is a way of "joining" with them, and we need as many ways of joining with parents as possible to build the bridge of trust. ❖

Spiritual Development
of the Adult:
Beginning the Journey

||||||||||||||||||||||||||||||||||||||||||||||||||||||||||||||||||||||||||||||||||||||||||||||||||||||||||||||||||

When we choose to work in Montessori, what are we choosing? Surely, we are not just taking a job, for a job comes with boundaries and clearly defined scope that our work simply does not have. We *are* entering a profession, insofar as our work demands the cultivation of good work habits, mastery of a specialized body of knowledge, strong communication skills, commitment to basic ethical practices, continuous improvement, and other capacities that all professionals must develop.

And yet, there is more to our work than any of this. I do not know a better way to say it, a way that I believe is congruent with my own experience and Dr. Montessori's point of view, than to say that when we commit to working with children in the Montessori way, we are taking on a spiritual discipline, beginning a spiritual quest. Like any authentic spiritual quest, the work we do has the capacity to transform us to our core, if we approach it in the right way. It is far more than the mere application of brilliant educational methods and technology, because we are—or can be—far more than mere teachers, by virtue of the way we work with the children.

Dr. Montessori spoke often, and always with a sense of wonder, about her own personal transformation from a young woman who had since her youth single-mindedly pursued and attained a career in medicine to one who left all of that behind to pursue a deeper understanding both of the "mystery of the child" and of her own relationship to it. Leaving behind her medical career was in a very real sense an act of renunciation, and renunciation—the setting aside of a settled, conventional life in the pursuit of spiritual development and insight—is the classic beginning of any spiritual quest.

We, as the inheritors of Montessori's legacy, must not let this part of her experience be obscured by the distance of time and cultural change. And yet, it seems to me that we are presently in danger of doing that—in danger of allowing the work to become just another educational philosophy among many, something that cannot even in principle provide the transformation of individual and society that Dr. Montessori spoke so urgently about to her first followers. Rarely do I hear, in the many Montessori forums that I monitor, open discussion of what it means to spiritually prepare oneself for Montessori work. When it is discussed, the conversation often remains vague and platitudinous, as if we all completely understood what it meant to be "spiritually prepared" and were fully equipped to carry out such preparation over and over at increasingly deeper levels throughout our careers.

I am particularly concerned that we begin to bring such discussions to the forefront as Montessori moves more and more confidently into the public sector, where government funding, government regulation, and constitutional restraints rightly require that we check our personal spiritual views at the door as we serve our secular, highly pluralistic communities. We need to understand more specifically what it means to "spiritually prepare" ourselves and to be able to articulate this to others who need to understand its importance in our practice.

Such discussions, should we have them, would also greatly benefit practitioners in the private sector who, more often than not, also serve pluralistic communities and who share many of the same cultural pressures to reframe their work as merely professional. I do not think there is a single answer or approach, but that the many possible approaches must be in dialogue in order to remain fresh, strong, and relevant.

While Dr. Montessori did not provide a detailed roadmap for spiritual preparation, she did offer much advice and many personal anecdotes that indicate a certain direction. We can use these as touchstones for our reflection.

We might begin by asking what is the relationship of religious practice to the spiritual preparation of the Montessori educator. It is clear that in Dr. Montessori's mind the two, while related, are not synonymous. Although she was a deeply religious person, she also understood that what the children had to teach us was not adequately represented in any religion, and that religious commitment per se did not guarantee the spiritual preparation she found necessary in her work. In *The Absorbent Mind,* she wrote "Spiritual life is perpetual life from one morning to the next morning. It is to live at a spiritual level, not merely to say prayers."

Granted! But what does it mean to "live at a spiritual level"? Does it mean to distance oneself from mundane experience, to float one inch off the ground with one's head in the clouds, contemplating the eternal verities? Here is Dr. Montessori's idea of spirituality:

> In all human beings there is a tendency, though sometimes vague and subconscious, to better themselves, a trend towards spirituality. Indeed these actions on the defects of character, have, later on, the quality of stimulating improvement. Both individuals and society have this in common: continued progress. This is a fact both externally and internally speaking and means that there is a little lamp in the subconscious of humanity which leads it to betterment. In other words the behavior of humanity is not fixed as in other animals, but can progress, so it is natural that human beings have this urge to progress. (*AM*)

This is a very rich passage, and we should spend a little time unpacking it. First, we see that spirituality is not an otherworldly pursuit, but a fully embodied practice of self-development. We also see that there is an unbreakable link—today we might call it a feedback loop—between the inner work of spiritual development that manifests in transformation of character and view and the outer work of spiritual development that manifests as the progress of society toward greater freedom, harmony, opportunity, happiness, and wisdom. The "betterment" toward which spirituality aims is, at least in part, the accurate diagnosis and development away from "defects of character" that get in the way of our work.

Most importantly, we see that the impetus toward spiritual development is not something foreign to our nature that must be imposed from without, or that depends necessarily on external authorities or institutions, but that it is something inborn in every human being, something rooted in our very biological nature as human beings, a Human Tendency, a "little lamp" in us that leads us on to personal and societal progress. This is immensely important to our understanding of what it means to work in the Montessori way.

It means, for one thing, that we as individuals are always works in progress; the little lamp always lights up the next bit of the unending path. Many of the qualities we must cultivate have no a priori upper bound; they can be cultivated endlessly to greater and greater levels of refinement. It also means that we see and celebrate the children in our care as lamp-bearers in their own right. We cultivate openness and receptivity to the light their lamps may shed on our own path. It means that we must fully embrace the truth that human beings are open-ended, always changing, always capable of bettering themselves—and we must not only embrace it intellectually but find ways to fully embody it in our practice. This is not to say that everyone will take the same path, encounter the same obstacles, or overcome them with the same ease or speed, but that the path to progress is always there and that we can choose to walk it at any time.

We must take this fluidity and innate freedom of the human spirit as our foundational principle and learn to sense even the slightest dissonance between this principle and other ways of thinking that we easily inherit from cultural conditioning, religious formation, scientific hypotheses misrepresented as fact, or misunderstood personal experience. If we bring to this work any point of view that would tend to lock human beings, especially children or ourselves, into rigid categories, castes, personality types, "learning styles," DSM-5 diagnoses, social or ethnic stereotypes, or other boxes of our own design, this is where we must begin the work of transformation. If we do not deeply trust that all human beings can change for the better, including ourselves, then it is pointless to talk about spiritual preparation or spiritual development.

On the other hand, taking this as our point of departure, we have great freedom to energetically explore this field of "human betterment" and its specific relationship to our Montessori work. ❖

Caring for Our Children by Caring for Ourselves

||||||||||||||||||||||||||||||||||||||||||||||||||||||||||||||||||||||||||||||||||||||||||||||||||||||||||

At present there is rapidly growing interest in "mindfulness in education"—bringing mindfulness practices into the classroom and into the life of the teacher. My own interest in this began in 2004 when I started to explore mindfulness practice in my personal life. In this article from 2008 I share one application of it that was great help to me as a Montessori guide. The article also appeared in the journal The Mindfulness Bell.

On the occasions when I slow down enough to actually think about it, it occurs to me that my job as a Montessori teacher is too hard for someone of my limited abilities—that is, someone who is still dependent on food, sleep, and occasional recreation. The demands never seem to stop, and if they do happen to slow down from time to time, I have a huge backlog of practice-improvement projects to fill the gaps.

Parents sometimes ask with a certain awe, "How do you do it?" How, indeed? How does one not only keep going, but do so with good cheer, grace, a sense of perspective, and, more often than not, a calm presence in the classroom?

I am happy to share at least part of "how I do it." I suspect that behind every successful teacher is a similar practice of self-care and reflection, although we seldom talk about these things with each other. Perhaps we should.

The crux of the matter is that less is more. At the center of the hurricane of teacherly activity, there must be a still center, a place of repose in the heart and the mind. This, I am convinced, can only be maintained through the regular, disciplined practice of stopping, paying quiet attention to one's inner voices, and reconnecting with one's highest self. One could call it a practice of prayer, or meditation, or affirmation, or self-reflection—the point is that it must be a regular period of quiet time, free from interruptions, an appointment one keeps with oneself.

I think of this quiet time both as a gift to myself and as a period of spiritual conditioning that keeps me emotionally prepared for whatever comes my way, in and out of the classroom. Although the children do not know of my practice of reflection, I am certain they could tell you which days I have failed to keep my appointment with myself.

My anchor, the backbone of my daily preparation for the classroom, is a practice found in Thich Nhat Hahn's book *Teachings on Love.* It is his version of a 1500-year-old text from Sri Lanka.

> May I be peaceful, happy, and light in body and spirit.
> May I be safe and free from injury.
> May I be free from anger, afflictions, fear, and anxiety.
>
> May I learn to look at myself with the eyes of understanding and love.
> May I be able to touch the seeds of joy and happiness in myself.
> May I learn to see the sources of anger, craving, and delusion in myself.
>
> May I know how to nourish the seeds of joy in myself every day.
> May I be able to live fresh, solid, and free.
> May I be free from attachment and aversion without being indifferent.

Just as a good weightlifting routine works all of the major muscle groups, I find that these nine lines exercise all of the psycho-spiritual "muscles" I need to strengthen for my work with children, parents and colleagues. I start my day with it, and I keep a copy in the front cover of my lesson-planning book, so that when I feel myself slipping away, I can read it to re-center and refresh myself.

May I be peaceful, happy, and light in body and spirit. I appreciate that this meditation starts with a clear statement of the desired state, the end-result of the practice. Sitting quietly, following my breath, I can bring my body and mind back from its habitual agitation and anxiety to the place of peace, happiness, and lightness that it is gradually learning to inhabit through years of this practice. Like a tennis player mentally rehearsing their stroke, I can mentally rehearse noticing the places of tension and disconnection in me and shifting them to calm connectedness. What could be more useful and important to someone working intensively with children?

May I be safe and free from injury. I have come to realize over the years that every kind of progress in the classroom depends upon all members of the community feeling safe and free from injury. This line reminds me of that and allows me to renew my intent to provide that physical and emotional safety for myself so that I can better provide it for the community. This hallows the many mundane things I do every day to insure the safety of the community, from lessons on safe use of science equipment, to keeping the first-aid kit well stocked, to mediating conflict on the playground, to honoring the children's efforts instead of their products. Looking a little more deeply, I also see that part of my practice is to know how to take care of myself and others when injuries do happen. Having the confidence that comes from being prepared, I believe, allows me to take appropriate risks on behalf of the community. So, far from being an invitation to always "play it safe," this line stretches me and allows me to walk away from fearful states of mind.

May I be free from anger, afflictions, fear, and anxiety. It is so helpful to have such a clear list of the major obstacles I face in my relationships with children, parents, and colleagues. It is even more helpful to have time to envision myself free of them and to look calmly at the roots of these problems. I can, for example, rededicate myself to my practice of noticing when anger and fear are arising in me and not acting on them until I have had a chance to calm myself and inquire what the emotion is telling me. My experience has been that simply acknowledging the presence of anger, fear, anxiety, craving, jealousy, and the like in myself greatly diminishes the urgency and force with which they batter my body and mind. The function of these emotions is to call my attention to something I need to take care of, and when I calmly give them my full attention, their job is done and they can relax.

May I learn to look at myself with the eyes of understanding and love. This line is priceless because it goes straight to the heart of so much self-inflicted pain, and it also helps to remove one of the biggest obstacles between me and the relationships that I need to build in a peaceful classroom. Behind this line is the wisdom that until we understand, accept and love ourselves, we cannot adequately understand, accept and love others. Indeed, whenever we think that other people are making us miserable with their foolishness and bad behavior, it is very likely that we are projecting some self-criticism or fearful insecurity that has taken root in us onto them. To our chagrin, we find those hypercritical, perfectionistic voices that chatter in our own heads speaking through our mouths to inflict harm on others. How wonderful to be able to practice stepping out of that cycle of injury by beginning to extend to ourselves the compassion that will allow us to connect compassionately with others!

May I be able to touch the seeds of joy and happiness in myself. This line comes from a view of human nature as being like a garden in which all kinds of seeds are planted—each one representing a capacity of body and mind. In each of us are the seeds of great evil, suffering, and destruction, side by side with the seeds of great goodness, joy, courage, and the highest states of being. Some of these seeds we inherited; some have been planted by our culture and personal histories. The seeds we water and tend, whether wholesome or otherwise, grow to crowd out the others, coming to dominate our internal gardens and our very lives. I find this outlook to be completely aligned with Dr. Montessori's views on the richness and essential goodness of human nature and the importance of the environment in the self-construction of the human being. The salient point in this line is that, although it is easy to lose sight of it when we are in the grip of a negative emotion, the seeds of joy and happiness are still there. We do not have to wait for our lives (or even just our classrooms!) to be perfect before we can be genuinely happy.

May I learn to see the sources of anger, craving, and delusion in myself. Now we go beyond a clear intent to be free of anger, fear, and anxiety to search for the roots of these negative forces in our lives. Quietly, deeply, consistently looking at these things while we are not being carried away by them, gives us the chance to see the patterns, to understand the ways these things work in our particular minds.

Seeing clearly, we have a chance to reorient our thinking and rebuild our habits into something more positive and free. To me, this line moves beyond intending and visualizing to doing something about the situation.

May I know how to nourish the seeds of joy in myself every day. Continuing the metaphor of seeds and the intent to learn to view and treat ourselves with compassion, this line invites us to take concrete action on our own behalf. The positive seeds are there, so how can I water them? I have gradually developed a mental list of very concrete ways that I can touch the seeds of joy and peace in myself, and I try to do some of these things every day. Here are a few of my touchstones: taking a slow walk in nature; really seeing and experiencing a blue sky, a flower, a stone, or a child's face; thinking of someone I love; enjoying a quiet cup of tea; giving my full attention to a great piece of music or art; holding my dog in my lap; reading a good poem or science magazine. Your list might be very different, but you can make one by noticing the things that give you joy. In particular, instead of reacting mindlessly out of anger, irritability, or fear, I try to stop and do one or more of my "joy things" to ground myself again in my best nature before responding to the situation.

May I be able to live fresh, solid, and free. As a teacher, I often think of this line as a description of the opposite of burnout. Surrounded as I am by the freshness of children, may I be able to find that freshness in myself. May I be solid enough to withstand the wind and waves of experience, stable enough to provide the consistent strength of purpose that it takes to build a good community. May I live as a free person, not in thrall to my faulty perceptions, fearful attachments and aversions, public personae, or life history.

May I be free from attachment and aversion without being indifferent. Montessorians are passionate people, the idealistic followers of a passionate and visionary leader. We have great expectations and bold plans. We have strong feelings about many things, strong likes and dislikes, long lists of both shibboleths and taboos. And yet, these attachments and aversions are often our undoing, the very things that get in the way of our realizing our vision. This line, when regularly rehearsed, helps me let go of my certainties, both positive and negative, and helps me live instead with the kind of openness to experience that

Montessori herself exhibited as she allowed a group of young children from the Roman slums to completely change her culturally conditioned views of who children are and what they are capable of. It reminds me that the opposite of passionate attachment and ego investment is not indifference but mindfulness, holding my perceptions and beliefs lightly, and being fully present to whatever the moment brings.

Now for the best part. Having taken good care of myself, I take the time to traverse these nine lines again, but this time the energy is directed outward to the community:

> May the children [or a specific child] be peaceful, happy, and light in body and spirit.
> May the children be safe and free from injury.
> May the children be free from anger, afflictions, fear, and anxiety.
> Et cetera.

For me, this closes the circle, and I am ready to enter the classroom again to see what great good can be wrought from whatever raw materials the day brings. ❖

Appreciating and Supporting the Nine- to Twelve-Year-Old

||||||||||||||||||||||||||||||||||||||||||||||||||||||||||||||||||||||||||||||||||||||||||||||||||||||||||||||||||||||||||

I came to Montessori education expecting to work with adolescents; as it happened, I spent my whole career with nine- to twelve-year-olds. I came to deeply appreciate this tricky, in–between time of life, as individuals would enter my classroom as children and leave as adolescents. In this 2010 essay, I share some of what I learned about working with them.

Anyone coming to work with nine- to twelve-year-olds after working with six- to nine-year-olds, as I did, will already know that although Montessori's Second Plane of Development is one continuous developmental plane, the two halves of it have a very different look and feel.

I have come to think of the elementary child as being on a journey from the Planet of the First Plane to the Planet of the Third Plane. When children first enter the elementary school, they are still very much feeling the "gravitational attraction" of the First Plane. Indeed, some of them may not have yet achieved escape velocity! As time goes on, the pull of the First Plane diminishes, and the children are increasingly pulled along by the gravitational attraction of the Third Plane. Our task as elementary guides is to see that the children arrive at their destination on time—but not before—and with no crash landings.

Understanding the Elementary Child

If we want to move beyond analogy and metaphor, we must understand where the second-plane children have come from and where they are headed. Then we must focus on the characteristics of the six- to twelve-year-old child and inquire into the nuances and emphases that shift during these six years. These evidence-based characteristics are the design criteria for our way of working with the child of this age, and we discount them at our, and the children's, peril.

Montessori speaks of each plane as being a "new birth." The Second Plane is the birth of the social being. The gestation period for this birth began with the First Plane, during which the child constructed an individual self, ready to present itself to the society of its peers. The young child's absorbent mind soaked up vast quantities of sense impressions of all sorts and unconsciously organized them as the experience of a human self.

Working directly with sense impressions, their organization, and classification made the younger child a very concrete thinker and a being that expressed its sense of order externally, in the world of objects. Cause and effect were often opaque to this young child and things experienced in the same time or place became unconsciously linked, often through mere association.

From this beginning the elementary child aims for adolescence, where the self, so carefully constructed, is reconstructed in community; where fully abstract, self-reflective thinking is the norm; where the rebirth of self-identity is achieved through imaginative exploration in the context of a community of peers and mentors; where individuals increasingly experience themselves as powerful in the world beyond the family, the social group, the "tribe."

What resources does the Second Plane child have for this journey? The reasoning mind, a newfound capacity and desire for relationships outside of the family, a growing capacity for abstract thinking, robust health and an increasingly skillful and trustworthy body and hand, and an expansive new power of imagination. The elementary child's expression of order moves inside in the now overpowering need to order the flood of ideas. Sensorial experiences no longer remain merely sensorial but become catapults into the world of ideas, explanations, and reasons.

Dr. Montessori told the story of a personal "aha!" moment in which a first-plane child whom a teacher was trying to help with his clothing looked at her in frustration and said, "Help me to do it by myself!" The child of the Second Plane, childhood's Age of Reason, demands of us,

"Help me think my own thoughts!" This we do by providing a free, peaceful, and rich intellectual environment for the child's explorations both at school and at home.

The Last Half of the Second Plane

The years nine to twelve are the flowering of childhood. All of the preparation and hard work done in the Children's House and the first three years of the elementary come to fruition. All of the characteristics that we see in the first half of the elementary are present in the second half, but they are typically intensified or more complex in some way. The attraction to peers becomes an obsession, the impatience with not knowing becomes an impatience with faulty reasoning and explanations, the enthusiasm for trying out new things becomes a need to test and challenge oneself physically and mentally.

The trend toward interiority and "hidden powers" which we saw as the child moved from the First Plane to the Second Plane continues, and the older child often delights in presenting themselves to us as an enigma. They are, after all, increasingly an enigma to themselves—a riddle that must wait to be solved in adolescence.

Above all, older children are astonishingly capable and need opportunities to demonstrate to themselves and others just how capable they are. This is the time of Great Work; of impossibly ambitious projects, often undertaken with a group; of whole-class projects, including camping trips organized by the children, plays, community service, art or science fairs, field days organized for the younger elementary children, and the like.

The children's ever-increasing capacity for abstract thinking and self-reflection make the last half of the elementary a good time to focus less on factual knowledge and more on learning how to learn. (This emphasis will only continue and intensify in adolescence.) The stellar results we see from Montessori children in high school and young adulthood owe much to the development of these high-level thinking skills, what neuroscientists call *executive functions*.

The Montessori elementary supports the children's higher-level thinking by providing frameworks for learning and exploration (e.g., history question charts, biological classification materials, templates for writing various kinds of essays, the scientific method); strategies for achieving one's goals (e.g., research skills, collaboration skills, getting and giving feedback); processes for effective workflow (e.g., time management skills, project management skills, experience with the full writing cycle); and habits of mind that characterize the life-long learner (e.g., self-regulation and evaluation, goal setting, open-mindedness, flexible attention, pacing oneself, confidence in one's abilities, resilience, and friendliness with error).

Finishing the Work of the Second Plane

As they near the end of childhood, when the tug of adolescence is so keenly and inescapably felt, children need strong support to slow down and give themselves the time to complete the work of childhood. The Montessori Upper Elementary, with its mix of three age groups, is the perfect place to do this. The developmental work of childhood is brought to completion in the sixth year of the elementary, when the highly capable, newly self-reflective, almost-adolescents can ground themselves by taking on the roles of leaders in a community of children. Then, from a position of strength and with a sense of full completion, they can launch into the unknowns of adolescence.

This is another important reason for ambitious whole-class projects such as camping trips and science fairs. As guides, our best contribution to these efforts is to step back and let the oldest children step up. We become their consultants and mentors, and in the process help them experience us as adults giving them new responsibility, adults beginning to see them as adolescent. This work of shifting the relationship we have had together prepares them for the new kinds of relationships they will need to forge with their families and future teachers. They see themselves as different because we see them as different.

Sometime near the beginning of the twelve-year-olds' last semester of elementary, I would meet with them to talk about beginnings and endings. I always looked forward to this conversation. I would begin by asking them how they were feeling. Feeling a little restless? A little impatient with the younger children? Boxed in by all the silly rules and customs of the classroom? A little angry or put out with me? Great! This means you are right where you ought to be. This environment that is so perfectly designed for the elementary child is no longer the ideal environment for the person you are becoming. All of these feelings are just you getting yourself ready for something new. This is just you doing your real work. (I learned early on not to wax poetic at this point about chrysalis and butterfly.) Now, let's talk about the next four months.

The sense of relief and new energy for work would be quite palpable after this conversation. The children would be eager to try new things that they saw as direct preparation for middle school: goal setting; new methods of time management; experimenting with assignments and deadlines; boys and girls who may have clustered by gender beginning to work together again, as they had as young children.

Throwing Away the Ladder

Part of the challenge of working with second-plane children is that the results are by nature ephemeral, indirect and somewhat hidden. Our job is to help the children build a ladder that they can climb from infancy to adolescence; once there, their maturation to adulthood requires that they throw away the ladder we so carefully constructed together. Nothing is permanent about the elementary child, so we guides must fall in love with change. Maybe we shouldn't speak of throwing away ladders. Maybe we should say, *Give a child a ladder, and they will climb to the next grade. Teach the child to build their own ladders, and they will climb to the stars.* ❖

Structure and Spontaneous Learning

||||||||||||||||||||||||||||||||||||||||||||||||||||||||||||||||||||||||||||||||||||||||||||||||||||||||||||||||||

This essay draws on material presented as a keynote address for a NAMTA conference in 2010 and again in Vienna for a symposium organized by the Austrian Montessori Society in 2012. It attempts to answer the perennial question, If Montessori education is a pedagogy of freedom, what is the role of structure in our pedagogy, and what kind of structure best supports the child's project of self-construction?

As an educational philosophy and practice, Montessori education stands somewhere between the rigidly structured Prussian factory model and the Romantic "free school" model that prides itself on how little structure it provides children. But there is still a lot of territory in this "middle ground" and many ways to misunderstand what sorts of structure are helpful to children and what sorts are stultifying.

How we think about structure and our role in providing it makes a big difference in the many little pedagogical decisions we make every day, and these, in turn, make a big difference in the experience of the children in our care.

As Montessorians we know that whatever structure we provide must start with an understanding of the child and their needs. We start where Dr. Montessori started: by asking who these children really are.

Whole Children or "Learners"?

At Austin Montessori School we talk a lot about language. We think language matters—that it subtly shapes how we think about our work, each other, and the children with whom we live. For example, what shall we call these children? Are they "children"? Are they "students"? Are they "learners"? We think that calling them simply "children" does the most justice to all of who they are.

We have noticed that when we see ourselves surrounded by "learners" or "students" then we more easily come to see ourselves as teachers, in the sense of professional practitioners of educational technique. The signature Montessori lessons and materials then risk ceasing to be invitations to open-ended exploration and inquiry and become mere didactic aids—"what to do in lieu of a worksheet."

The prepared environment itself may then become for us an elaborate bit of educational technology, full as it is of ingenious and efficacious educational devices. We may begin to buy into metrics related to "quantity of learning" instead of observing broadly the development of the whole child.

In this world of educational technique, a phantasmagoria of problems arises, all connected to the children's perverse insistence on being whole children and not merely "learners." We begin to look for ways to force the children to be learners, and, tragically, we may miss what they are actually revealing to us. The circle of ironies is then complete, since it is precisely through Dr. Montessori's willingness to let children be children and to deconstruct her own prejudices in light of the revelations they had for her that our work has its roots!

The spirit of Montessori is then lost to the world as we join the ranks of educators who are conditioned not to see the environment as something to prepare for the children but the children as something to prepare for the environment. Whether we call that environment "the next grade" or "the next Plane" is of little significance.

Learning Is Not a Role

We can see the tautological nature of the psycho-educational concept of "learner" when we recognize (with educational philosopher Frank Smith) that *children are always learning.*

Learning is not a role, not something that human beings switch on and off, not a choice. Rather, it is a name for a necessary relationship between a conscious organism and its world. It refers specifically to the changes that organism and the world create in each other by virtue of their relationship of mutual information exchange.

The question then is never "Are the children learning?" but "*What* are the children learning?" and "To what extent can I influence the direction of that learning?"

The answer to this question of influence is sometimes "Not at all," and often "Probably to some extent, but in ways I cannot predict." This reality of the prepared environment is a far cry from the conventional fantasy of a deterministic world of efficacious educational technology and measurable inputs and outputs.

As Sir Ken Robinson puts it, "Life is not linear; it's organic. We create our lives symbiotically as we explore our talents in relation to the circumstances they helped to create for us." This is what is to be discovered and rediscovered in the Montessori elementary, and it is a fine metaphor to live by.

So, Dr. Montessori's poetic mode of expression may ultimately be the most helpful:

> Our care of the child should be governed, not by the desire to "make him learn things," but by the endeavor always to keep burning within him that light which is called the intelligence. (*AMM* vol. 1)

Structures for Spontaneous, Intelligent Activity

But what sort of environment encourages and enables "that light which is called the intelligence" to burn brightly within the child?

One necessary element is the presence of a guide who holds the conceptual structure of the Montessori intellectual disciplines and their Key Lessons firmly in mind for the community of children. Such a guide can work flexibly, accepting opportunities where they arise and creating them where they do not.

Yet, there is more to the environment than the well-ordered physical space and the well-prepared guide with their structure and their frameworks for interpreting what they observe in the community of children. There is also the culture of the community, tended and built over years by the guide and children working together.

Of this much has been said over the decades and much is yet to be said, but in the works of Frank Smith and Daniel Pink, two creative and provocative non-Montessori thinkers, I have found two ways of thinking about the role of structure in the prepared environment that help me avoid thinking of myself as a "teacher" and the children as "learners" or "students."

Frank Smith's "Clubs" Metaphor

Frank Smith, in *The Book of Learning and Forgetting*, presents a view of learning that I found to be an invaluable complement to the structure of my Montessori elementary training. Smith argues that what we often refer to as "traditional education" is anything but traditional—tradition being properly reserved as a description for something more than 150 years old. He calls this innovation in education of the nineteenth and twentieth centuries "the official theory" and contrasts it with the truly "traditional" way of learning that had been a part of human experience and culture since time immemorial.

This truly traditional way of learning was to watch people do things that you would like to do and then to try those things out, perhaps with the more experienced person's help and advice. Certainly, in preliterate societies this has been the norm, and it continues to be the norm in contemporary non-literate societies. One thinks of certain cultural institutions that have served as environments for such learning, including the family business or farm, the master-apprentice system, and the trade guilds. However, most such learning happened and continues to happen outside even relatively relaxed structures such as these.

Once we have "left school" (conventional terminology for having finished our formal education) we often revert to the traditional method for further learning. For example, when as a new elementary guide I wanted to know more about telescopes and their uses and how to organize star parties for children, I did not just read books. I joined the Austin Astronomical Society, started going to their events, and gradually formed relationships with some of the members who were most knowledgeable and most willing to help a novice amateur astronomer.

Some of these individuals were professional astronomers or graduate students, others were just very experienced amateurs, and all of them taught me the same way: by showing and telling, letting me watch, letting me try things out under their supervision, and encouraging me to keep going.

You can probably think of many examples of similar learning situations in your own life. Here is one more: When you buy a new computer or software application or other piece of complex technology, do you make sure to thoroughly read the instruction manual before touching the device? Or do you fire it up and play around with it until you get stuck and have to look up something very specific in the manual? Or do you dispense with the manual altogether and instead get an experienced user to show you and tell you how it works?

Smith follows scenarios like my informal astronomy apprenticeship to their logical conclusions and says, metaphorically, that the traditional way of human learning is to join "clubs" full of people who have the knowledge we want and are willing to help us get it by showing, telling, and letting us try.

Keeper of the Clubs

Working in the prepared environment with the metaphor of clubs, I came to see my task as creating an environment in which it was natural, expected, encouraged, and frequent for children to join as many *metaphorical* clubs as they could during the three years they were with me: the math "club," the history "club," the camping "club," the biology "club," the cooking "club," the geometry "club," the essay "club," the acting "club," the chess "club" (there actually was an elementary Chess Club, but its only purpose was to help people join the chess "club" in Smith's sense), and many others.

I further saw it as my role to insure that each metaphorical club offered a wide variety of learning opportunities to its members, to establish a culture in which there was a palpable open invitation to join any club at any time, and to insure that visitors to any club were received with open arms, shown, told, and allowed to try.

It was also understood that "membership" in the "club" did not depend on attendance at every club meeting, that it was expected that people who were members of many clubs would sometimes spend more time with one club than with the other club, and that one rose in status in a club by offering help to newer or less experienced members.

Self-Image is Key

What makes this metaphor of joining clubs so powerful? For one thing, visitors and new members are motivated by their own interest and by being in the presence of those who know what they would like to know. One willingly places oneself in the hands of the master. Members set their own level of challenge and keep themselves interested by raising the bar at their own pace—and they know what is possible by watching the masters. The club does not see failure as personal but as part of the learning process, and it celebrates its members successes with them—the success of the individual redounds to the strength of the club.

Through much observation and reflection I came to see one more aspect of the club experience as perhaps the most important: One's self-image becomes intimately bound up with one's membership in various clubs. Children came to see themselves as "the sort of person who likes" whatever it is the club does. By the same token, if a child consistently refused invitations to visit or join a particular club, the reason almost invariably had to do with the child's self-image as "someone who doesn't like" or "someone who cannot do" what that club does.

But because of the culture of encouragement, the gregarious nature of the elementary child, and the wide variety of learning opportunities offered by each club, over time most children would happily join most clubs. This, in turn, would change their self-image.

Ultimately, the clubs metaphor works because, like Montessori education, it is rooted in the nature of human learning itself. Metaphors like these can help us understand our role as the stewards of prepared environments that provide structure that helps, not structure that hinders.

AMPs, the Energy of Learning

Daniel Pink, in his book *Drive: the Surprising Truth About What Motivates Us,* offers another way of thinking about the kind of environment that keeps the "light of intelligence" burning brightly in children. Unintentionally, he also provides another way of seeing why the club metaphor is so powerful.

Pink sets out to demolish a set of entrenched beliefs of corporate managers (and traditional educators) about what motivates people and how to motivate them if motivation seems lacking. Reviewing the research literature, he finds ample evidence that standard motivational strategies such as rewards, punishments, monetary incentives (including tying pay to performance), lavish praise, grades, rating and ranking, and so forth were not only ineffective motivators over the long term, but that they could actually cause lasting damage to an individual's ability to self-motivate—an ability that Pink sees as crucial to success in the contemporary world of work.

Pink writes:

> Ultimately, [intrinsically motivated] behavior depends on three nutrients: autonomy, mastery, and purpose. [This] behavior is self-directed. It is devoted to becoming better and better at something that matters. And it connects that quest for excellence to a larger purpose.

So, the three things Pink would have us look for in an environment in which children were motivated to join as many clubs as possible are autonomy, mastery, and purpose. With apologies to Mr. Pink for the pun, I would like to say that like electricity, the energy of learning is measured in AMPs!

Let us look at each of these three things in turn.

Autonomy

Autonomy in the context of the "club world" and the Montessori prepared environment is the opportunity and ability to choose and the opportunity and ability to choose how to choose. But what is chosen? What work to do at a given time; how long to do it; the scope of work (setting one's own level of challenge); the pace of work; the tools one uses; and how one evaluates the success of the endeavor.

If we accept that the energy of learning is measured in AMPs, we see that when we as teachers limit the autonomy of the child in any of these dimensions, we risk disconnecting them from the very things that would energize them for work. Yet, we Montessorians do offer structures for each of these dimensions. Is there a contradiction or paradox here?

I see the resolution in a more careful examination of the definition of autonomy as both the *opportunity* and the *ability* to choose in each dimension. This is also an insight of Dr. Montessori's, as when she defined obedience as comprising both the *will* and the *ability* to do what is asked of one. Our inclusion of autonomy in the design of the prepared environment involves many acts of restraint on our part as teachers who do not want to give unnecessary help, and our offering structure in each dimension of choice is to be seen only as *making it possible* for the child to exercise authentic autonomy. We offer the children structures that they can make their own and within which they can innovate, just as the musical world of the eighteenth century "offered" Beethoven the structure of the classical symphony within which he was able to innovate and express what could not have otherwise been expressed.

When we see in this pragmatic way the structures we employ for ourselves and that we offer to the children, we can hold them lightly and offer them lightly. We can "jam" in the manner of a good jazz group, improvising together to find what works in the moment, not hesitating to discard, or to at least temporarily set aside, the known to make room for the unknown that is trying timidly, or in an unexpected guise, to reveal itself to us. We can use structure as an aid to life, not a distortion or truncation of it.

With this attitude and way of working we can ensure that Albert Einstein's indictment of Prussian-inspired education will never be true of our schools:

> It is nothing short of a miracle that the modern methods of instruction have not yet entirely strangled the holy curiosity of inquiry; for this delicate little plant, aside from stimulation, stands mainly in need of freedom; without this it goes to wreck and ruin. It is a very grave mistake to think that the enjoyment of seeing and searching can be promoted by means of coercion and a sense of duty. ("Formative Years")

Mastery

As Dan Pink says, mastery is "getting better and better at something that matters." It is in the Second Plane of Development that we human beings first experience "mastery" as a conscious project with all of the elements of the adult experience of it.

The American psychologist Mihalyi Csikszentmihalyi is famous for his concept of "flow," and Montessorians have rightly seen flow as a contemporary name for what Dr. Montessori described as "concentrated work," with all its unique capacities for transformation of the worker's cognitive abilities, character, emotional regulation and all the rest. What we may not know is that Csikszentmihalyi's original term for flow was "autotelic experience." "Auto," meaning "self" and "telic," meaning "purposeful." Autotelic activity is activity that is its own reward, activity that, although it may produce a tangible result, does not depend for its meaning or enjoyment on that result.

It is in the context of autotelic experience that we should understand the so-called Human Tendencies that are so central to our pedagogical theory. Working? Repeating? Perfecting? Being exact? Manipulating? Controlling oneself? Yes, all these, all directed toward mastery via autotelic experience.

In the Second Plane, we also see the coming to consciousness of moral concerns. Understanding right and wrong and one's own relationship to each are major projects of the second-plane child. Understanding who one is in the community of one's peers begins in the elementary and extends into adolescence. And what do we see time and time again, both in the classroom and in our own personal lives? That we discover who we are by forgetting ourselves in meaningful work.

It is vital that children in our care regularly have flow experiences and that they grow over time in their self-awareness of these flow experiences and in their ability to create such experiences for themselves. Nevertheless, this is clearly a case of "helping them do it themselves"— helping children find a path to flow in whatever they do. The structures we provide must be ladders of a sort that can easily be discarded once the child has climbed up.

Csikszentmihalyi, Montessori, Pink, and Lev Vygotsky all agree that the greatest developmental aid we can give our children is to help them find meaningful things to do that are not too easy and not too hard—tasks in the "sweet spot" that Vygotsky somewhat ponderously called the Zone of Proximal Development. Here is Daniel Pink on the subject:

One source of frustration in the workplace is the frequent mismatch between what people *must* do and what people *can* do. When what they must do exceeds their capabilities, the result is anxiety. When what they must do falls short of their capabilities, the result is boredom. (Indeed Csikszentmihalyi titled his first book on autotelic experiences *Beyond Boredom and Anxiety*.) But when the match is just right, the results can be glorious. This is the essence of flow.

Most of our encounters with the child, then, are either for the purpose of arousing interest and engagement with a new topic or for the purpose of providing intellectual tools and resources that the engaged child will need on their journey of exploration. Dr. Montessori wrote:

> We are trying to arouse the child's interest. Should we fail to arouse it immediately, we must still trust the same principle while we make our presentations in a specific environment and await the reaction. If the enthusiasm is not shown, we do not delay but pass on. If the enthusiasm is shown, we have apparently opened a door. We are at the beginning of a long road, along which we will travel with the child. (*FCA*)

Dr. Montessori's brilliant insight was that this crucial setting of the bar between "too hard" (frustration) and "too easy" (boredom) could be entrusted to the children to do for themselves *if* they were genuinely engaged and *if* the materials they were given were properly constructed. The beautiful sequences of activities with, for example, the Trinomial Cube, or the Constructive Triangles, or the Tone Bars are exemplars of the sort of liberating structure we can hope to create as we travel along with the child in their explorations of things not so well mapped out for us as the Trinomial Cube.

Purpose

To create a context in which the energy of learning flows freely, we need a third ingredient: purpose. To Pink, purpose means knowing that one's work contributes to something of value beyond oneself. Having a sense of purpose, in this sense, keeps the search for flow from becoming narcissistic and constrained by the limits of one's current set of likes and dislikes. Purpose leads us to look for flow in areas where we would not otherwise venture.

The Montessori elementary is the perfect place for children to learn with purpose. The culture of the community gives ample opportunity for these newly social children to begin to experience themselves and define themselves as servant-leaders, to contribute to something larger than themselves, but not so large as to obscure the consequences to the community of individuals' actions and decisions.

The help the children give each other becomes for them a form of enlightened self-interest as they see themselves learning and relearning past lessons through the eyes of their beneficiaries. Tasks that would not normally attract them take on new value and meaning when accepted on behalf of the community of their peers.

Nevertheless, it must also be said that, unlike the adult business managers who are Daniel Pink's primary audience, for our elementary children, self-construction is a legitimate and ever-present purpose. This is the purpose which has always driven them and will continue to drive them through the Second Plane and into the Third Plane. Indeed, the elementary child's self-construction is an invaluable form of service not only to the proximal community, but to the future of humanity—and the elementary child can come to a consciousness of that with only a little help from us.

These elementary children are increasingly capable, through their growing powers of imagination and abstraction, of setting big goals for themselves and for each other. What they need from us is the provision of practical tools for scoping, planning, resourcing, and organizing their efforts. We often find ourselves acting as project management consultants to the children's projects.

There is another aspect of the Montessori classroom that I think speaks to the issue of purpose in learning. Montessori said that the first thing the elementary teacher must do, the preparation out of which everything else in the work flows, is to fall in love with the universe. She modeled that love so well for us, and we can model it for the children.

Conclusion

As we return again and again to consider the dialectic of structure and freedom in our work, we pledge ourselves not to surrender to the cultural and historical forces that would have us approach our work as technicians implementing a method full of deadening structure. Instead, we will approach our work as lovers of the universe travelling again and again the long path of organic human development with each new child that comes to us, ready to offer help in the form of structure where structure is needed, holding our structures lightly and provisionally, ready to reinvent, to adapt, to improvise where the needs of the child dictate.

Our passionate love of the universe will not be a vacillating, half-hearted, or fair-weather love, but it will be a love that inspires in us a vigorous and joyous pursuit of knowledge, for as Dr. Montessori, Albert Joosten, and many sages throughout time have acknowledged, true love comes only from deeply understanding that which is loved. Therefore, we will passionately pursue knowledge, and we will hold in mind as a kind of trust for the children all the beautiful structure that the children have yet to discover in the universe, even while we stand aside to let them discover it—and their discoveries will be our greatest joy and our most profound source of energy for mastery of our chosen work.

We will come to a deeper and deeper knowledge of ourselves, our children, our materials, our purpose, and we will therefore come to understand the many uses of structure-in-context—the function and fit of each potential learning encounter in the prepared environment. We will skillfully select and use a range of metaphors to guide our own work with the children, and we will remain alert and receptive to new ways of thinking about and structuring experience that may come to us from other disciplines and, indeed, other cultures.

In this way we will prepare an environment that is a generous source of aesthetic, captivating, autotelic learning encounters for our children. In this way, we will continue to develop well into the future the work of art and science that is Dr. Montessori's legacy, that monumental structure that in the whole and in its many contextualized parts—our classrooms—serves the cause of authentic freedom. ❖

Four Ways of Learning: An Explanatory Framework

||||||||||||||||||||||||||||||||||||||||||||||||||||||||||||||||||||||||||||||||||||||||||||||||||||||||||||||||||||||||||||

To partner effectively with parents, we must be able to explain the principles and practices of Montessori education to them in terms that they can understand from their own typically non-Montessori experience. This essay presents one approach that I have employed successfully over the years.

All of us who guide Montessori classrooms are frequently called upon to justify our very unusual methods to those whose ideas about education have been shaped by conventional schooling. Often we lead off with our Montessori theory, and often our dialogue partners hear only confusing jargon: prepared environment, auto-didactic materials, three-hour work period, Cosmic Education, practical life, control of error, sensorial materials, sensitive periods, Planes of Development, Human Tendencies, engrams, psychological characteristics, spiritual embryo, inner guide, even (heaven forbid!) *mneme* and *horme*.

All of these ideas which Maria Montessori appropriated or invented to explain her work to a curious world are still useful concepts among Montessorians, yet our unthinking use of them can actually serve to wall ourselves off from the surrounding culture even as we endeavor to build new bridges of understanding.

Another more difficult, yet more rewarding, approach is to reinterpret some of these ideas in light of current research and contemporary language. For example, the work of Kevin Rathunde and Mihaly Czikszentmihalyi on "flow" has given us new ways to talk about the central role of concentration in the development of the psyche.

Another non-Montessori thinker whose books offer us a different way of explaining our work is Frank Smith, a psycholinguist who taught and researched at the University of Toronto, the Ontario Center for Studies in Education, the University of Witwatersrand, South Africa, and elsewhere. A novelist and journalist before he was a professor, Smith writes about teaching and learning with precise, straightforward language and a keen instinct for what is important in the learner's experience. I have incorporated many of his metaphors and explanations into my own talks with parents and others to whom I need to explain my Montessori practice.

In his beautifully written, deeply thoughtful book *The Book of Learning and Forgetting*, he introduces the very helpful language "forgettable learning" and "unforgettable learning" (or "permanent learning"). I have incorporated this language into a simple four-part framework that speaks directly to every listener's personal experience of learning. It is one strategy I use to help parents think about Montessori education without resorting to Montessori jargon. Here is my explanatory strategy.

Imagine a two by two grid titled "Four Ways of Learning." The columns are labeled "Forgettable" and "Unforgettable"; the rows are "Painful" and "Pleasurable." Into these four quadrants, one can place just about any learning experience, and the crux of the approach is to interactively fill in the grid with examples drawn from the audience's experience.

	Forgettable	Unforgettable
Painful		
Pleasurable		

The facilitated discussion proceeds through six major steps:

1. Enumerate the educational, developmental outcomes we seek in Montessori.

2. Display the "Ways of Learning" grid and discuss each quadrant, working interactively with the audience to find examples of each from their personal experience.

3. Identify the "pleasurable, unforgettable learning" quadrant as the "home base" for Montessori learning.

4. Outline the tools we have as Montessorians for helping children stay near "home base." These include the Human Tendencies, choice (intrinsic motivation), and the psychological characteristics of the age, all of which help us create a classroom full of experiences that lead to pleasurable, unforgettable learning and the achievement of our desired outcomes.

5. List (and discuss as time permits) some of the methods of conventional education that conflict with our goals, largely because they lead away from pleasurable, unforgettable learning. Examples include assignments, rating and ranking, rewards and punishments, traditional testing, predetermined lockstep curricula, and age-segregated classrooms.

6. If I am talking to parents, I wrap up by discussing how the home environment can either support or undermine the way the children work in the classroom.

With that process in mind, let us look more closely at the content of some of the steps.

Step One: Our Montessori Goals

In Montessori we look for certain characteristics in a healthy, well-functioning learning community and in each individual in that community.

We want to see *enthusiastic learning*. Whether the children are quiet and deeply engrossed in work or actively exploring and discussing together, there should be an aura of happy, spontaneous expression of their natural drive to learn.

We know, both from classroom experience and from decades of educational research, that this kind of learning only comes about when the learner is *intrinsically motivated*.

We want to see children developing at their own pace on all fronts: strengthening *concentration*, gaining *self-confidence* to take on greater challenges, developing *perseverance*, increasing *self-knowledge*, gaining *knowledge in all areas* while exploring deeply and joyfully in some areas.

We want to see children growing in the knowledge and practice of *social relationships* and the *morality* that is rooted in community living.

Step Two: Four Ways of Learning

Sometimes we wonder aloud if our children are "learning anything." In fact, both we and our children are always learning. Short of extreme situations of deprivation and abuse, it is impossible to keep a child from learning. Learning is what a human mind does whenever it is awake and encountering the world.

The question is *what* is being learned—and learning is always happening on different levels, which we sometimes refer to as "cognition" (thinking and learning) and "meta-cognition" (thinking about thinking and learning about learning).

Most of our learning is *forgettable*, and that's both natural and fortunate. We learn things, use them while there is a need and then let them go. I remember my own phone number; I remember my office phone number as long as I work there; but I don't try to remember every phone number I dial.

However, our most important learning is *unforgettable* or *permanent* learning—learning that becomes a part of who we are, learning that "sticks with us" even when we have no immediate need for that skill or knowledge. My one-hundred-year-old grandmother can still remember precise details of her childhood experience, even though her present circumstances and needs are completely different.

A moment's reflection on a list of one's unforgettable learning will reveal that invariably this learning is attached to some strong emotion or feeling. This connection between the "cognitive" or thinking mind and the "affective" or feeling mind is well known to all good teachers (and brain researchers). Various educational reformers have attempted to codify and capitalize on this connection, as in the "confluent learning" movement of the 1970s and 1980s. In ways that we will see later, the Montessori classroom is a place in which the connection between thinking and feeling arises constantly and naturally in the children's work.

When it comes to the permanence of learning, it does not seem to matter whether the associated emotion is painful or pleasurable. This leads us to four possibilities: painful forgettable learning, pleasurable forgettable learning, painful unforgettable learning, and pleasurable unforgettable learning.

If all painful learning were unforgettable, we would presumably never make the same bad mistake twice. Whatever the case, for designers of an educational system it would be nonsensical to employ painful means to force learning that will soon be forgotten anyway. Yet, this seems to happen in many educational settings.

I suspect that painful learning becomes forgettable when the meta-cognitive learning is painful and the content learning is eminently forgettable. So, a child who is learning multiplication tables under duress may be learning a number of things: (1) multiplication tables, (2) that they hate math, (3) that they hate the teacher, (4) that learning is something they must be forced to do, and so on. They may still forget their multiplication tables, but what they learned about learning may be near permanent.

And what if they do remember their multiplication tables? Then we have painful unforgettable learning, in the same category with learning not to pick up a hot frying pan with your bare hand or remembering where you were when you first heard about the destruction of the World Trade Center or the assassination of John Kennedy.

Sadly, this is about the best that one can hope for in a school system based on coercion, fear, and punishment. The incremental improvements in academic performance that can be measured by standardized testing comes at the cost of much permanent negative meta-cognitive learning that will only show up decades later as a spectrum of societal and individual ill-being.

As Montessori said of the conventional schools she knew, "Study such as it is today, is a work against nature, so the students carry it out aridly and under compulsion without animation. [...] Other needs exist, which if not satisfied always cause inner conflicts that influence the mental state and confuse the clarity of the mind" (*FCA*).

In a classroom where learning is routinely pleasurable, its permanence or impermanence will be dictated by the child's perceived need for it and for its usefulness to the child's own purposes. This is why Montessori spoke of a good education as an "aid to life" and worked to make her schools just that—relevant to the child's life as it currently was and as it soon could be. In Montessori, there is little space for "memorizing it now because you might need it when you grow up." However true such an adult need may be, if the learning does not connect with the child as they presently are, it will very likely be impermanent. This is not the perversity of the child, but the nature of human learning.

It is the fourth possibility—pleasurable unforgettable learning—that is "home base" for the Montessori classroom. This is not so much because Montessori guides tend to be kind people (we do!) but because we know that this is the only way that we can successfully educate on both the content and meta-cognitive levels. That is, it is the only way to help children learn both what they need to know to function in our society and to simultaneously develop positive, healthy attitudes about learning, community, and their own abilities.

Pleasurable, unforgettable learning is what stands behind Montessori's famous claim that graduates of her elementary schools would know "at least as much as the finished High School product of several years' seniority" and that, most importantly, this learning would have been "at no cost of pain or distortion to body or mind" (*TEHP*).

Step Three: Tools for Unforgettable Learning

By the end of her career, Montessori was able to see that one of the keys to the success of her methods was that in her classrooms children were given the freedoms they needed to express the basic tendencies or characteristics of the healthy human of any age or race. Among these *Human Tendencies* are the tendency to explore; to orient oneself physically, temporally, and socially; to create order; to imagine; to think conceptually and abstractly; to move, use one's hands, and work; to perfect a skill through repetition and to find one's own errors along the way; to freely communicate with others; to belong; and to create meaning through symbols and rituals.

Montessori guides are trained to see all the children's activity as expressions of such universal tendencies, and the Human Tendencies are also our guide for furnishing the classroom environment with a rich assortment of activities and materials.

Along with the Human Tendencies, each age group displays certain physical, psychological, and cognitive characteristics distinct from those of younger and older groups. For example, the elementary child is gregarious, imaginative, independent, fascinated by extremes, worshipful of heroes, interested in questions of morality, and developing greater capacity for responsibility and abstract thinking. Montessori guides use their knowledge of these characteristics to help elementary children create the personal emotional connection with their studies that results in unforgettable learning.

Universal tendencies and characteristics of age groups aside, every child is a unique package of abilities, propensities, and energies. The Montessori way of working with children allows and, indeed, requires the adult to get to know each child's personal idiosyncrasies and to work with them as they really are, not as we imagine them to be or statistically predict them to be. In particular, for learning to be pleasurable and unforgettable, children must work at their own pace, with allowances for their personal social maturity, their personal cognitive strengths and weaknesses, their relative need for closure, and their personal history.

If you are, as I am, often astonished by the wisdom of Maria Montessori, it is perhaps only a vindication of Emerson's observation that "Nothing astonishes men so much as common sense and plain dealing." ❖

Developing
Spiritual Order through
Responsibility to a Community

||||||||||||||||||||||||||||||||||||||||||||||||||||||||||||||||||||||||||||||||||||||||||||||||||||||||||||||||||||||||||||||||||||||||||||||||||||

Although this article predates the article on structure and freedom in this volume, it can be seen as an exploration into another area where the relationship between structure and freedom must be understood, namely, what is termed "classroom management" in adult-centered methods of education. For the Montessori elementary guide, the question is how to help the children build a just, orderly community in a way that respects the psychological and moral characteristics of the Second Plane.

In *The Advanced Montessori Method,* Dr. Montessori sets out a list of things to look for in the behavior of the child that to her signal "the evolution of spiritual order" (vol. 1). They are, in essence, the desired outcomes of Montessori education. She divides them into three clusters: behaviors related to the child's work, behaviors related to the child's conduct, and behaviors related to the child's obedience to the adults in the environment.

Within the cluster related to work, the looked-for behaviors can be summarized as regular engagement in concentrated work and the display of enthusiasm or joy in the act of work.

With regard to conduct, one is primarily looking for correlations between periods of concentrated, joyful work and orderly behavior. One is also looking for altruistic or pro-social behavior ("the part the child takes in the development of his companions").

Spiritual order increases in the child when he or she moves from one level of obedience to another until finally the child "obeys eagerly and joyously." One also looks for correlations between improvements in work, conduct, and obedience.

Establishing an Orderly Environment

It is the adult's role to prepare an environment for the child in which their inner order and outer manifestations of inner order can evolve along the lines laid out by Montessori. Part of this preparation involves the physical provision of the classroom, and another equally important part involves the establishment of a secure, healthy social environment in which the child can thrive. What does this entail?

In my work with nine- to twelve-year-olds, I prefer not to use the language of "rules" or its euphemistic cousin "guidelines." Instead I use the language of *responsibility, community,* and *purpose.* In the 9–12 class, even more so than in the 6–9 class, an important part of the work in which the child should be actively and passionately engaged is to use the reasoning mind to probe, analyze, and comprehend both concretely and abstractly the concept and practice of responsible participation in a purposeful community. I want to establish a community of learning, and the relation I wish the individual to have to this community is one of participation and care, not rule following.

The approach begins with the axioms that we as a class constitute a community, and that our class community is part of a larger school community. Moreover, we are not a community merely thrown together by an accident of birth or geography; we are instead a community that comes together for certain *purposes.*

The *purposes* of the community are these:

- To support all of its members in learning;

- to support all of its members in developing moral character;

- and to continue far into the future (beyond the tenure of its present members).

The community operates to realize its purposes according to two *beliefs*:

- People learn and develop best when they have freedom of choice, freedom of movement, freedom to communicate, freedom to find and correct their own errors, and freedom to explore.

- Freedom must always be in balance with responsibility.

The *responsibilities* which all members of the community have for the community are:

- To advance the purposes of the community;

- to abide by the customs and decisions of the classroom community and of the school community as a whole;

- and to question the customs of the community when they seem to be causing suffering or injustice or when they seem to conflict with the purposes of the community.

The Evolution of Spiritual Order in an Orderly Environment

This framework, understood and shared by the community, creates an orderly environment in which individuals can develop what Montessori called "spiritual order" and what we might call "psycho-spiritual order." Behaviors that tend to foster an environment of concentrated, joyful work, self-control, compassionate action on behalf of others, and cooperation with legitimate authority are tied directly to the shared purposes and responsibilities. Conversely, behaviors that obstruct one's own learning or that of others, behaviors that violate the morality of the community, and behaviors that harm the physical or social environment are in conflict with the specific purposes, beliefs, and responsibilities of the community. In those cases, the adult plays an important role in helping the child to see how their behavior is in conflict with the purposes or fails to honor one or more of the responsibilities. Over time, the child can do more and more of this sort of analysis for themselves; this is the development of consciousness and moral reasoning. It is another dimension of independence, leading to more personal power and the readiness to accept more freedom and responsibility.

This framework makes visible the responsibility the children have for making the community work smoothly and for addressing problems that come up in the community. This level of responsibility is possible because the children have the freedom to act on behalf of themselves and others. Conversely, the level of freedom in the classroom is kept in balance with the children's ability to use it responsibly, *as demonstrated by the best efforts of the children.*

Montessori writes in *The Advanced Montessori Method*, "*freedom in intellectual work* is found to *be the basis of internal discipline*" (vol. 1). This is also the thinking behind the framework of purposes and responsibilities. Instead of a list of rules to be followed, there is a list of purposes to be advanced, and the chief of these is to support all members of the community in their intellectual work. The underlying belief is that if the children are joyfully working, the disorderly behaviors that appear to require rules and sanctions will simply not be frequent enough to warrant them.

The framework intends to form the habit in the children of looking to and relying on each other for help. It also speaks of the responsibility that each has for all and that all have for each. It understands that living out these purposes may stretch the community's abilities and patience in surprising and unpredictable ways as the community struggles to aid and assimilate certain children who have immense difficulties developing psycho-spiritual order.

Montessori often makes the point in her discussions of obedience that a child who does not yet have the physical and intellectual abilities necessary for obedience cannot properly be said to be disobedient. Although I would not argue that none exist, I have yet to meet a nine-year-old that did not have the ability to obey. For the nine-to-twelve age group, cooperation and obedience are closely tied to understanding and moral reasoning. The framework reflects the belief that children of this age often need to know the reasons behind what they are being asked to do and that most of them cheerfully obey adults who are willing to take their questions seriously, even as they resist adults who expect to be obeyed simply by virtue of their adulthood. In the case that a child believes a command to be unjust or unreasonable, the worst thing is for the child to silently obey. The alternative provided by the framework is for the child to question the command. Then there can be a discussion in which either the child comes to understand the command to be just and reasonable (although not necessarily pleasant), or the adult comes to understand that the command was indeed unjust or unreasonable. Both outcomes are positive for the community.

Living purposefully and responsibly requires more creativity than following rules. For nine- to twelve-year-olds, it specifically (although unbeknownst to them) challenges them to stretch into the next level of moral reasoning and development, to go beyond the rule-based morality which is their natural comfort zone (as described by moral development theorist Lawrence Kohlberg and his followers). It invites them to put their energy and formidable mental abilities into creating something strong and beautiful, instead of into finding and exploiting loopholes in a legal system.

It is important to the success of such a framework that children understand what they do and do not have the power to change about the framework. In this case, the purposes cannot be changed since they are the purposes of a school. Likewise, the beliefs cannot be changed because they are part of what makes the school a *Montessori* school. The responsibilities are open to discussion but are not easily changed since they are the logical and pragmatic consequences of attempting to be a Montessori community. What is open to debate and revision are those lower level procedures and norms that the framework calls "customs." In practice, children frequently *are* in a position to see flaws in these that the teacher cannot see. Here, there are wonderful opportunities to learn from the children—another way to "follow the child." ❖

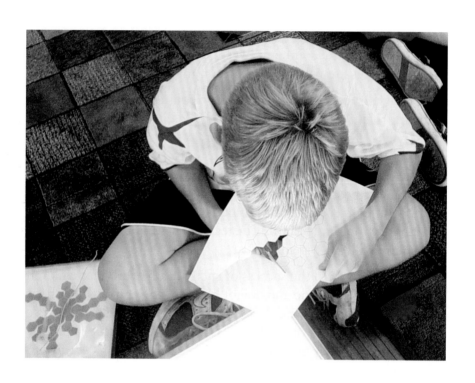

On Criteria for Evaluation

||||||||||||||||||||||||||||||||||||||||||||||||||||||||||||||||||||||||||||||||||||||||||||||||||||||||||||||||||||||||||||||||||||||||||||||||

An elementary colleague at another school wrote to say that he had been given the task of designing objective criteria by which he would measure his students' progress. He said he thought he would keep it as vague as possible. Here is my response.

I very much like the advice to keep it "as vague as possible." Whenever I tried making performance criteria more specific, I found I ended up limiting my own practice and the development of the children. Even worse, in any kind of objective-based specific evaluation system, I found that there is an almost irresistible gravitational pull toward choosing specifics that can be easily measured—which is not only a very different exercise than choosing what really matters, but actually irrelevant to the overall goal of optimizing children's development.

Nobody wants to hear this, but evaluation of any kind is much less important that we usually think. What's important is understanding the complete arc of human development and having unshakable confidence that if we remove what we without a doubt know are the big obstacles in the child's developmental environment, children will not deviate from it. In short, I believe that there should be constant, serious evaluation going on, but it should be evaluation of our practices as teachers, not of the children's performance vis-à-vis some predetermined curricular rubric.

Having said that, here are the two approaches to "criteria" with which I had the most success. Both were, in a sense, given to me in training and not something I had to invent. I did have to mature in my practice to the point where I could actually hear what my trainers had said, but when the time came I found it was all there waiting for me. Both approaches rely on Montessori's idea of "Human Tendencies."

First, I learned to love this quote from *The Advanced Montessori Method*:

> Our care of the child should be governed, not by the desire "to make him learn things" but by the endeavor always to keep burning within him that light which is called the intelligence. (vol. 1)

When this really sunk in, I stopped worrying about whether or not all my twelve-year-olds could remember the formula for the lateral surface area of a sphere, for example, and started focusing more on whether or not they could figure it out for themselves when they could not remember it.

"Intelligence" is something worth paying careful attention to; the minutiae of objective-based instruction really are not. I also found it useful to contemplate (and I still do) what intelligence actually is, what it looks like, how it shows up in various contexts. The more I looked at it, the more it started looking like context-dependent synergistic manifestations of the Human Tendencies all working together like a well-oiled machine. So, I would suggest that at a first approximation looking for the Human Tendencies—not in isolation, but as an integrated system—is a good way to spot intelligence. And intelligence is a good star to steer by.

Another thing I noticed along the way is that intelligence is inherently creative. In human beings, the two cannot be separated. One vague but very fruitful criterion for me was: are the children (is this child) regularly surprising me? Authentic development of the mind has that quality at any age. Am I regularly having to revise my view of the child's capabilities and rethink what I thought were their limits? If so, we are both on track. If not, one or more of us is off track and the default assumption is that that it is I—at least that's where I would start the analysis. Usually, the problem was that there was something about the child I was not understanding. So, if anything I did for the child helped, it was purely accidental. More often, it didn't help or even made things worse—like treating hypothermia with ice packs.

This meant I also had to learn better how to observe. If I was not being surprised, I had to ask whether it was because there was nothing surprising to observe or because my own observational skills were too dull or two rigidified to see it. Of course, the nature of that question is that it cannot be definitively answered by the same mind that asked it, but I do think asking it creates a certain positive pressure toward growth.

The second approach to evaluation that helped me stay centered without creating problems for the children was to spend a good deal of time thinking through what manifestations of the Human Tendencies would look like in each of the album disciplines. That is, I tried to develop and mentally rehearse specific scenarios involving each Human Tendency in each discipline and sub-discipline. Also, I asked what are the functions of each Human Tendency in each discipline—because, I think, different disciplines recruit the Human Tendencies in different ways and in different proportions.

For example, "abstracting" in geometry has a different form and flavor than "abstracting" in reading, music, art, history, or the natural sciences. I find it most useful to spend time thinking about the tendencies that are not normally associated with a certain discipline; e.g., how does "abstracting" function in the world of dance or sport? Or consider "communicating" in the world of mathematics or logic—very different from in the world of debate or poetry, but no less critical.

This kind of intentional reflection broadened my categories and helped me see Human Tendencies happening around me that I had not seen before. It also helped me understand why they were not happening in a given discipline for a given child.

In any case, I found I had more success and was a happier guide when I thought of myself not as "helping Susie with long division" but as "removing obstacles and/or shoring up support for Susie to joyfully reconnect with her innate ability to explore, repeat, abstract, and work exactly" in the domain of basic number operations. It really does have quite a different feel and leads to sets of quite different interactions and partnerships with the child. Sometimes all it took was for Susie to see that I genuinely saw in her those innate abilities and that I was quietly but unshakably confident that she, perhaps with my help, would be able to connect to them and surprise herself with how intelligent and capable she was in this area. Sometimes it took more careful, step-by-step explorations and experiments for us to find the key that worked for her. Always it involved a change in how the child viewed themselves and a deepening of my understanding of them both as an individual and as a representative of the species that exhibits Human Tendencies.

Ultimately, I think that's what one is looking for—deeper understanding between two human beings—and the way one approaches criteria of evaluation can either lead to that or to something that masquerades as that but is actually only the projection of more or less arbitrary mental permutations of sterile, preconceived notions having little to do with reality and even less to do with keeping alive the light of intelligence.

P. S. Although we usually talk about the Human Tendencies as nouns (abstraction, order, communication, etc.), I've come to think that's a nasty trick of the English language that helps us miss an important point; namely, that one cannot peer into the head of another and see a "quality" or "property" or "characteristic" called, say, Abstraction. The Human Tendencies never show up as nouns. One can only observe them in behavior; that is, as a process, as action. Look as hard as you like, you will never see Exploration; you will only see exploring. So, it is really helpful to think of all the Human Tendencies as verbs: exploring, ordering, abstracting, communicating, repeating, working, exacting, et cetera. This may seem like a minor point, but I don't think so. It's the difference between looking for what can be observed versus entertaining a theory about human psychology or nature. ❖

Working without Specialists Works for Children

‖‖‖

I have had both the opportunity to teach at a school that has for almost fifty years held firmly to the principle of not using specialists or scheduling parts of the work period for special subjects and the opportunity to visit and observe in schools that do use specialists. The title of this article has already telegraphed my conclusions. The article was written in 2009, when the economic downturn was threatening the viability of many of our tuition-based schools.

In this time of economic contraction and uncertainty, school administrators and boards are confronting difficult decisions. If we must cut back, what part of our program will we sacrifice? If we, as private school administrators, discontinue the special enrichment programs that seem to attract families to our school, will we further endanger our already shaky enrollment? If we, as public school administrators, must plan for shrinking local and state revenues, where will we find cost savings in our already lean budgets? It looks like "back to basics" once again.

Although I have never weathered an economic storm quite like the one we are in, my life experience and my ingrained Montessori optimism tell me to look for the silver lining, even as the clouds continue to gather. Times of adversity can also be times of focusing one's energies, clarifying one's principles, and deeply examining questionable habits that have taken root when times were easier.

This refocusing, I believe, is one way to reframe for our parent community and ourselves the loss of program specialists in our schools. Losing the foreign language specialists, the art, drama and music specialists, or the dance and P.E. specialists does not have to mean the loss of those subjects and experiences from our classrooms and the lives of our children. Times when my class and I have had to "do for ourselves or do without" have usually been the times when the children (and I) have discovered a new depth of creativity and independence in each other.

From my experience, I see four reasons why working without specialists—letting the classroom guides learn to present all areas of knowledge to the children—will not only decrease costs but actually improve the children's educational experience.

1. Uninterrupted work periods foster flow. "Flow" is the modern psychological word for the timeless, "in the zone", concentration that Montessori observed when children were given uninterrupted time to work on things of their own choice. She strongly believed that it was these regular episodes of "flow" that were responsible for the amazing transformations that she saw in her children. Non-Montessori psychologists Mihaly Czikszentmihalyi and Kevin Rathunde discovered the Montessori movement precisely because they were looking for educational environments that fostered flow. In contrast, fragmenting work periods with scheduled specialist time disrupts flow. When I talk to parents about the importance of the uninterrupted work period, I appeal to parents' own experience of work. When do they feel best about their work, most fulfilled, happiest? Is it when they can find uninterrupted time to get into flow, or when their time is fragmented by meetings, interruptions, and other things in their calendar over which they have no control?

2. Working without specialists allows us to reduce the number of difficult transitions children face. One of the best things that adults can do for the children with whom they live and work is to become aware of children's experience of transitions from one activity to the next, one environment to the next, one adult to the next. For good developmental reasons, transitions are more difficult for children than for many adults (although many adults also have problems with transitions—perhaps this is related to our Human Tendency for orientation). Our most vulnerable, developmentally struggling children are precisely the ones that have the most trouble with transitions. These children in particular will spend most of the hour or so of specialty time just trying to cope with the transition; they could learn more about the subject staying in the organic flow of the prepared environment than they can in a "pull out." If the parents of these special "weathervane" children understood the issue of transitions and how their vulnerable children are affected, they could potentially become a strong anti-specialist voice within the parent community. There are unavoidable transitions throughout the school day—arrival, lunch, outdoor time, departure, interruptions for lessons, and changes of work or activity. This is plenty for the children to handle; creating artificial transitions is unhelpful to the children (and the guide!), and one has to ask, "Is this really necessary?"

3. When we work without specialists, children get to make their learning their own and integrate it with their other classroom explorations. Mandatory specialist-based programs are work choices made by adults, not children. They may deprive the children of an opportunity to "own" their learning and encourage them to think of cultural and self-expression as separate compartments of knowledge more like "hobbies" than integral parts of what it means to be human. Unless working with specialists is offered as an invitation which the children may decline without negative consequences, and unless the specialist has Montessori training and knows how to support auto-education by preparing an environment, linking the children's own explorations to it, and standing back, specialist time is time away from Montessori and the main benefits of Montessori education. We cannot have Cosmic Education when various parts of the cosmos are missing from the education. All subjects need to be in the same room, organically related to everything else in the room. Only then can the guide model what it means to be a cosmically educated human being, one that need not be fluent in all areas but joyfully exploring all areas along with the rest of the learning community. When we simply hand off this or that subject to experts, we are inviting the children to internalize the very epistemological split that is such a deep wound in our culture. We are encouraging them to see their own efforts as we are showing them we see our own: I'm not good enough to do this; that's for experts.

4. Working without specialists allows us to work in deep alignment with Montessori's discoveries and principles. Aside from the more mundane, concrete problems with specialty programs, there are deeper issues of philosophy. Reliance on specialists often proceeds from a deep misunderstanding of Montessori education. It is easy for a school and parent community to devolve into the perspective that Montessori is a superior, more efficient, perhaps more humane way to *teach*—a better way to deliver curriculum. The truth is that the Montessori elementary has no curriculum, so our work with the children cannot be seen as a better way to take children through it. I am using words very precisely here; we certainly do have lessons, and the choices about what we present and do not present constrain and guide the children's inquiry, but (as discussed in Part One of this book) we do not have a curriculum in the conventional sense. "Curriculum" and "course" come from the Latin *currere*, to run. The idea is that there is a set path or course that everyone moves along or through to reach the goal at the other end. That is precisely what we do not have. In the world of curriculum, it makes sense to cordon off periods of time for each subject and to have specialists who can skillfully manage the academic obstacle course and coach people through it. In contrast, Dr. Montessori presents our work as taking children safely into a vast landscape of knowledge, where they are free to explore and blaze their own paths, guided by our prior knowledge of the territory and our accumulated experience of what parts of the terrain will likely appeal to children of their age. We focus on giving the children the tools they need in order to explore the world for themselves. The children are driven from within by the dual desires to learn all about the world and to become competent members of the culture in which they find themselves. If we want to offer them reading, we surround them with writing and the tools for writing and reading. If we want to offer them Spanish or art or music or math, we surround them with those things, give them the links they need, give the inspiration and encouragement they may need, and leave the rest to them.

For these and other reasons, I believe that the best way to use specialists is to make them resource people and consultants to the classroom guides. Guides without formal training in music, foreign language, art, and other specialized areas, can benefit from tutoring and consultation with a specialist, and any associated costs are true investments because lasting value is being added as the guides learn.

At first, a guide's presentations in the specialty in question will not be as polished as either the specialist's presentations or as the guide's own presentations in other areas. This is usually more a problem for the guide than it is for the children. Elementary children love to work with adults who are vulnerable enough to let their own rough edges show, and they delight in and take inspiration from the adults' little successes and progress in learning. When we can join the children in their learning—join them where they live—then all of our lives are better. ❖

Bringing the World of Artistic Expression to the Child

This article began as a response to an email from a parent who had recently attended a presentation in which I spoke about "refinement" as one of the characteristics we look for and support in the children. She wondered if I was advocating cultural snobbishness or elitism. It was a wonderful opportunity to clarify both for her and for myself exactly what I did mean.

When I speak to parents who are just learning about the Montessori elementary, I sometimes tell them that there are many ways for children to learn "the three R's." To be sure, they will learn them in a very special way in the Montessori classroom, but it is not this sort of academic learning that makes Montessori education unique. I tell them that Montessori education is different because our children exhibit "the seven R's": they are resilient, responsible, resourceful, respectful, rational, refined, and ready—these are characteristics we look for and support in the children.

Parents readily understand and appreciate the importance of the seven R's, but sometimes I get questions about "refined." What does that actually mean? Is it really important? Does it imply some sort of cultural elitism or snobbishness? Good questions!

I maintain that refinement is an important goal of Montessori education, but we have to understand it properly. In the Primary, it is well understood that the children use the sensorial materials to refine their senses and to learn the words that describe various sensations. As children move into the Second Plane of Development, their work increasingly becomes less about the outside world and more about the inner world—the world of ideas, concepts, imagination, and reasoning.

Just as the elementary child loses his attraction to physical order and finds satisfaction in the ordering of ideas, the refinement of the senses that was so satisfying to him in earlier years now becomes refinement of experience, refinement of taste and judgment. The reasoning mind is less and less satisfied with merely liking or disliking things; it wants to understand and justify its judgments of experience. This is where the Montessori elementary prepared environment can be of great service to the child.

Bringing the World of Culture to the Child

Maria Montessori said that it was the job of the elementary guide to "bring the world to the children." That's a tall order. Moreover, she wanted us to do it in a way that was "an aid to life," by which we understand her to mean that what we bring should have some relevance to the child's present life, not just some hypothetical future; that it should meet the developmental needs of children that age; and that it should at least indirectly help the child stay on a trajectory toward becoming the kind of adult that could join with others to improve the conditions of life for all humanity. Dr. Montessori wanted us to bring the very best of the whole world to the child in a way that is positive and immediately helpful to the child in their big work of both understanding the world and adapting to the specific culture in which they are growing up.

As we choose which cultural experiences to offer the elementary child, we must also keep in mind our practice of offering keys that open doors into new areas of knowledge. Always, we work to broaden the field of choice for the individual, now and in the future. To me, there is a big difference between not choosing a certain cultural experience because it is not one's cup of tea at the moment and not choosing it because one has no idea that it even exists. The first is a form of freedom; the second is a form of oppression.

In choosing which "seeds of culture" to sow in the classroom, the elementary guide is limited only by their own knowledge and experience and in their ability to discern what is and is not quality in a particular art form or genre.

There is also a practical limitation, namely, that there aren't enough hours in the day to sow all of the seeds, to bring the whole world into the classroom. Guides will therefore want to use their time very wisely. For me, there was always a calculation to be made that involved just how eye-opening or mind-expanding a particular experience might be for the children and an estimate of the probability that the children might not have the experience unless I introduced it to them.

So, there were always many good activities to be done, much good music to be listened to, much good art to be seen, and many good books to be read that the children were not going to hear about from me, because they did not have to. Instead, I chose to offer what was new to the children, what was inspiring, and what was often inaccessible to the layman. Of course, all of these decisions were contingent on the needs of the particular group of children I had with me. In different years, with different groups of children, my choices could be quite different.

Inspiration and Gratitude

Dr. Montessori was wise enough not to have ensured the immediate obsolescence of her work by giving us lists of specific cultural experiences the children should have, but she did give us advice about the orientation we should model for the children with respect to culture, both current and past. This advice can be summed up in two words: inspiration and gratitude.

One of the main themes—arguably, *the* main theme—of the elementary is that we who are alive right now are the living edge of human civilization poised between the past and the future. We were born into a world and into a specific culture and a specific family that preexisted us, and from the moment of birth until the moment we die, all that makes our life and our accomplishments possible is a gift, a gift purchased at incalculable expense of human life, labor, creativity, courage, and passion. Gratitude is the natural response to this awareness. We the living preserve, embellish, and improve the gift of culture we have received and pass it along to our children and future generations.

The role of the guide is not so much to teach as it is to inspire, and nowhere is that more the case than it is with the arts. Art, music, and literature have the capacity to touch and transform us very deeply, and I know from personal experience and my experience of working with many children that such deep impressions can stay with one for a lifetime.

Carefully selected and skillfully presented, encounters with artistic expressions of all times and cultures afford the children the opportunity to experience creativity as something belonging to humanity, not just to a few or to a specific time and place. Such an experience invites the children into the ongoing stream of culture, invites and inspires them to see themselves as people who can make their own art, music, dance, and literature. Such self-expression not only strengthens their self-confidence and sense of belonging to the world, it also becomes a means by which they explore other areas of knowledge—geometry, geography, science, math, history, economics, and all the rest.

As we explore music and the other arts across time and space, we do so with an open mind and a sense of humility, knowing that the artistic expressions of others arise from their life experiences, which may be very different from ours. We know that we may not easily understand or know how to appreciate the art of times and places very different from our own. Nevertheless, we also know that to understand a culture's art is to understand something essential about that culture. So, we persist; we work hard to understand more and more about art and those who made it.

This necessarily takes us into studies of history, religion, philosophy, social organization, and even technology. When we know who made a particular piece of music or art, we learn the stories of that person's life and practice, trying to hear or see that person's work from the perspective of the person's time and place. When we see how often great artists of all times and cultures have had to struggle and sacrifice to create the beautiful and inspiring works we still enjoy, we once again connect to gratitude and inspiration.

There is, then, no room for narrow-mindedness or snobbery in the Montessori environment—whether it be the snobbery of elevating the Western artistic canon above all others or the reverse snobbery of thinking that we can somehow skip or depreciate the artistic achievements of what some have foolishly and spitefully termed DWEMs (dead white European males). If it is the skillful product of human minds, hands, and hearts, we receive it gladly and without discrimination.

Children Deserve the Best

Because we approach the arts of other times and places with humility, gratitude and respect, we want to bring the very best artistic expressions of those cultures to the children. Each culture, each genre, each artist deserves to be represented by the very best work available. This can be difficult and time-consuming work for those of us adults who were not helped as children to refine our own tastes and to learn about the artistic expressions of other cultures and times, but it is what the children need from us and what we must do.

Commercial collections of music and art marketed to teachers and parents for use with children are often thrown together from low-budget material, poorly performed or reproduced, and are often selected based on condescending underestimations of children's intelligence, taste, and abilities. Instead, adults working with children in the Montessori way will educate themselves enough to know which works are most representative and how to tell a high quality, authentic version from a cheap knockoff.

When children are helped to experience the very best and highest quality works of art, they have benchmarks against which to measure the pop culture in which they are immersed. They begin to understand what it means to be innovative and highly skilled in the different genres. They come to know that there has been great art and mediocre art in every time and place and that we are not living in a "fallen age," doomed to look back longingly to some golden age when artistic giants walked the earth.

Above all, children who are helped to refine their taste and broaden their experience are better able to accept the many explicit and implicit invitations we give them to join the great stream of human creativity, better able to evaluate their own progress, and better able to appreciate the efforts of others. These habits of mind are gifts that will keep on giving through a whole lifetime of cultural experience and exploration. ❖

The Story of Human Creativity in Cosmic Education: Including a Story to Tell the Children

||||||||||||||||||||||||||||||||||||||||||||||||||||||||||||||||||||||||||||||||||||||||||||||||||||||||||||||

Montessori guides are first and foremost storytellers. The five Great Stories are the backbone of the saga of the cosmos that we tell the children. From this foundation, we present many stories to inspire the children's thinking and work. This article, based on a presentation given at the 2011 AMI-EAA Summer Conference, provides an example of one such extension.

Why do people tell stories? For many reasons: to entertain, to preserve history, to pass along important cultural norms and knowledge, to impel others to thought and action. Following Dr. Montessori's key insight into working with children of elementary age, we also know that the way to reach and teach these children is through engagement with their very active imaginations. And this is the special gift of the good storyteller.

As people who consciously and diligently cultivate our storytelling skills, it is helpful for us to have a way of thinking about all the many stories we tell and the purpose for which we are telling them. Dr. Kay Baker, former Director of Training for the elementary course at Washington Montessori Institute, suggests a tripartite classification: the five Great Stories; stories that introduce a major area of study (for example, the introduction of geometry with the story of the Egyptian rope-stretchers or the introduction of human body studies with the Story of the Great River); and stories that introduce topics in a major area of study (for example, stories about the history of pi;

the Pythagorean Brotherhood; the story of Ferdinand Magellan; the Three Kings in the cubing sequence; or the origins of the Fahrenheit, Celsius and Kelvin temperature scales).

However we classify our stories, I think you will agree that we tell them, for the most part, to impel the children to thought and action. We want our stories to open up something that was previously unknown or opaque to the children, inspiring them to explore new territory.

Only One Story

While it is helpful to classify our stories to get them straight in our own minds, it is also helpful to step back and ask, "How many stories are there really?" If we do that, we see that all of our stories are really part of a greater narrative. Whether we are working with a truly cosmic topic or with the details of a discipline or sub-discipline, we are always trying to tell the story of the cosmos.

There really is only one story—and that is the story of the cosmos and the continuing unfolding of the cosmos. This is a story that we can never fully tell, a story that has infinite mystery and no end, a story that we are helping to make even as we tell it. Yet, it is the only story that there is to tell, and the human race is, as far as we know, the only means of its telling.

You may know the parable that the Buddha told about the blind men who chanced upon an elephant—one grasping the tail, one a leg, one the side, one the trunk—, each coming to believe that the totality of the elephant was the little bit he was touching.

What if we are *all* blind and what we have chanced upon is the *universe*—something too big and open-ended to grasp, to wrap our arms or minds around, to experience in its totality? What will we do then? We will have to tell this story of the universe to each other in bits and pieces, looking together for the patterns, the meanings, the whispers of the past and the future.

Some of those patterns and meanings and experiences will become the most important stories that we tell and retell—the "great stories" of our culture. These foundational stories will become our myths, our cultural narratives into which all the other little stories fit and from which the little stories derive their deepest meanings. (At the same time, we will need to remember the point that the Buddha was making in his parable—don't mistake your partial perceptions for the whole elephant!)

This is how I think we must approach storytelling in the Montessori elementary. The Great Stories are our foundational myths, and in them we must search for the meanings of all the other stories we tell. Taken together, they are the great, infinitely generous sun that shines in the heaven of Cosmic Education, giving the energy for the life of the mind that we cultivate in our communities of children.

In other words, we always start with the Great Stories and everything else we do is the discovery of the latent potentials in them, the elaboration and celebration of their themes, their hints, their implications, their mysteries, their narrative trajectory. There is only One Story, told from many different perspectives, and we are characters in it.

I think it is crucial that we think of our presentation of Cosmic Education in this way. There are many strong forces working in our culture and especially in our schools against our seeing and presenting the "big picture." If we slip into thinking of our many stories as separate little entertainments for the children, forgetting they are all sub-plots and complications of the One Story, our children will miss the opportunity that Montessori education gives them to glimpse the wonderful interdependence of the Cosmos—and then how will they ever find their home, their place in it? How will they resist the alternative cultural narrative that reduces everything to acquisition, consumption and individual pleasure seeking?

Let me give an example of how we might go prospecting for gold in the Great Stories, developing stories that highlight, extend or unlock latent potentials in them. Consider the third Great Story, "The Coming of Human Beings." In this story, we discover that humans have *minds* that can imagine new things, *hands* (and technology) that can bring these new things into being, and hearts to love the other people in the world—when these three things combine, we call it *"creativity."* Here is a story we might tell the children about human creativity.

THE STORY OF HUMAN CREATIVITY

Children, do you remember the story of the coming of human beings upon the earth? Perhaps you remember the three gifts that this new creature had that made life possible for it in the sometimes difficult and dangerous world in which it found itself. The human being had a *mind* that could imagine things that didn't yet exist and skillful *hands* to bring those ideas into existence. And the human being had a deep need to be with other human beings, to find a life together, to share ideas and to work together to build and create and enjoy life—and so, the human being had one more gift: the gift of a *loving heart*. Because of its wonderful capacity to imagine things, the human being could even love others who were not in its own family—even others whom it had never met. So, this is part of what it means to be human: to have these gifts. And we do all have them today, just as the first humans did!

Even before humans had the idea of writing things down, they were imagining and making and sharing. Sometimes we still find things they made tens or even hundreds of thousands of years ago—tools, shelter, clothing, jewelry, and even art and musical instruments. Even though these ancient people did not speak directly to us through writing, the things of theirs we find tell us much about them. For one thing, they tell us how very much like us they were. And we can also see how many things our ancient ancestors first imagined that are still part of our lives today—their gifts to us.

When someone thinks of something to make that is new—something that has never been made before or never been made in just that way, we say that the person who imagined it and made it is showing their human gift of *creativity*—because they have created something new.

Human creativity is expressed in many different ways. Sometimes people make new stories, and they become known as *bards* or *storytellers*; and if they know how to write, they write them down and become *authors*. People who make poems are called *poets*. *Playwrights* write new plays.

Sometimes people make up new music and become *composers*. Sometimes people draw or paint new images and become *visual artists*. Others know how to take clay or a big stone or a log and shape it into an interesting new shape—these we call *sculptors*. Still others train their bodies to become instruments of expression through movement and are called *dancers*. *Architects* are the people who think of new ways to make buildings of all kinds—and some of their creations last for thousands of years!

Creativity has been highly valued by people down through time, and highly creative people—people with lots of good ideas—have often been admired and supported by their society. Many civilizations have stories about their gods creating the universe, and human creativity has often been thought to be a gift of G-d or the gods—something that makes human beings almost god-like.

Nevertheless, people sometimes become very attached to their usual ways of thinking and doing things, and they may be startled or frightened or puzzled or even angry when a person comes along with a new idea. There are many stories of people having to wait a long time before their creations are fully appreciated by their communities.

Most people's creativity doesn't make them famous. They just create for the joy of it, because they enjoy the feeling of having a new idea or making something new, and because they want to contribute something valuable to their community or to the world. Everyone is creative *sometime* about *something*. One special kind of creativity that many people have is called *resourcefulness*; that's the ability to use whatever materials are at hand to solve a problem or get something done.

Can you think of a time when you were resourceful? How does your own creativity like to express itself? What areas of creativity have you not tried yet? ❖

Introduction to the First Great Story for Older Children

|||||||||||||||||||||||||||||||||||||||||||||||||||||||||||||||||||||||||||||||||||||||||||||||||||||||||||||||||||||||||||||||||||||||||||||||||||||||||||||

Older elementary children still love to hear the First Great Story again and again, but their minds are hungry for more detail and a broader perspective on Cosmic Education. There is an opportunity to sow more seeds, to pique their interest in more in-depth studies. Here is how I began the First Great Story for the older children each year.

From the very beginning people have wondered where everything came from. Every group of people—the earliest Stone Age people, the people of ancient Mesopotamia (the Sumerians and Babylonians), the ancient Greeks and Romans, the native peoples of Australia, the ancient Israelites (whose descendants are today's Jews), the people of the Indus Valley, the Mayans, the Germanic peoples of Europe, the people of Eastern Asia and their descendants the Native Americans—every civilization has had stories to explain how the world began.

People looked around and saw many amazing things in their world. They saw that everything around them had a beginning, a middle, and an end. They wondered, "What was the beginning of the world?" People tried to imagine what it was like before anything existed. They imagined a great emptiness, where there was nothing to be seen or heard or touched because nothing existed!

One of the oldest creation stories was told in India for many ages before it was written down three thousand years ago in a book called the *Rigveda*. This Indian story says:

Who Can Say How Creation Happened?

Then even nothingness was not, nor existence.
There was no air then, nor the heavens beyond it.
What covered it? Where was it? In whose keeping?
Was there a cosmic water, in depths unfathomed?

[...]

At first there was only darkness wrapped in darkness.
All this was only unillumined water.
That One [Creator] which came to be, enclosed in nothing,
arose at last, born of the power of heat. (X: 129: 1, 3)

The story of the Mayan peoples of Central America was told for ages before it was written down in a book called the *Popol Vuh*. The Mayan story says:

Before the world was created, Calm and Silence were the great kings that ruled. Nothing existed, there was nothing. Things had not yet been drawn together, the face of the earth was unseen. There was only motionless, and a great emptiness of sky. There were no humans anywhere, or animals, no birds or fish, no crabs. Trees, stones, caves, grass, forests, none of those existed yet. There was nothing that could roar or run, nothing that could tremble or cry in the air. Flatness and emptiness, only the sea, alone and breathless. It was night; silence stood in the dark.

The story of the ancient Israelites is similar in some ways to the stories of the Babylonians who lived nearby, but very different in other ways. The story of the Israelites was told for ages before it was written down about twenty-five hundred years ago in a book that came to be part of the Jewish *Torah* and the Christian *Bible*. The Israelite story says:

In the beginning God created the heavens and the earth.
But the earth became chaos and emptiness and darkness came over the face of the Deep—yet the Spirit of God was moving over the face of the waters.

Then God said, "Let there be light!" and light was. (Genesis 1.1–3)

So you see how all these ancient stories—and there are many others—imagine the world coming out of nothingness and chaos, coming out of a place of no order and no laws.

Yet, people looked around them and saw that everything worked according to its laws. The rocks didn't try to be trees. The trees didn't try to grow feathers like the birds. The rivers didn't try to flow uphill. Spring always followed winter. The sun always came up in the east.

Today we have another creation story in addition to our beloved ancient ones. That is the story told by the scientists from all around the world. This story is different from the old stories in some ways. For one thing, the old stories changed very slowly. They have been told in more or less the same way for thousands of years. The story told by the scientists is always changing. Every year it changes a bit! But like the old stories, it depends on people being able to look around and see the order in the universe and observe the laws that things follow. Also, this story does not belong to just one culture or tribe or religion, but to all of humanity. Scientists from all over the world—Europe, Asia, America, Africa, and Australia—have helped to write this story. It goes something like this... ❖

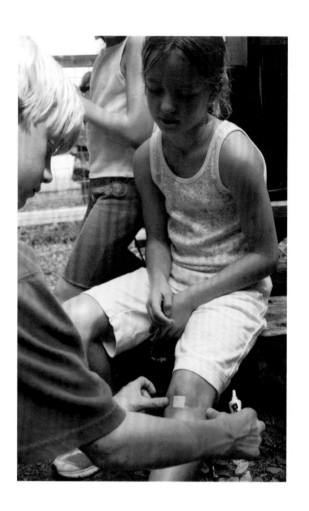

And the Greatest of These is Love:
A Story for the Children

||||||||||||||||||||||||||||||||||||||||||||||||||||||||||||||||||||||||||||||||||||||||||||||||||||||||||||||||||||||||||||||||||||||||

A mong the Great Stories of Cosmic Education that are told at the beginning of each year in the elementary, one of the most wonderful is the story of humanity and its three gifts. Coming after the stories of "God With No Hands" and "The Coming of Life," each of which has exciting demonstrations, inspiring charts, or fascinating timelines to accompany it, this short story introduces the human being with a touching and profound simplicity.

In this story Dr. Montessori sets the advent of human beings in its biological, evolutionary context. This newcomer, the human being, is shown surrounded by its creaturely elder brothers and sisters, and its place in nature, sharing the earth with other living things, is firmly established.

The human being's powers are contrasted with those of its fellow creatures, and its relative weaknesses are gently but clearly exposed: it lacks the strength, the speed, the agility, the endurance, the ferocity, the camouflage, the sheer numbers of other animals. How then will this unlikely new creature survive? By virtue of three unique gifts: the human mind, the human hands, and the human capacity to love.

The story then explores the ramifications of these three gifts. With its unique mind, the human being is able to *learn* from its experience in ways that other animals cannot. It can *communicate* in unique ways. The human mind can rise above the urges of instinct and evolutionary programming to *choose* how to act, how to live. Above all, it can *imagine* things that do not exist—things that cannot be directly experienced.

With its unique hands, the human being is able to fashion tools, to explore its environment in new ways, and, eventually, to produce things of great beauty and utility. Because its hands work together with its mind, it can imagine things that do not exist and then bring them into existence. Unlike other animals, it need not be completely dependent on the vicissitudes of nature, but it can begin even from the earliest times to shape its own world—the beginnings of "supra-natura," the constructed world of human culture.

With these two awe-inspiring gifts alone, the human being could perhaps survive, but it is the third and last gift that makes possible what we know as truly human life. It happens that the human being has a great heart—a unique capacity to love that goes far beyond that of other animals. Whereas other animals may, in their own ways, love their mates or their offspring or their pack or herd, the human being's love is so great that it can extend to human beings well outside its family, human beings that it has never seen, even to other non-human creatures that are radically unlike it in many ways.

If told with dignity and a sense of wonder appropriate to the subject, this story never fails to rivet the elementary child. I have come to see it as a pivot around which everything else in Cosmic Education turns, and the moment of its telling as one of the most important moments of the school year.

In this simple story Dr. Montessori accomplishes a number of very profound things. It is, for one thing, the subtle presentation to the child of the foundation of her whole pedagogy: The human being is the creature who exercises these three unique gifts for the elevation of life and the betterment of the world. The education of the human being must address its defining characteristics of mind, hand, and heart.

In the plan for Cosmic Education, the mind is supported by the many intellectual explorations the children are guided to undertake. The hand and mind work together with the carefully crafted materials to call forth, each from the other, the best potentials inherent in the individual. The community of children, guided by adults who have given themselves to the highest possible development of the three gifts in their own lives, provides fertile ground for the development of uniquely human love.

As adults, people with the sometimes bitter perspectives of personal and human history, we may wonder as we tell this story to the children whether or not we may be deceiving them by telling them only half of the story about human beings. What about the mystery of human evil and folly, the great failures and perversions of mind, hand, and heart? Are we encouraging a dangerous naiveté in the children?

To think so is to miss an important purpose of Dr. Montessori's story. By defining the human being as the creature who has been given these three unprecedented powers to use for the good of all, she is doing on a cosmic level what she calls us to do every day in our interactions with the children, namely, to see past the deviations of behavior and thinking in the children and to penetrate to the true nature of the child as a perfected being endowed with powers that both we and the child may only dimly glimpse at present.

Just as the individual child is helped to achieve her full potential when we mirror for her the perfected being we see her to be, the human race is helped to achieve its potential when it can firmly hold in consciousness the conviction, knowledge, and vision of its own deep goodness and unique value. This is the vision that Montessori hoped to impart to the elementary child.

Subsequent lessons and materials, such as the Hand Timeline, reinforce and elaborate the themes introduced in the story of the three gifts. Likewise, discussions of human love and the failures of human love begin to give texture and nuance to the bright but simple vision of the original story. Discussions of morality can nearly always hark back to the shared story of the three gifts.

What follows is my latest attempt to put into words some of the ideas about human love that elementary children naturally want to explore as they become more and more aware of the world outside their family, their school, and their historical period. This story can be told to the children anytime after the telling of the third Great Story. It can also be retold whenever the community needs a reminder to cultivate love and inclusion or when the community needs to process some great and disturbing evil, such as the beginning of a new war or the murder of a class parent.

THE STORY OF HUMAN LOVE

Remember the story I told you about how we humans first came to live on earth and about our three special gifts of human intelligence, human hands, and human love? We humans have intelligence instead of instinct to guide us through life. Unlike the animals that are driven by instinct, we can *choose* how to live, depending on our circumstances.

Many times we make wrong choices! Sometimes our love grows weak, perhaps overcome by fear or greed or anger, and we fall back into the practice of slavery or war or vengeance. Sometimes we make things better for ourselves but worse for other people, plants and animals, air and water. Sometimes we unfairly take more and more for ourselves—much more than we need—leaving less and less for others. Sometimes we exclude people who are different or difficult, treating them as though they were not human, with the same need for love and friendship that we have.

Yet, often our love joins with our intelligence to make something beautiful and wholesome. Nothing we know in the universe is as powerful as great intelligence guided by great love.

What have we learned about our gift of human love? We humans love our families, friends, and neighbors; we have even learned to love them as much as we love ourselves. We have a special love for our children and would give our lives for them. Some of us would even give our lives for a friend or for the people of our country.

We have also learned to love those who we cannot see, those who live far away. We have learned to love those who came before us and those who will come in the future.

With practice and strong intent, we have learned to love those we don't understand, those whose ways and ideas upset us. We have learned to love those we cannot even like, those who are so sick and wounded in their minds and hearts that they hurt or even kill other people. We have even been learning to love our enemies, those who wish us harm, but that takes our greatest effort and constant practice. We are willing to give this effort because we know that hatred has never yet been overcome by hatred, only by love.

We humans have learned that love is not just a feeling; it's not just liking someone very much. Love is also an action; it's acting for the good of the loved one. This is how we can love people we haven't met or don't like. This is why love is measured by what we do, not by what we feel or what we say.

We humans love our earth with all its plants and animals, its lands and waters, and its skies. We like to think new thoughts and ideas, exploring, discovering, and inventing. Sometimes we get so excited about loving things and ideas that we forget about loving people. We are learning to remember.

Our human hands are the tools of our love and intelligence. With our minds and hearts we imagine a better world, and with our hands we work together to make it so! The more we make and the more we do, the more skillful our hands become and the more intelligent our minds become.

Our gifts are so strong! We continue to work together to know how to use them wisely and for the good of all. Little by little, we human beings are learning to use our gift of love as it was truly meant to be used. ❖

Talking to Children about Peace in a Time of War

||||||||||||||||||||||||||||||||||||||||||||||||||||||||||||||||||||||||||||||||||||||||||||||||||||||||||||||||||||

A conversation with older children following the terrorist attacks of September 11, 2001.

Children, we have talked about human beings and the special gifts they bring to the world of living creatures: a mind that can imagine wonderful things—things of great beauty that have never before existed; a heart that can hold an infinite amount of love—love even for people we have never seen, people who live far away and have different ways of life; and miraculously skillful hands that can take those ideas from the mind and, through the power of love, make them real, a gift for all humanity.

And yet, my dear friends, I have to tell you the sad part of the story as well. If a child is not loved or has nowhere safe to live or has nothing to eat while others have too much, or is taught by misguided adults to hate those different from himself, then that wonderful human heart that was made to grow a garden of love, can start to grow seeds of fear and hate. Those seeds may even grow into a tangled vine of violence, choking out the love altogether. This is why we care for and guard each other's hearts so carefully in this community of ours. We are helping each other to grow the love in our hearts and not the fear and hate. I am very sorry to tell you that not all children in the world have this kind of help from adults and each other to grow love instead of fear and hate.

When a person's heart is no longer full of love, as it was meant to be and longs to be, then the person's mind and imagination may turn to evil things—things that destroy and hurt and take away the freedoms of others instead of things that make people stronger, more caring, and more able to enjoy their lives. This is a great tragedy, and many wise human beings in all ages and all places have looked for ways to still grow love in their hearts for all people and yet keep their communities safe from those who would harm them.

This is a very hard thing: how to stop people with confused, suffering hearts from harming others and yet continue to love them at the same time. I have to tell you that we adults do not have very good answers to this question. Most of us either do nothing to stop the evil or we begin to hate the people doing the evil and think of them as our enemies. We are trying hard to figure this out, and we are getting better little by little.

One of the great human beings who has shown us adults a new way lived in India about sixty years ago. His name was Mohandas K. Gandhi, and he taught the world more about peace than anyone had for thousands of years. Gandhi said that the worst possible thing for human beings to do is to see some evil in the world, to see some harm being done to other people—and do nothing to stop it. Even though he loved peace, he said that it was better to use force and weapons to stop the evil than to do nothing at all to stop it.

Sometimes we adults cannot think of any way to stop the evil without using force and weapons. We are trying, but we sometimes cannot think of any other way. It is so sad for us adults when this happens. We know we must protect our communities from harm, but we also feel very sad when we have to use weapons to do it. We wonder, "What will our children think? These children whose hearts are so full of love and whose minds are so used to thinking about beauty and order and peace—what will they think when they see us taking up weapons?" We hope you will understand that we are doing it to protect our communities so that you can grow up to be adults who may be able to think of ways to stay safe without using weapons.

When you see someone using weapons to protect your community, you can think about how brave this person is. Think about how good it is that this person is trying to stop the evil instead of just pretending that it is not there or saying, "Well, it's not my problem that other people are getting hurt; it's not my problem that those other people have no freedom to enjoy their lives." I think you can see that the true strength of the soldiers who use weapons does not come from the weapons but from the love they have for their communities, their families, and their children whom they are trying to protect.

Yet Gandhi said there was an even greater kind of strength. You remember he said that the worst thing was to do nothing to stop evil. He also said that there was a better way than using weapons. He said there is a way to stop evil just by using the strength of nonviolent truth. He said that nonviolent truth was the most powerful thing in the universe, even powerful enough to stop evil.

If he was right, then why don't we just use the power of nonviolent truth all the time? Why do we still use weapons at all? Because to use the power of nonviolent truth, people have to be so strong that they are willing to stand up for the truth *without the protection of weapons.* The greater the evil, the greater the number of strong nonviolent people it takes to stop it. They have to build a wall of love and truth that the evil cannot break through. They have to be willing to be hurt or even to die for the truth without striking back at those who are hurting them.

We know this works when there are enough strong nonviolent people who will work together. Every time in history we have been able to find enough people strong enough to use the power of nonviolent truth, they have won against evil without having to use guns and bombs and other such weapons. But right now in human history we often have trouble finding enough people who are strong enough and brave enough to make it work.

This is one of the reasons Maria Montessori started the Montessori schools. She wanted the children in her schools to have every possible chance to become the kind of person strong enough to use the power of nonviolent truth.

Right now our country is thinking about what to do to stop the people we call "terrorists"—people who are so wounded inside, who are in so much pain in their hearts and minds that all they can think of to do is to make other people feel the same pain. These terrorists are our fellow human beings, and we must try to love them as we love all people. But we cannot let them continue to cause death and destruction in the world.

Some people are saying we must use guns and bombs to stop them. Perhaps this is true. Perhaps there are not enough of us adults who are strong enough to use the power of nonviolent truth. Or perhaps we are giving up on nonviolent truth too fast. Maybe we are stronger than we think. It is confusing even to us.

There is one thing we are not confused about. We are going to do whatever we can to keep all the children safe and healthy. And we are going to keep trying to create a world in which guns and bombs are not needed—a world where everyone has freedom, respect, safe houses, enough food, an education, a place to worship if they like, and friends to love them. When you children are adults, you will be stronger and know more about peace than we do. When *your* children are adults, they will be even stronger and more knowledgeable than you are.

Think of it! We have known about the power of nonviolent truth for less than one hundred years, yet we have already used it to make right some powerful wrongs and to bring freedom to many people. When you think of how old the earth is (remember the Black Strip?) and how short human history is, it is really remarkable how fast we are building a peaceful world. We must remember that in the days ahead if we are tempted to think that violence and death are winning out over peace and life. ❖

Designing Key Lessons for Inquiry

This article draws on material from a workshop first presented for NAMTA in 2010 and again for the Austrian Montessori Society in 2012. As I explain it, I see the craft of designing new pedagogically sound key lessons as critically important for both guide and children—far more important than anything that can be left to chance.

AMI elementary teachers are trained in two arts: the art of presenting inspired versions of time-tested stories and lessons given in our albums, and the art of creating new pedagogically sound stories, key lessons, and extensions for topics of interest to specific groups of children or topics mandated by state or national curriculum standards.

In truth, many of us are so consumed with the challenges of mastering the first art that we fail to master the second. Instead, we fall into the trap of bringing into the prepared environment off-the-shelf instructional materials based on theories of learning and pedagogical practices inconsistent with those of the Montessori prepared environment. Once we start down this road, we can find ourselves a number of years later working in classrooms cluttered with non-Montessori materials, relying on worksheets and other disempowering methods, while the Montessori materials languish on the shelves untouched. We may then come to the erroneous conclusion that "children these days just don't respond to the Montessori materials."

Alternatively, if we are committed to the purity of our method and have not mastered the creation of new key lessons, we may find ourselves in what traditional educators refer to as "yellow note syndrome"—giving the same lessons in the same way over and over, year after year, while the world in which our children live and in which our parents parent slowly passes us by. Symptoms of this syndrome would include continuing to teach mid–twentieth century science and geography, not being prepared to support older children who finish all of the Montessori lessons and extensions in one part of our albums (such as math) as they continue building on what they know in a logical progression that connects with what they will be studying as adolescents, or feeling that we need to regulate how quickly children move through their studies so that we will not run out of lessons from our albums.

In short, these are all ways of failing to "aid the life of the child" as that life currently manifests in our classrooms. In one case we actually "help" the children to disconnect from their intrinsic motivation to learn and to take on the view of the dominant culture that learning is something that adults make you do at school, not something that has personal meaning for you. In the other case, we miss opportunities to help today's children make sense of the world in which they are growing up and prepare for the world that is coming.

Given that we are responsible for offering information and activities to support state and national curriculum standards, what's a poor teacher to do? First, we can look back at our albums, not as finished products that we present over and over by rote, but as inspired and ingenious examples of how to present the full array of human knowledge to the elementary child. We can then use the same structures and techniques in our new lessons, and we can preserve the vital essence of our old lessons even as we bring the content up to date. Second, we can challenge ourselves to find new ways of using materials already on the shelves to meet our curricular needs. The math and geometry materials are especially amenable to new uses because, for the most part, as "concretized abstractions," they are brilliant physical incarnations of fundamental principles of mathematics. But other materials, such as the grammar materials, also have much untapped potential.

Before we begin to look at the specifics of designing key lessons that lead to spontaneous activity and child-directed inquiry, it would be good to ground ourselves in what Maria and Mario Montessori had to say on the subject. I know of no place where the Montessoris definitively laid out their thinking on "key lessons." Nevertheless, the following collection of quotes gives a very strong indication of the direction of their thinking and will be more than enough than we need to do our work:

> Here [the teacher] must be sure of what he ought to do, of what he ought to say, and of the extent to which he must reply to questions. He must be clearly conscious that his duty is to say little; to say only what is true, but not the whole truth in all its details. He must now also *say what is "necessary and sufficient."* (*FCA*)

> The point of view from which we present to the [elementary] children these sciences [chemistry, mineralogy, etc.] in their embryonic development must be well understood. Our presentations must be *sensorial* and *imaginative*, given by means of clear visual symbols which permit details to be determined.

> We are trying to arouse the child's interest. Should we fail to arouse it immediately, we must still trust the same principle while we make our presentations in a specific environment and await the reaction. If the enthusiasm is not shown, we do not delay but pass on. *If the enthusiasm is shown, we have apparently opened a door. We are at the beginning of a long road, along which we will travel with the child.* But what we would most like to recommend is *not to begin too late.* Thus, the presentation of chemistry may be made at nine years of age. The interest may even manifest itself sooner.
>
> We recommend above all *not to give too many explanations* but rather to *give precise names* [terminology, nomenclature]. [...] We must have the courage to give as many names a possible. The more difficult the names are, the more attractive they are to the child. And then one may say that hydrogen is univalent, that oxygen is bivalent, etc. (*FCA*)
>
> We have touched on several cycles [of nature], as, for example, that of calcium carbonate. But all is interrelated. And what is interesting is to be able to *orient ourselves among these correlations.* To present detached notions is to bring confusion. We need to determine the bonds that exist between them. When the correlation among the notions, by now linked to one another, has been established, the details may be found to tie together among themselves. The mind, then, is satisfied and the desire to go on with research is born.
>
> Here is an essential principle of education: *to teach details is to bring confusion; to establish the relationship between things is to bring knowledge.* (*FCA*)

"Great Stories," in the elementary class, are to set the scene for the mind to act. They give an over-all picture, they open up a view, they should 'fire the imagination,' 'open up a door' as Dr. Montessori asks. [...] "Key lessons" take up the details, item by item. Each gives *some new information, presents new material, shows another exercise in a progression which allows the mind to build up knowledge and to continue searching on its own for what it does not know.* "Key lessons" are limited to *essential presentations, giving only that information without which the mind of the child would find it very difficult to understand a new concept.* Other exercises may be interesting and offer *variations,* but if not absolutely essential to understanding, can be an obstacle to the mind's own investigation. Dr. Montessori expressed this very well when she said: "Any unnecessary help is a hindrance." (Mario Montessori, Sr., from a letter to Karen Saltzmann, 1970s)

Practical Considerations

From these passages, we can see that a key lesson is a short lesson, usually given to a small group of children (sometimes one child) that specifically addresses a key concept or skill that the child needs in order to work independently in a given subject area. It is pithy, spare, economical—"a point of departure in the study of the whole." Sequences of key lessons may be designed to lead the children along a certain path of discovery, each lesson in the sequence extending the one before and preparing the next—but always with the child's own exploration and activity in mind.

How do we know a new key lesson is called for? In one case, we see a child or a group of children whose interest has taken them into intellectual waters too deep for them to cross alone. They need a key lesson or a sequence of key lessons to introduce key concepts or skills they will need in further expirations. For example, I once had a group of children whose interest in chemistry greatly exceeded what I was prepared to present. Despite their own efforts to tutor themselves from textbooks, the task was too formidable. Not only could they not recognize the major landmarks in the new territory they were exploring, they did not know what to look for or even what country they were in. I followed them one key lesson at a time into their explorations, giving only the next set of ideas and hints. Over time, we went very far together into organic chemistry.

It is also time for a key lesson when we see that the world around us has created a need for children to understand something that previous generations of children did not. A good example of this is the electromagnetic spectrum. Today's world is incomprehensible without a basic understanding of the electromagnetic spectrum and the many ways it intersects with our lives. In previous generations, it could have safely been considered an elegant and abstract physical theory with an interesting history of development—something to occupy the minds of adolescence or young adults. Because of the explosion of knowledge in biology, there are many additional examples of this to be drawn from that subject.

Finally, for whatever reason, some new topic may have been added to state or national curricula to which we as elementary teachers are beholden. In this case, it is particularly important to resist the temptation to adopt "off-the-shelf" non-Montessori materials, since developers of those will be heavily marketing them to all teachers under the purview of the new regulations. On the other hand, it is particularly rewarding to be able to find a way to accommodate the new topics with existing materials.

It is equally important to note that development of new key lessons should be driven by the children's real need, not by the teacher's predilection for developing new lessons and materials. It is just as easy to clutter the prepared environment with "Montessori-like" teacher-made materials as it is with prepackaged materials. So we ask ourselves some sober questions and expect truthful answers: Am I creating this lesson just because I'm very interested in the topic and think it would be great fun to teach the children? Am I sure (because I regularly read my albums) that there is not already a key lesson or an extension in my albums that meets this need? Do the children really need a new lesson from me, or can I help them continue their explorations with even less help or perhaps a well-chosen outside resource? Are there other children in the classroom who could help these children progress in their explorations?

Our Toolbox

When we undertake to create a new key lesson or a sequence of them, we can draw on a powerful set of tools and environmental conditions available to us through our training and classroom experience. The first of these is the set of Human Tendencies: exploring, communicating, abstracting, being exact, imagining, manipulating with the hands, ordering, orienting, repeating, perfecting, exercising self-control, and finding meaning in purposeful work. We know that these are the hallmark of human beings of all ages whose developmental needs are being met. As we design our lessons, we can explicitly look for ways to build in opportunities for the children to express as many of these tendencies as possible, both in the lesson and in the activity that follows. This one practice alone is enough to prevent us from creating "key lessons" in the form of lectures, handouts, or reading to children out of books while they passively listen.

Another ace we have up our sleeve is a thorough understanding of the psychological characteristics of the elementary Plane. Any lesson we give, whether from our album or something that we have designed ourselves, has to appeal to our elementary audience, otherwise there will be no spontaneous activity or joyful follow-up. So what do we know about our audience? We know that they are increasingly living and expressing their Human Tendencies in the world of ideas, imagination, and reasoning—but not to the exclusion of the senses and the hand. We know they are highly social, highly communicative, and want to work together in groups. They have already built and are continuing to build collaboration and teamwork skills. They are full of energy and need ways to work that involve purposeful movement. They are physically and emotionally resilient and resent being "babied" or underestimated. They relate to and are inspired by stories of people who have overcome great obstacles in order to achieve a worthy goal, to make a lasting contribution to the world. As they advance through the Second Plane, they are increasingly capable of and drawn to self-reflection. As they near and then enter adolescence they are fascinated by the things they are beginning to notice about themselves and others—differences and similarities that seem to define who individuals are. All of these new powers are given to them by nature, like treasures left on one's doorstep, but they do not immediately understand how to use them.

A great deal of behavior at this age can be seen as "experiments" the children are running to find the limits, capabilities, capacities, and dynamics of their new powers. Their imaginations generally run far ahead of their abilities, and the elementary child often lives, sometimes painfully, in the tension between what they can imagine and what they can actually produce. Part of the attraction to working in groups is the discovery that they can achieve more with a good team then they can as individuals.

We have seen in a previous article Daniel Pink's summary of the research on what supports intrinsic motivation: autonomy, working for mastery, and purpose. This is yet another lens through which to evaluate new lessons we might design. What autonomy does the child have? How does the lesson engage the child's natural drive to master things? Will the child see a clear link between this new work and what matters to them as children of the Second Plane?

Finally, there is a set of features that we can build into our lessons that I like to think of as the "attention magnets." In a key lesson, we only have a few minutes in which to engage the children's full attention, impart what little information we need to impart, and leave them with a clear idea of where they could go from here. We need to be savvy about what will quickly grab their attention, hold it throughout the duration of the lesson, and then continue to call out to them on subsequent days as they are making their work choices. Here is a quick list of the most effective attention magnets. It will be seen that many of these attentional strategies are based on a calculated, intentional playing with expectation. Human beings are evolutionarily programmed to notice differences, especially things that are different than they are expected to be.

- *Association.* This usually happens with that... but then it doesn't. That difference catches one's attention. We experience it as a little burst of surprise.

- *Contrasts* of mood, energy, complexity, or simplicity. Again, these changes are noticed. They can be skillfully used to highlight a point that we want to make. Sometimes direct attention can be drawn to them: "This seems pretty complicated, but see how easy it is to think of it this way."

- *Modulation* of voice or expression. This is the main way human beings communicate affect. Any lesson, no matter how skillfully designed, can be easily killed by a monotone presentation that essentially says to the listener, "Everything I'm saying is of equal importance."

- *Tempo.* Related to modulation of expression, tempo is a critical factor that moves the whole stream of experience along. Changing tempi create qualitative changes in the student's experience. Sometimes, we may slow down to emphasize a point or speed up to increase the energy and excitement of the moment as a way of highlighting a key point.

- *Juxtaposition.* Another way to create surprise is through extreme contrast. *Interruption* can also be seen as a form of juxtaposition, as when we establish a certain pattern or tone and then suddenly interrupt it with something quite different.

- *Novelty.* This could take the form of new, attractive materials to offer or new experiences—perhaps a new idea for Going Out after the lesson. It could even be giving a lesson in a new place where lessons are rarely given. (Teachers who give all of their lessons at a special "lesson table" give up this important attention magnet.)

- *Control of error.* Materials that provide a natural control of error create more interest because they highlight a difference between what was expected and what actually happened.

Creating the New Lesson

With these initial considerations and the toolkit in mind, we can now consider strategies for creating a lesson. Start with an existing Great Story, story, or key lesson, and look for natural extensions. Cosmic Education, as it comes down to us, is a more or less seamlessly integrated structure of knowledge, and it can stay that way if we are careful to create key lessons that are natural extensions or that have clear links to the lessons in our albums: "To teach details is to create confusion; to establish the relationship between things is to bring knowledge." As a rule of thumb, you are not ready to present a new key lesson to children unless you can clearly link it in your own mind to at least three other strands in the curriculum.

Unless the topic is one in which you are thoroughly and professionally educated, your own research and reading comes first. To effectively create and deliver new lessons, you must know much more about the subject than you will ever present—and present only a small fraction of what you know. This is because a great deal of the value you will bring to the children in the creation of a new lesson is determining what is critical to understanding (and must be presented) and what is secondary. For example, the average college chemistry textbook consists of perhaps twenty-five to thirty pages of vital information, surrounded by five hundred pages of detail and elaboration. Unfortunately, the book will not be organized this way. An important part of what it means to be thoroughly educated in any subject is to know how to extract the highly important from the not-so-important.

Like a chess master who is always looking ahead several moves, you also need to be able to look down the road toward potential key lessons that you may in fact never create or present in order to design the one at hand. That is, the new key lesson must be set in a larger context that is clear in your mind. Incidentally, this self-study and research stage of development is the time to examine pre-existing non-Montessori materials to get an idea about what others have done. Use them to educate yourself, but keep them off the shelves of your prepared environment.

Once you know enough about the subject area, whether through prior education or your own self-study, do not immediately turn your knowledge into a whole curriculum in that subject area. Instead, follow the children's interest. Create the new lessons only when you see that there will be some demand for them—indicated primarily by the children's enthusiastic follow-up work from the previous lesson. This will allow you to create just the right lesson for the children with whom you are working, following their interest and letting them set the pace.

Keep ever present in your mind the Montessori dictum to give as much to the hand as you give to the mind. This is particularly important when designing follow-up activities in creating new materials through which the children can explore the new topic. For example, if the topic is electrical circuits in series and in parallel, the children need to have wires, switches, lamps, alligator clips, and batteries with which to build circuits, draw them, and observe their properties. If the topic is the Iroquois Confederation, perhaps the children undertaking that study would enjoy creating a short play about a particularly important leader or a critical moment in the Confederation's history to present to the class.

Since it may be difficult to keep all of these moving parts in mind as you are creating the lesson, you may want to employ the strategy of drafts and revisions. Create the first draft focusing on logical flow, careful choice of material, and working out clear language for explanations. In a later draft, read through the lesson asking yourself at each point, "Is this something the children could reasonably discover for themselves? Is there some way I could make it possible for them to discover it for themselves?" Take those parts out or modify them as appropriate. Then take out just a bit more. You can always give more information later, but you cannot give back the work you should have left for the children.

As you create materials, pay attention to important design features or strategies such as the three-period lesson, control of error, and intentional incompleteness. Challenge yourself to find a way to present the new lesson using only materials you already have on the shelves. This will not always be possible or optimal, but it is a wonderful exercise that can lead to very successful results. (In the next article I will give an example of such a lesson that uses the pegboard to illustrate fundamental notions about Cartesian coordinates.) Try to introduce the lesson with a short story or a recollection of prior knowledge on which the lesson will build.

Finally, keep the lessons short. Minimalism is a good quality in a key lesson. As you give the lesson once, twice, three times, pay close attention to the children's response to each part of the lesson and to their follow-up work, and use that feedback to hone your lesson and your presentation practice to create future success. And always keep in mind that in the elementary, we are sowing seeds. It is not necessary that the children master every part of a topic or "get to the end" of a sequence of lessons we have designed. If they have learned a little, stayed in touch with their own intrinsic motivation, exercised their Human Tendencies, and had fun doing it, this will build a positive foundation for future, more thorough studies of the subject. ❖

Cartesian Plane Activities
with the Pegboard

|||||||||||||||||||||||||||||||||||||||||||||||||||||||||||||||||||||||||||||||||||||||||||||||||||||||||||||||

This article presents a key lesson of great practical value to those working with older children. It is also intended as an example of a key lesson developed according to the principles of the previous article.

I n the previous article, we have suggested that creating new key lessons having the "look and feel" of the time-tested lessons in our albums is an essential art for the Montessori educator—especially one who wants a long teaching career.

As an illustration, I would like to share how I came to present activities supporting understanding of the Cartesian plane to children of the Upper Elementary. The concepts involved are not difficult, and there is a plethora of non-Montessori instructional materials I could have adopted, but since I set myself the challenge of re-using existing materials, I realized that the trusty pegboard could be pressed into service. In retrospect, this is hardly surprising since the pegboard is already used in so many different ways across the math curriculum.

Think of the pegboard as a small section of the infinite plane. Now think of the holes in the pegboard as points (x, y) on the plane where x and y are integers. Then the hole in the lower left corner is the origin $(0, 0)$. This is already enough to allow introduction of the major ideas behind Cartesian coordinates: the x- and y-axes (named and labeled with paper strips), ordered pairs of numbers as "addresses" of unique points on the plane (marked with green pegs and labeled with small paper tickets), and the origin as a privileged point defining the coordinate system being imposed on the plane (perhaps highlighted with a red peg).

But this can be improved. We need a way to place the origin anywhere on our little sample of the plane. The axes will then, of course, no longer be the wooden edges of the pegboard, but the two orthogonal lines intersecting at our specified origin. To accommodate this, we need only make laminated black poster board strips sized to our particular brand of pegboard and punched with holes that exactly align with our pegboard's holes. These axes can then be moved up and down, back and forth, as needed (figure 1). The movable axes now allow us to introduce one other key concept: the quadrants of the Cartesian plane.

You may want to begin the introductory presentation by showing a picture of René Descartes and telling the well-known story about him watching a fly crawling on his ceiling and thinking about how to describe the fly's position as the distance between two intersecting walls. You may go on to say that although this was a simple idea, it was enormously important because it allowed Descartes to connect two ancient branches of mathematics: geometry and algebra.

During the presentation introducing the Cartesian plane, place a few green pegs in the first quadrant. Show the children how to find the (x, y) coordinates of each point by counting first along the x-axis, starting at the origin, to find the x-coordinate, and then along the y-axis to find the y-coordinate. Label each point with its coordinates.

Place a few green pegs in other quadrants and show the children how to label them. Mark and label (4, 4), (-4, 4), (-4, -4), and (4, -4) so that the children can see how each quadrant is characterized by a consistent pattern of negative and positive coordinates.

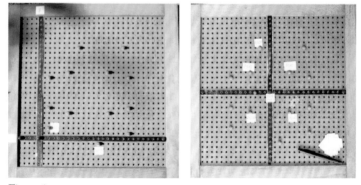

Figure 1

The children can then be shown two related activities that support the two skills involved with using Cartesian coordinates: labeling a given point with its coordinates, and finding the point corresponding to given coordinates.

Prepare ahead of time a few cards listing the coordinates for interesting patterns that can be built with the pegs. For example, a square wave pattern, a smiley face, or a word or short phrase. Do not label the card with the pattern, but allow the children to discover the pattern through building it on the pegboard. This plants the seed for them to build their own patterns, record all of the coordinates, and trade them with their partners. Allow the children to discover for themselves that they can make more intricate patterns by also using the blue and red pegs.

After children have worked with the Cartesian coordinates on the pegboard, they are ready to move to grid paper for further work with pencil and ruler. Among the applications I regularly introduced to the children were these:

- *Graphing linear equations,* such as y = x, y = 2x, y = x + 4, y = 4x −2, et cetera

- *Slope of a line,* measured by rise/run

- *Distance between two points on the Cartesian Plane,* using their coordinates and the Pythagorean theorem to derive the distance formula (for children who had already done significant work solving problems with the Pythagorean theorem)

- *Data plotting,* for scatterplots, line graphs, et cetera ❖

The Children's Play,
the Children's Way

||||||||||||||||||||||||||||||||||||||||||||||||||||||||||||||||||||||||||||||||||||||||||

After a number of experiences of making plays with children, it seemed to me that this important part of the elementary experience was one that needed a lot of rethinking. In our child-centered environment, it often appeared as the last bastion of adult-centered activity. The children and I found a better way.

Anyone who has worked with elementary age children knows how important drama is to them. Making and performing plays intersects with many of their most important developmental imperatives. In making plays, they hone their narrative skills, explore cause and effect, and gain insights into human psychology. In acting out plays, they practice taking on different personae—an important psychological experience at this age—in a safe and socially sanctioned context. The perspective taking required in both writing and performing plays is not qualitatively different from that required to be a good friend or to understand people from different cultures. Finally, the production of plays is necessarily a group activity, a challenging and intricate collaboration of just the sort that captivates and inspires the gregarious second-plane child.

Given the importance of drama to the elementary-age child, how can we best offer opportunities for playmaking in our Montessori environments? Like everything else we offer in the prepared environment, the way playmaking is presented and supported is almost as important as the actual playmaking itself. Like Montessori children who say "Nobody taught me to read; I taught myself," our children can come away from theatrical productions saying, "Nobody taught us how to make a play; we just did it ourselves!"

In order to achieve this result, we adults have to let go of some of our notions about children and theater, and we have to find new ways to work with children that lead them gently and lightly in the right direction as they go about making their own plays.

We will not go very far with this until we are clear in our own minds and hearts that the children's plays *belong to the children*, not to us, the school, or the children's families. Let's face it, we all love to watch children on stage, and class plays are an immensely popular way to showcase the class for other adults. (I can vouch that even the late Walter Cronkite showed up for his nine-year-old grandson's class play at our school.) However, if we allow our desire to impress other adults to consciously or unconsciously govern how we work with the children, theater will always seem an adult-centered incongruity in a child-centered environment.

When we let the play belong to the children, we also have to recalibrate our expectations about how elaborate and polished the production should be. There is no doubt that a small army of enthusiastic, creative adults—whether they be parent volunteers or children's theater specialists—can work miracles with the sets, props, costumes, lighting, music, special effects, and programs for a children's play. And there is no doubt that the children can learn a few things looking over the shoulders of the adults as they put together the children's play for them. Nevertheless, as Montessori educators, we are called by the children to "help them do it themselves," and this means we will need to learn to judge the success of a production by the children's standards, not our own. Our success as guides hinges on how little we do for the children, not how well the children do for us.

Another cherished tradition we may need to give up for the good of the children is the tradition of adapting adult plays for child actors—or even of using adult-written plays at all. What?! No elementary productions of *Midsummer Night's Dream* or *Our Town* or *The Sound of Music*? This is certainly a hard pill to swallow, but after seeing what children can do when they are given creative freedom to make plays out of their own life experiences and perspectives, I have come to think that it is not such a difficult trade off. Children who learn to love drama through making plays will take opportunities later in life to act out the classics. Children who are force-marched through the classics may never again darken the door of a theater.

How the Children Make a Play

We start out with a class meeting to discuss ideas for a play. What stories do we already know that might make a good play? What other stories might we make up for ourselves? From this brainstorming comes a list of books or stories to read, and perhaps a group or two will spontaneously form to work on ideas for an original play. If there are many stories or books to consider, groups of children might want to read one selection and present it to the class for further discussion.

After a period of reading, discussing, and thinking together, the children converge on a story that can serve as the basis of our play. This could be an adaptation of an existing story or myth, or it could be an original work. Our last play was based on three episodes from Homer's *Odyssey*; the play before that, entitled *The Director Disaster*, was completely original, growing out of the children's prior experiences with a traditional theater specialist.

If we are basing the play on a pre-existing story, we read the story again a few times, noticing different aspects of it: how characters are introduced, how the plot moves along, how the time and place affect the plot and other particulars of the story, how the characters change during the story. Depending on the length and complexity of the story, we may need to leave some parts and some characters out, and we begin to debate how to do that so that the end result is coherent and still captures the themes and mood of the original. A group of children then volunteer to write a plot summary and develop a list of characters. The plot summary only describes the major events in the story, without description or details.

From the plot summary, the children develop a framework of acts and scenes, noting briefly the major events that happen in each scene. If there are too many short scenes (as is usually the case), there is an intermediate step of consolidation and perhaps another round of selection and editing of the plot.

Children are now given a chance to say how they would like to contribute to the play. Who would like an acting part? With or without lines? Who would like to work on the sets, props, and costumes? Who would like to be co-directors?

The co-directors, assisted by the guide unless they have previous experience with this play-making process, think carefully about the characters and the available actors and draft a plan for casting. They call each actor one at a time and offer them the role that the co-directors think most suited to them, always having an option or two held in reserve in case the actor declines the proffered role. Characters are described to the prospective actor only in the sketchiest of terms. "Jason is a boy who is crazy about peanut butter." "Celina is a shy girl who is worried that her best friend Rita may abandon her for the new girl Angie."

Once the cast is set, each actor is invited to write a full character sketch of their character. A list of questions is available on the language shelf to aid in writing character sketches. All that is asked of the children is that they stay true to the minimalist description of the character given them when they agreed to take on that character. The character's other attributes are entirely the product of the actor's imagination. In this way, the children start to identify with and understand their character even before they do any acting.

The co-directors may now start calling rehearsals of specific scenes. At first, only the major characters in that scene are called to the rehearsal. The directors remind the actors what happens in the scene and then watch as the actors, staying in character as much as possible, improvise the scene. The actors and directors together note what worked and what didn't work, and they continue to practice the scene repeatedly until they have all converged on a satisfactory rendition.

The scene is then "frozen" and all practice from that time on focuses on polishing the scene and helping individual actors with the fine points of acting out their characters. It is astonishing (to adults) how quickly the children can work out a scene, and how well they can remember from day to day the lines and blocking they have improvised. In this way, the play comes to life in the minds and bodies of the children *without ever being written down.*

Scene by scene, act by act, the play takes shape through this process of guided group improvisation. Because of the prior framework of plot summary and character sketches, the play as a whole hangs together. Little issues of continuity that arise between scenes are worked out in the later rehearsals when the children begin to run through the whole play.

At this point performance dates can be set. Delaying the scheduling of performances is an important, if somewhat unconventional, practice. When dates are set ahead of time and maybe even put on the school calendar at the beginning of the year, the children's natural way of working is disrupted as they attempt to race the clock to get ready for their performance.

As the scenes and acts come together, the directors and actors capture important information about the play such as what props are needed, what sets are needed, what costumes are required, how the lighting should work, what special effects there should be, and so forth. The guide can help as needed and may be particularly helpful in putting the children in touch with outside resources for the things they need for the play. As this information starts to gel, groups of children can begin to work on sets, props, costumes, and other elements. Children love to dress up and will probably want to be designing costumes even before the plot is completely worked out, but it is important to delay costume and set design until the children can run all the way through the play. At that point, it will be very clear what costumes and sets are needed.

Far from intruding on the regular life of the Montessori classroom, plays made in this way are organic creations that flow out of the life of the community. No longer is the class play a spectacle of children pretending to be little adults. Instead, the children's authentic literary voices emerge in ways both moving and enlightening—but only if we have the faith and courage to let it be the children's play, the children's way. ❖

花
桜

Nancy C. Kinstler
Van Gogh's Almond Blossom

Call Me by My True Name

||||||||||||||||||||||||||||||||||||||||||||||||||||||||||||||||||||||||||||||||||||||||||||||||||||||||||||||||||||||||||||||||||||||||||

This article draws on material written for a 2008 NAMTA co-presentation with Donna Bryant Goertz titled "Support and Engagement for All Students." This is been a defining theme at Austin Montessori School throughout its fifty-year history, and I was happy to have the opportunity to write a little about the importance of seeing children as they are and not as they are labeled.[1]

There is a large and growing literature in the anthropology and sociology of so-called "learning disabilities." Montessorians would be wise to acquaint themselves with this literature, its history, and its goals.

One point of departure shared by virtually all of this research is the understanding that the categories used to sort the competent from the incompetent are socially constructed. In his book *Questions of Competence*, sociologist Richard Jenkins writes:

> "Competence" is the capacity or potential for adequate functioning-in-context as a socialized human. [...] Neither incompetence nor intellectual disability—nor indeed disability more generally—are consistent, "natural" or self-evident categories. This is not to ignore the fact that, for a range of reasons, individuals differ in their intellectual or physical capacities. Nor is it to overlook the likelihood that some distinction between competence and incompetence is drawn in all societies. However, *where* the line is drawn, and what it *means*, varies enormously.

One line of Jenkins's research compares cultures all over the world with respect to what competences are important to the culture, where the line is drawn between competence and incompetence, and what

---

[1]Donna explores the theme thoroughly in her inspiring book *Children Who Are Not Yet Peaceful*.

the culture does with those deemed incompetent. A vast range of different answers to these questions has been found by Jenkins and other researchers. The same person, if transposed from one culture to another, would be seen very differently, with very different consequences for their quality of life. The inescapable conclusion is that, as Jenkins goes on to say, "all models are local models."

Having this perspective is therapeutic for those of us who work with complex, challenging children. It reminds us to recognize the somewhat arbitrary nature of our judgments of competence or normality. It hovers in the background whenever we are sure we have seen and named the true nature of the child's "problems," asking "Are you sure? Are you sure?" In Montessori terms, it gives us another way to understand why our work is always with the periphery of the child's being, not its core.

Jenkins notes that where he grew up, having a good ear for music, a good sense of rhythm, or artistic talent were considered positive but by no means necessary attributes. He then comments that "The practical aptitudes that are identified as (in)competencies in any given local or cultural setting are always, at least to some extent, an arbitrary selection from the spectrum of aptitudes and potentialities that make up the human behavioral portfolio. The degree to which they are marked or emphasized is also—once again, to some extent—arbitrary."

Our Language Misleads Us

Very much related to the issues of the social constructedness of our views of (in)competence, is the issue of language. We can learn from anthropologists, linguists, and philosophers of language how much our thinking and our very perception of the world is conditioned by our language. Thinking is, to a great extent, "languaging," and this is yet another complicating factor in our work with complex, unusual children.

Consider the never-ending debate on labels in special education. James W. Trent, in his 1994 history of mental retardation, notes that in the United States, "*defectives* became *mental defectives, imbeciles* became *high-grade* and *low-grade imbeciles, moron* became the *higher-functioning mentally retarded.* More recently, the *mentally retarded* have become *mentally retarded persons* and now *persons with mental retardation* and, in some circles, *persons with developmental disabilities* or *persons specially challenged.*"

In this progression and in analogous progressions for all manner of learning differences and putative disabilities, we can see the labels shifting along with the shifting influence of medical, sociological, and political points of view. The constantly shifting labels are the tip of the iceberg of controversy and confusion about the phenomena they label.

In Trent's progression we can also see a growing uneasiness with the acts of labeling and categorization themselves. But to have a diagnosis is already to have a label. In this sense, labeling is inherent in the medical model of learning differences. The rest is degree of politeness.

This is much more than a philosophical point. Labels have consequences; sometimes they imply whole lives. Anthropologist Michael Angrosino describes the operational meaning of diagnostic labels in our culture: "Because the United States lacks universal health insurance, virtually the only way many people—particularly the indigent, but also the working poor—can receive medical and associated services is by accepting a designation of disability. [...] It is simply not in the best economic, legal or political interest of most persons defined as disabled to contest their designation" (Jenkins).

In our work, we see many parents who end up seeking a label for their child because it is the entrance ticket or the passport to the bureaucratic maze of social and educational services.

For English speakers, there is an even deeper problem: English is a label-making language. Marshall Rosenberg, the developer of Non-Violent Communication, tells of a communication workshop he held in Malaysia. The interpreter with whom he was working, came to him before the workshop expressing some concern about how to translate much of what Rosenberg meant to talk about. Apparently, in the language of Malaysia, there is no way to directly translate "So-and-so is such-and-such"; e.g., "John is lazy." Surprised, Rosenberg asked what would they say instead. The interpreter explained that it would have to be translated something like "John rests a lot and does not do as much work as others." This sort of non-judgmental description was, of course, exactly what Rosenberg had intended to advocate in place of labels.

When we say in English (or in many other languages) "John is lazy" or "Sue is a borderline personality disorder" or "Mark is dyslexic," structurally, the utterance appears to be defining something essential about the named person. The copula "is" is the verb of definition. "Snow is frozen water" and "John is lazy" are two very different speech acts, but they can both be taken as definitions. If we stop to think about it, we know that John is not our judgment of his work ethic; he is much, much more. But the language obscures that.

Labeling language reinforces the medical model's view of the labeled condition as belonging to the individual. (Dyslexia is of the essence of Mark.) But Montessorians and many non-Montessori critics of the medical model know that the individual is always an individual-in-context, that it makes no sense to speak of "learning differences" in a context-free way. That was the message from the cross-cultural studies mentioned above.

Call Me by My Name

Sofia Cavaletti, co-developer of the Montessori-inspired religious education curriculum the Catechesis of the Good Shepherd, tells the story of a physically handicapped boy who participated in the Catechesis. There he heard the story from the Gospel of John in which the Good Shepherd "calls his own sheep by name." This made such an impression on the boy that from that day on he would never wilt under the teasing or cruel name-calling of other children, but would reply with great dignity, "The Good Shepherd has called me by my name."

This touching story speaks to the importance of being seen, accepted, and valued for the totality of who one is. As Montessorians, we have a chance to see who the child is even more clearly than other observers because in our free environments filled with materials that appeal directly to the child's inner needs, they reveal themselves as in no other place. Having seen the child for who they are, why would we ever then fall back on the misleading labels assigned them by those whose only perspective is that of a diagnostic test? Instead, let us call them by their true names. ❖

Lyle's Tale:
Exclusion and Inclusion
in the Upper Elementary

Steeped in theory and practice though we be, it is ultimately the stories we accumulate through our shared life with the children that most deeply inform our practice. Lyle's story, which dates from my earliest years as a guide, was one of those for me. I am happy to share it with you, knowing that it will resonate with anyone who works with elementary children. "Lyle" is now grown and doing amazing things.

Anyone could see that Lyle was different. For one thing, although he was nine years old, he had the physical appearance of a six-year-old. He was tall, but his face, hands, arms, and legs still had a soft, chubby, little boy look. He walked on tiptoe much of the time, and he had that kind of rolling gait that in a younger child might be called "toddling." When Lyle ran, he was slow and ungainly, arms and legs flapping out to the sides like a fledgling just learning to fly. Lyle was acutely sensitive to touch; he could hardly bear anything as coarse as denim jeans against his skin. He usually wore soft cotton clothing that accentuated his little-boy appearance.

Lyle looked out at the world through half-closed eyes under canopies of long, thick eyelashes. Although he was acutely intelligent, what he saw often made no sense to him. He was often baffled by people and how they communicated. The facial expressions, body language, tone of voice, and other social cues that most children intuitively understand frequently escaped him. He either failed to notice them or could not interpret them. Why would someone smile at you unless they were making fun of you? Being touched was uncomfortable. Why would someone touch you unless they wanted to hurt you? Lyle was also alarmingly literal. Sally must be evil because she said she was hungry enough to eat a horse, and it is wrong to eat such intelligent animals. Why did that boy ask me if the cat got my tongue? Doesn't he know that there are no cats here?

When Lyle spoke, it was often hard to understand him. He spoke quickly, indistinctly, and almost entirely without inflection. What Lyle had to say was often very surprising. Lyle had an encyclopedic knowledge of certain subjects: the solar system, butterflies, parakeets, fish behavior. He could lecture non-stop for an hour on these and other subjects, leaving even adult listeners exhausted, albeit impressed. After hearing his discourse on the solar system, an astronomer from the local university remarked with appreciation, "There was nothing I could add to what he said!"

Unfortunately, Lyle did not understand why other people were not as interested as he in these subjects, nor did he understand their frustration when he talked about them again and again, often interrupting other conversations or activities by launching into one of his esoteric lectures. After exhausting all of the socially acceptable ways to stop the lectures, people would often just walk away in desperation while Lyle continued to talk to their empty chairs.

His first few months in fourth grade were a real struggle. Lyle depended on rigid routine to orient himself in time and space, and in his new classroom everything was different—the children, the teacher, the furniture, the bathrooms, the playground—everything. He spent the first few weeks in terror and frustration. If he needed to go to the bathroom, would he be able to remember which door was the supply closet, which the girls' bathroom, and which the boys' bathroom? Lyle particularly dreaded lunch. The teacher would find him wandering aimlessly around the room, flapping his hands, and crying, "I'm not used to getting my placemat before my lunchbox! I'm not used to getting my placemat first!"

It was heartbreaking to see how lonely Lyle was. His odd behavior, unusual interests, and inability to join in the games of the other children made it difficult for them to befriend him. Lyle had learned to misinterpret almost every peer interaction as a kind of teasing or bullying. The normal curiosity and playfulness with which children approach a potential new friend were to Lyle just confirmation that people were out to get him. More than one curiously friendly child was sent packing by Lyle's defensive response or loud wails to the teacher that so-and-so was "bullying him." The more isolated Lyle felt, the more prone he was to interrupt the other children's activities with his erudite, monotone lectures about things they could not understand. It was a vicious circle.

There were two older boys in Lyle's class, Vince and Patrick. Vince and Patrick were best friends. They loved each other with that intense, single-minded devotion that pre-adolescent children can have. They shared an interest in basketball, and at recess Vince and Patrick were always to be found together on the basketball court, no matter what the rest of the children were doing.

Lyle, on the other hand, spent recess wandering around by himself or trying to lecture the adult playground attendants on one of his obsessions. Lyle had learned long ago that he could not play the games the other children played. He found it difficult to keep track of what seemed to him meaningless and arbitrary rules, and being in a group of children all running in different directions confused and paralyzed him.

Most people, not knowing what else to do, just ignored Lyle, but there were a couple of children who were beginning to realize that Lyle was advertising in neon letters "I'm an outcast! Persecute me!" and they were beginning to accept the invitation. Little things began to happen in the classroom. A nudge, a bump, a hard look, a whispered remark. At first the maltreatment was spontaneous and coincidental. Was Lyle at the water fountain? Oh, no problem, you can cut in front of Lyle. He won't do anything. Was Lyle giving somebody one of his crazy lectures again? Well, it's fun to mock that. Was Lyle crying about the placemats again? Boy, what a baby!

As time went by, more and more children were learning that Lyle was the class outcast. Everyone had a role in class, a way that they fit into the community, and that was Lyle's role: outcast. Children who hardly knew Lyle and who certainly bore him no particular ill will followed the lead of those who had already discovered the guilty pleasure of exercising illicit power, the little thrill of seeing the power of one's words and actions over another. They began to like the very real, if double-edged, sense of belonging that comes when one group defines itself against another. And Lyle always came through with a big reaction. Lyle was different, but he was certainly consistent!

A few of the girls in the class, always eager to write notes, tried writing notes to Lyle. "Lyle, you're stupid." "Lyle, I hate you!" The teacher knew something had to be done, but it wasn't clear what would work. It wasn't always easy to tell who was involved. Coming down hard on the "ring leaders" when so many of the children were implicated might just make martyrs out of the leaders and drive the teasing even farther underground. It was already hard enough to know which of Lyle's complaints were justified and which were misinterpretations of everyday human interaction.

Many times the teacher took Lyle and one of his persecutors aside and mediated a discussion about unacceptable behavior, the importance of understanding each other, the underlying values of the classroom community, and so forth. There were class discussions. All the same, the teacher knew the situation would not likely shift as long as the victim/oppressor system was in place—even a strong child would be dragged back into the system and the dynamics of exclusion. The teacher also knew that ultimately he could not socially engineer a solution. The maltreatment of a fellow student was a problem in the community of children, and although the teacher could be a catalyst, any lasting solution would have to come from the hearts and minds of the children themselves. Somehow, these fundamentally kind, empathic children had to be called back to their better selves, and some children had to take the lead to make it safe for the others.

The teacher also knew very well that what the community was experiencing was a universal human dynamic. The community of children was a microcosm reflecting in its own way the very deepest and most intractable problems of adult society. How the children worked through this, what they learned about themselves and about their peers, what they learned about the challenges and joys of living in community—these experiences and insights could become life-changing foundations for lives of peacemaking. Because this was real, with real risks on all sides—and not a curriculum module on character building—it could be authentic education for peace. But there were no guarantees.

Even Vince and Patrick, usually compassionate boys, and in any case too involved with each other to pay much attention to Lyle, began to join the game. They joined in the jokes and the laughter. When Lyle came to sit by Vince on the school bus, Vince and Patrick showed their solidarity with the other children by screaming and scooting as far away on the bench as possible, so as not to be "contaminated."

When Vince's father heard about this, he was very upset. He knew he had to do something, and he also knew that this could be a pivotal moment in Vince's life—a moment that Vince might come back to many times as he made decisions about how to treat other people. Because the father was angry, disappointed, and afraid, he waited a while to say anything to Vince about it. He wanted to find the right approach, and he needed time to sort out his own strong emotions—emotions he knew were linked directly to his own childhood memories of at times being excluded and at other times joining in the exclusion of another. He finally found a quiet moment with Vince. He sat down by Vince, put his arms around him from behind, and let Vince lean back on his chest. He somehow knew that what he had to say would be hard for Vince to hear—and hard for him to say—if they were face to face. He did not want to shame Vince, just to speak to his heart.

"Vince, I'm feeling very sad about something I've heard. I heard that you and Patrick were being mean to Lyle on the bus this week. Is that right?" Vince nodded his head, "Yeah, I guess so." Silence.

"Well, Vince, I want to tell you a story. When I was in school, there was a boy named Terry. He was really different. He dressed in rags. He had no manners. He smelled bad. His desk was always a rat's nest of papers and junk, and the teacher was always yelling at him about it. He talked funny, and all the kids made a lot of fun of him. We used to play this game at recess called "Terry germs." It was like tag, only Terry was always "it." Terry would chase us around, and we would run away screaming 'Arrrgh! Terry germs!'" I knew it was wrong to treat Terry this way. It was against my family's beliefs and values, and it just felt wrong. But, you know what? I did it anyway. Not as much as some other kids, but I did it. Sometimes it was hard for me to relate to the other kids, too, and when we were all making fun of Terry together, it felt good to be a part of the group and the game. Even so, when I was alone, I wasn't proud of it, and I felt guilty about it. Vince, you know what? Even today, thirty-five years later, I still think of Terry and feel awful about how I treated him. I sometimes wonder whatever became of him and if he ever found a better life among kinder people. Vince, the feeling I have when I remember how I treated Terry is still one of the worst feelings I have ever had. I really, really don't want you to have to have those feelings when you grow up.

"Vince, do you understand that story?" Vince nodded. "Do you understand why I told you that story?" Again, a nod. Vince and his father didn't mention Lyle after that.

About a week after Vince and his father talked, Lyle came running into the classroom during recess. He was flushed and panting. The teacher thought, "Oh, boy. Here we go again. Who is it this time?" But Lyle burst out, "Vince and Patrick are teaching me basketball! I used to be a wimp in basketball, but now they're teaching me to be a pro!" He ran back outside, leaving the teacher slack-jawed, staring at his disappearing back.

The lesson lasted for the whole recess period. The playground attendant reported later that both older boys were heroically patient with their new pupil. Lyle was too weak and uncoordinated to heave the ball more than six feet off the ground—some four feet short of hitting even the rim of the basketball goal. Nor could he dribble. He knew none of the rules. Still, the boys showed him over and over, encouraging even the tiniest bit of improvement. Once, when Lyle heaved up a shot that almost hit the rim, the usually very quiet Patrick jumped up and down shouting, "Lyle, you almost made it! Awesome, Lyle!" All three boys were so exhilarated by the experience that the teacher let them go back out to the basketball court later during the afternoon work period and continue the lessons.

From that day on, Lyle was the third man on the court with Vince and Patrick. They would practice their behind-the-back passes and cool shots; he would practice dribbling and heaving the ball in the general direction of the basket. There were days when Vince and Patrick would look at each other and sigh, remembering the good old days when they could just be together in their friendship on the court. But they never ran Lyle off, and they saw that he got to touch the basketball from time to time.

Things quickly started to turn around for Lyle in the classroom. Many of the children recognized their own best impulses in what Vince and Patrick were doing with Lyle, and they quietly disengaged from the teasing. Different notes started appearing on Lyle's desk. "Lyle, I'm sorry." "Lyle, I think you know a lot about planets." A few children who were slower to let go of the old pattern stopped themselves when they realized that the community of their peers was no longer giving them tacit permission to mistreat Lyle. Things the teacher said about living in community were now heard with different ears.

Lyle himself never tired of talking about his new basketball prowess. "I used to be a wimp at basketball, but Vince and Patrick taught me." It sometimes got a bit tiresome, and the lectures continued, but now it was just Lyle being himself—something that every member of the community was entitled to do—and the community was on its way to being whole again. ❖

Emotions Like Clouds,
Thoughts Like Rain

||||||||||||||||||||||||||||||||||||||||||||||||||||||||||||||||||||||||||||||||||||||||||||||||||||||||

Many educators these days have gone much further than I did in introducing mindfulness practices into the classroom.[1] This 2009 article illustrates how mindful walking can be an effective self-calming tool for children.

"Calm, penetrating vision" is, I think, an apt description of the psychological flow that characterizes the Montessori child at work. It is also a mind/body state that people can learn to create for themselves even when the conditions are not otherwise right for flow to arise.

One of the self-calming tools I have sometimes given children is the practice of "mindful walking." This method has historical roots in the contemplative traditions of Asia, but it is in no way esoteric and is easily understood by children.

As in sitting meditation, mindful walking employs deep, relaxed breathing to calm the mind and focus the attention, but unlike sitting, it links the breath to movement. This makes it especially accessible to children.

Walking is usually a means to an end, a way of getting where we want to go. In mindful walking, we walk just to walk. That is, it is the experience of calm, relaxed walking itself that is the focus, not the destination or calculations about which path to take.

In its simplest form (and it has no complicated forms), mindful walking involves starting from a relaxed standing posture. One takes

---

[1] For an excellent example, see Meena Srinivasan's *Teach, Breathe, Learn: Mindfulness in and out of the Classroom.*

---

up the thread of the breath and begins to follow it—breathing in, breathing out. Then, when one is ready, stepping slowly with the left foot, one breathes in. Stepping with the right foot, one breathes out. Left, in; right, out. And so it goes.

The pace is set by the length of the breath. As one walks in this way, as attention is directed to the synchronized action of breath and steps and the felt sensations of walking, the breathing becomes slower and deeper and the pace slows down, as well.

I have found it most natural to introduce mindful walking to a few children at a time instead of to large groups. Once it is understood, large groups can practice it together. It is quite a beautiful and inspiring sight to see a large number of children walking mindfully through the places where they normally run and shout and play.

Mindful walking has been a great help to some children with whom I have worked. I will share the story of one such wonderful child, whom I will call Hans. I can hear Hans now; he's making quite a commotion over by my assistant's work space.

It Doesn't Make Sense!

Hans is upset because he can't understand a math problem he is trying to do. It involves dividing a fraction by a fraction. He hasn't actually had the lesson on how to do that kind of problem, but that never stops *this* boy from trying. Usually he can figure math out for himself. He's crying and raising his voice and repeating himself over and over to my assistant, who is trying to calm him. She is quite skillful and can usually help him get a grip on himself, but he is not responding to the usual approaches this time.

Hans easily gets into mental loops, carried away by thoughts he cannot stop. I can see that he is in a mental loop now, and it will be very hard for him to get out of it without help. All his carrying on has naturally attracted the attention of other children, and one boy makes a wry face. Hans kicks at him and yells for him to stop. I come over to be near Hans.

"Hans, you are very upset. I would like to hear how you think about this kind of math problem, and I would like to show you how I think about it, but first you will need to be calm."

"I can't calm down, because it doesn't make sense! I don't know how I could get the wrong answer when I'm just doing the logical thing! Everyone says it's the wrong answer! How can something be divided and get bigger? That can't make any sense! It should get smaller!"

"Hans, what can you do to calm yourself? Would a walk outside help? Get some fresh air away from all these people?"

He agrees to go outside, but once out, he walks around in a tight circle complaining loudly about things not making sense. I join him outside and lead him gently out to the playground, with him obsessing loudly the whole way.

"It doesn't make sense! You can't divide something and get something bigger! It doesn't make any sense! I don't know why anybody ever made that up! I can't stop thinking about it, and it doesn't make any sense! And then Jeff did that thing where he makes a face, and I lunged at him because it was like I was already to my breaking point and I couldn't take any more! Because you are supposed to get something smaller if you divide..."

"Hans, you're right: it doesn't make any sense at all based on what you already know very well about division, so when you are calm again, I will show you something new that will help it make sense."

"No, I can't! I can't stop thinking about how it doesn't make any sense! I can't calm down!"

"Hans, I'd like to show you something I do to calm myself down. I call it mindful walking..."

"It won't work! I can't ever calm down when things are not making sense. You can't divide and get something larger..."

"Hans, first I just pay attention to my breathing for a few breaths. Breathing in... Breathing out..."

"I can't think about *that*! Breathing doesn't work! I've tried breathing. Breathing just makes me think about not making sense. It will just make it worse, and I'll keep thinking about it!"

"Breathing in, I know I am breathing in... Breathing out, I know I am breathing out...

And then I step with my left foot, breathing in... And with my right foot, breathing out..." I begin to walk slowly onto the playground. Hans follows, muttering.

"This isn't working! This won't work, breathing doesn't work, I'll just keep thinking about other things!"

"It takes a little practice, but I'm confident you can do it... Left, breathing in... Right, breathing out..."

Hans starts to calm down a little. He is still agitated, but I can see that he is at least trying to do what I do. We walk a few more steps as I talk to him, with long pauses to let things sink in.

"Breathing in... breathing out... breathing in... breathing out... And then I can begin to look around... I see all those clouds... moving across the sky... That reminds me how everything changes, all the time... even my emotions... sometimes I'm really excited, but then it changes into something else... sometimes I'm really sad or really angry, but it doesn't last forever... I think our minds are like a big blue sky with all sorts of thoughts and feelings moving across them all the time.... I don't even know where all those thoughts come from or what causes them... they just move on by and change into something else..."

His energy shifts tangibly as we walk. He says in an almost dreamy voice, "Clouds move toward us and away from us."

"Yes, always moving, always changing."

"Emotions move toward us and away from us.... Emotions are like the clouds... and thoughts are like the rain."

"Oh, I like that! Emotions are like the clouds and thoughts are like the rain."

"Or some other kind of precipitation—it could be snow or hail or sleet."

"Ah! I see! Some thoughts are cold and crystalline; some are foggy and amorphous; some are hot and searing like the sun in summertime..."

We walk a bit more, and I notice that he is saying to himself sotto voce, "In... out... in... out..."

Smiling a little now, *getting* it, he says, "I feel like I'm walking mindfully on the cliff of anger. One foot on and one foot off."

"One foot on, one foot off... you're on the edge, but you're no longer falling off the cliff... You know, Hans, I like to come outside to walk mindfully whenever I'm feeling flooded by emotion. So, Hans, anytime you feel like walking mindfully just let me know. You can just say, 'John, I'm going outside to walk mindfully,' and that will be okay with me. And... let me know when you want that math lesson."

Later that day, we sat together on a bench watching some other children on the playground. Hans remarked, "It's funny how different thoughts *feel* different. Some feel shady and cool. That's how my thoughts feel right now. It's pleasant."

Later that week, with the help of Dr. Montessori's ingenious math materials, we made sense of division by fractions. It was very, very pleasant. ❖

Staying in Touch with the Wonder of Language

||||||||||||||||||||||||||||||||||||||||||||||||||||||||||||||||||||||||||||||||||||||||||||||||

This article draws on a keynote address "Exploring Language, Discovering the Mind" given for NAMTA in 2012.

In our literate, media-intense, hyper-connected world, we swim in a sea of words. We take them for granted, and when we stop to consider them, it is often with a clear instrumental purpose in mind; that is, we see them as tools and only stop to consider matters of technique. Is that expression clear? Is it correct? Is it cogent? Is it what I meant? Is it likely to be misunderstood? How could I say or write it better?

These are excellent questions to ask about language, and I fully intend to keep asking them about my speech and writing every day. But if we only relate to language instrumentally, we can lose touch with how truly astonishing it is that such a thing as language even exists. We can fail to ask deeper questions about language and miss the insights that our search for answers to these questions would provide.

As teachers and guides, we are especially susceptible to adopting a merely instrumental view of language. In our attempts to help children develop as readers and writers, we can easily become rigid and narrow in our views of language, seeing "right" and "wrong" where there are really only culturally-conditioned conventions, seeing our simple grammatical tools as the whole truth about language, losing the playfulness, expansiveness, and openness to experience that are the seeds of joy. If we fail to regularly water these seeds in ourselves, how will we connect with children exploring, playing with, and delighting in language? How can we offer inspiration if the spirit has gone out of us? We need to see language for the miracle it is and stay in touch with the sense of wonder this engenders.

The Montessori Connection

This question about what it means to be human is at the core of Montessori's Cosmic Education. And part of what it means to be human is to have language.

Among the great stories of Dr. Montessori that are told at the beginning of each year in the elementary, one of the most wonderful is the story of humanity and its three gifts. In the story this newcomer, the human being, is shown surrounded by its creaturely elder brothers and sisters, and its place in nature, sharing the earth with other living things, is firmly established. The question is posed: How will this unlikely new creature survive? By virtue of three unique gifts: the human mind, the human hands, and the human capacity to love.

With its unique mind, the human being is able to *learn* from its experience in ways that other animals cannot. It can *communicate* in unique ways. The human mind can rise above the urges of instinct and evolutionary programming to *choose* how to act, how to live. Above all, it can *imagine* things that do not exist—things that cannot be directly experienced.

With its unique hands, the human being is able to fashion tools, to explore its environment in new ways, and, eventually, to produce things of great beauty and utility. Because its hands work together with its mind, it can imagine things that do not exist and then bring them into existence.

The human being's third gift is its great heart—a unique capacity to love that goes far beyond that of other animals. Whereas other animals may, in their own ways, love their mates or their offspring or their pack or herd, the human being's love is so great that it can extend to human beings well outside its family, human beings that it has never seen, even to other non-human creatures that are radically unlike it in many ways.

So all things human to be explored in the Montessori elementary are to be found in the vast territory marked out by the mind, the hand and the heart. *Wonder*, I think, lives at the intersection of these three human capacities. It can arise as the response of the heart to the activity of the mind, or as the response of the mind to the activity of the heart, or as the response of either to the activity of the hand. Wonder is what philosophers would call a kind of aesthetic experience, a very close cousin to the experience of beauty. When we stand in awe of something, we are connected to it in a very deep and special way. It is a species of I-Thou relationship, even with inanimate things.

A Fourth Gift?

But what of language? I have sometimes felt that the story needs a fourth gift, the gift of language. After all, even with my human mind, hand, and heart, I am still not much without my community. It is in and through the quintessential human need for companionship, for a family, a tribe, a social matrix that the three gifts manifest in all their richness. And language is the primary medium of both that social matrix and that cultural richness. In the canonical story with its three gifts, communication is in the province of the mind. What my hand creates, my mind first imagines. But this imagining is full of language, and when I need the hands of others to help realize my imaginings, it is language that will knit us together in purpose and collaboration.

So this uniquely human mind is not left alone in its imaginings. Perhaps its very greatest creation is not something made by the hand, but the means by which it reaches out to touch other minds; namely, language. In one of those inexpressibly beautiful interpenetrations of the human being and its world, the brain both shapes and is shaped by the exercise of communication through language. Although we use the same verb, to "know" a language is a much more wondrous thing than to "know" any number of facts or even to "know" how to ride a bicycle or play a piano concerto.

Knowing a language is open-ended and creative in a way that nothing else I know is. It is a fully embodied kind of knowledge, a deep integration of body and mind, a full expression of the capacities of the human organism.

To have a capacity for speech, the raw materials we need are a healthy human brain; ears; a mouth with lips, teeth, palate, and tongue; a glottis and vocal chords; and the apparatus of respiration:

nose, trachea, lungs, diaphragm, and so on. Any one of these organs, should we look deeply at it and how it functions, is a wonder greater than any appearance of angels; equally remarkable is that all these organs, both separately and in various combinations, have other, older functions in the organism. Our capacity for linguistic competence is, as it were, cobbled together from borrowed materials. It rests on an anatomical substructure not of its own making. There is something that is, to me, very poignant about that and very inspiring.

Unscientific though it may be, I like to imagine that this human animal that we are, having stood up on its hind legs and achieved self-awareness, felt a deep unsatisfied longing to escape the prison of its own skull. I hear it saying to itself, "Lips and teeth, no longer will you merely eat and grimace. Tongue and throat, no longer will you merely swallow. Lungs, no longer will you merely respire. Ears, no longer will you merely listen for prey or predator. Brain, no longer will you merely sense, react, and control movement. Together, we will now speak what is in my mind!"

The Wonder of Communication

Loren Eiseley, in his famous essay "The Long Loneliness" (1960), mourns our inability to communicate with other species, almost turning the miracle of human-to-human communication into a liability. I'm of a different mind. While it would no doubt be wonderful to communicate with dolphins, seeing the world through their eyes, I am more than content, through the wonderful gift of language, to see the world through the eyes of my human brothers and sisters throughout time and space—to think the thoughts of the Buddha or St. Hildegard, Voltaire or Basho, Darwin or Mary Oliver.

Dr. Montessori's own fascination with language and child development comes through powerfully whenever she writes about first language acquisition. We know that infants begin from the moment of birth, if not before, to reshape their brains to conform to the recognition and production of the language in their environment. Montessori was right to focus on first language acquisition as the paradigmatic case of untutored, child-initiated learning.

At first there is for the infant only an undifferentiated stream of sound. The sounds of speech are mixed together with all other sounds in the environment. But almost immediately infants begin to distinguish between the sounds of speech and other sounds, and they show a particular interest in speech sounds.

Researchers have discovered that even newborns are sensitive to the prosodic features—that is, the tone and rhythms—of their native language. They rapidly begin to learn where the boundaries of words occur. By 4½ months American infants can detect clause boundaries; by 9 months, the boundaries of major phrases and sentences.

By the end of the first year infants can distinguish between the basic properties of their own languages and those of other languages. The one-year-old already knows a great deal about the phonology of their native language, including what sounds can be put together to form words; the structure of vowel categories; and distributional properties of the language, that is, the relative commonness of sounds and sound combinations.

As Montessori wrote, "There is in every child a painstaking teacher, so skillful that he obtains identical results in all children in all parts of the world. The only language men ever speak perfectly is the one they learn in babyhood, when no one can teach them anything!" (*AM*).

How wonderful that is! And what a delight to share the wonder that children naturally have about language. ❖

Haiku: Windows on the World

||||||||||||||||||||||||||||||||||||||||||||||||||||||||||||||||||||||||||||||||||||||||||||||||||||||||||||||||||||||||||||||||||||||||||||||||||||||||||||||||||||||||||||

In 2002 I set myself the goal of learning the Japanese haiku form and how it was being brought into the literary life of the English-speaking world. I had some success over the years, publishing many haiku in journals around the world and winning the haiku competition at the 2005 World Haiku Festival in the Netherlands. This article captures some of the insights from a workshop given at the 2007 AMI-EAA Summer Conference.

In the aftermath of World War II, gazing at the rubble of his fire-bombed house and trying to comprehend the end of Japanese culture as he had known it, the poet Shuson Kato wrote,

> my house gone
> only the ground lies there
> with dew drops

Decades later, the New Zealand poet Linzy Forbes captured a rare but universally recognizable moment:

> patches of snow
> the finger-warming breath
> of a newborn lamb

Aida Braciu, a Romanian high school student, recently penned these bright, sweet lines (translated by her young friend Sonia Coman):

> golden leaves
> I've hidden his letter
> under our tree

And this little poem came to me while I was on spiritual retreat:

a thousand rivers
flow into this ocean
lifting the little boats

Each just a few words and only three lines, yet I know of no other poetic form that more naturally and powerfully serves such a remarkable range of emotions, purposes and cultural contexts as this—the haiku. This seven-hundred-year-old Japanese tradition, so firmly rooted in the Japanese perspective and way of life, has in the past twenty years been eagerly imported into the literary and linguistic traditions of nearly every country in the world, including those of the English-speaking countries.

The Internet has been the catalyst for much of the exponential growth of interest in serious haiku. A quick Internet search on "haiku journal" will turn up a surprising number of high-quality, well-edited online and print journals devoted to the practice of haiku. For the first time, non-Japanese poets can be in regular contact with Japanese poets and with each other, and the conversations and debates have been eye-opening for those of us who thought we knew what haiku was solely on the basis of a brief encounter with syllable counting in elementary or middle school.

The common misconception in English-speaking countries is that a poem is a haiku if and only if it is arranged in three lines with five, seven, and five syllables, respectively. In the new understanding and practice of English-language haiku poets (and most other non-Japanese haiku poets), no part of this definition survives! There is much, much more to writing a good haiku than counting syllables. In fact, for beginners, counting syllables very likely precludes any progress toward writing authentic haiku—poems with true "haiku spirit."

In retrospect, this is not too surprising a turn of events. Any serious poet knows that there is much more to writing a Shakespearean sonnet than three quatrains and a couplet in iambic pentameter with a certain rhyme scheme. Mere structural issues aside, to master the sonnet, it is necessary to enter into the tradition and culture of the sonnet; to come to understand the *spirit* of the sonnet; to come to intuit the organic, ineffable relationship between the structural elements and how they support or fail to support a specific poetic inspiration, context, or expression.

While this sort of project may well be beyond the capabilities of our young students, the beauty of the haiku is that it is a form eminently suited to the child. The child's direct but penetrating way of seeing and interpreting the world of concrete experience is exactly what is required. The child is a natural *haijin* (haiku poet), whereas we adults must often work hard to recover the fresh, childlike perspective that embodies the authentic haiku spirit.

Since we cannot give away what we do not possess, our first step toward bringing haiku to the children is to educate ourselves in the ways of haiku. There is no better way to do this than to spend quality time with some of those online journals, in parallel with a careful reading of Jane Reichhold's book *Writing and Enjoying Haiku: a Hands-on Guide*. While you wait for your copy to arrive, I would like to offer five tips that represent the distillation of my own years of teaching haiku to both adults and children.

1. Don't count syllables. Think shorter-longer-shorter.

In Japanese, haiku are written in one line that is usually divided into sections of five, seven, and five "syllables." When early Western admirers of the Japanese haiku imported the form into English, they thought the best way to honor the haiku tradition was to count 5-7-5 just as the Japanese did. Most serious English-language haiku poets and scholars now think this literal adoption of 5-7-5 overlooks some radical differences between the two languages.

To understand the differences, one needs to understand the two languages at the basic level of phonology—sound and rhythm. This can quickly become very technical, but the gist of it is that the "syllables" that the Japanese haijin counts are not the same as the English syllable. Japanese "syllables" are all of about the same duration and sonic "weight" or "richness." English syllables are not: compare "e" and "nough" in the word "enough". On average there are several Japanese "syllable" equivalents in one English syllable. So, counting 5-7-5 in English usually leads to verses that sound heavy, artificial and verbose—verses that lack both the elegance and the "punch" of traditional Japanese haiku.

Moreover, because of the great phonological differences between one English syllable and another, it has not proved practical to agree on some specific number of syllables to count in English—say, 4-6-4 or 3-4-3. The best results have come from just thinking "shorter-longer-shorter" and from *concentrating on making sure every word is doing some work in the poem.*

A parallel line of thought proceeds from the question "Why would the Japanese themselves fix on 5-7-5 as the structure of a verse?" The simple answer is that the natural rhythms of Japanese speech fall quite naturally and elegantly into those parameters, which is decidedly not the case in English.

2. Use simple, concrete language. Less is more.

Although masters such as Basho and Shiki raised haiku to greatness, it always was and still is a popular art form. It mines common experience for its insights. Good haiku capture the universal in the particular, and they do it by speaking plainly of direct experience. Poems that preach, teach, speak about philosophical or fantastic subjects, or use poetic rhetorical devices lack haiku spirit. The best haiku are great not because of their erudition or cleverness, but because they make us look again at the little mundane details of life to see with the poet's penetrating gaze something that we have habitually overlooked.

3. Pause and change the thought after the first (or second) line.

Traditional haiku typically comprise two sections separated by a meaningless "cutting word" (*kireji*). Since English does not have *kireji* in the same sense that Japanese does, we use punctuation and/or line breaks to show the separation between parts. When haiku are written in three lines, as is the custom in the English-speaking world, the break can come either after the first line or after the second line.

Poets often use the two sections to do different things. With a one-line/two-line poem, the first line often sets the scene (and season) and the other two lines describe what is happening (this means that there is often a verb—but only one—in the second section). An example by American poet Zhanna Rader:

Autumn wind ...
the widow sweeps the same leaves
again and again

In a two-line/one-line poem, the first section often gives a strong but ambiguous image that is then crystallized in a surprising way in the last line, as exemplified in this wonderful poem by the seventeenth-century master Basho:

whore and monk, we sleep
under one roof together—
moon in a field of clover

The culturally shocking image of an itinerant Buddhist monk and a woman sleeping under the same roof dissolves in the realization that the roof they share is the open sky and the precarious existence they both lead unites them in an undeniable way.

4. Show, don't tell; imply, don't assert.

In just a few words, the haiku poet must say something of significance. There is no room for long descriptions or explanations. Instead, a tiny glimpse must be offered, and the mind of the reader fills in the rest. Open-endedness, ambiguity, and indirect reference are an important part of the haiku aesthetic.

Reread Zhanna Rader's above. On the surface, it is quite mundane: a woman having trouble keeping the leaves swept in the autumn wind. However, in the hands of this very skillful poet, the image becomes a metaphor for the widow's persistent, frustrating experience of loss, and we get a deep but indirect insight into her life and experience a little of her grief. Good haiku often create this sort of empathic connection between reader and subject.

5. As part of nature, speak of the natural.

Although the admissible subject matter for haiku has been greatly expanded over the past century, most haiku continue to have a strong connection to nature: seasons, plants, animals, weather, land, mountains, sea, and so forth. In classical haiku, there is always a word or phrase (*kigo*) that firmly associates the poem with a particular season of the year. ("Cherry blossom" is the somewhat clichéd kigo for spring.)

In Western nature poetry, the poet often stands outside nature even while extolling it. Though haiku are about human experience, the haiku poet understands herself to be part of nature, with all its seasons, moods, and—above all—its impermanence. So, even when there is no seasonal or nature reference and the poem seems to be entirely about human affairs, this understanding of humanity as part of nature and the processes of nature is in the background.

A wonderful way to share haiku with children is to take them on a haiku nature walk. A haiku nature walk is a relaxed saunter through a beautiful natural area, enjoying the sights, smells, sounds, and embodied feelings that nature evokes. Everyone has a little notebook and a pencil. Whenever someone notices something or has an insight or new thought about their nature experience, they stop and jot it down. Experienced haiku poets write haiku right on the spot. Beginners can make a little note that can be developed later into a haiku. ❖

Bringing Experience to Conscious Awareness

||||||||||||||||||||||||||||||||||||||||||||||||||||||||||||||||||||||||||||||||||||||||||||||||||||||||||||||

"Bringing experience to conscious awareness" is how I would summarize the work of human maturation, beginning especially in the Second Plane. Here I describe a program at Austin Montessori School that helps older children reflect on and come to understand their Children's House experience in a new way appropriate to their reasoning minds.

The coming online of the Reasoning Mind of the Second Plane of Development has ramifications for our teaching—some of which we are well aware. In the Second Plane the child's sensitivity to physical order recedes, and there is a new drive and a new capacity to explore the world through ideas. Although the Third and Fourth Planes bring their own new powers and developmental emphases, important things change forever when the child enters the Second Plane and begins to develop the capacity for abstraction and self-reflection.

In the First Plane, our aid to the child's life is to surround it with sensorial and linguistic richness, facilitating the absorption of high-quality experience that becomes the child's raw material for self-construction. The young child's mind is immensely powerful, but its powers are mainly directed toward unselfconsciously experiencing the "what" of the world, not toward consciously ordering that experience. Consciously ordering the "what," "how," and "why" of experience is the life-long work that begins in earnest in the Second Plane.

Another way of saying this is that the long arc of human development is rooted from birth in sensorial experience and spirals up from that foundation in cycles of increasing consciousness. Our aid to life of the second- and third-plane child is to be midwives to this bringing-to-consciousness of felt, absorbed experience.

This is not to say that our work is to help children leave behind the world of matter and their bodies to live in their heads or in "spirit." But as Montessori educators, we are interested in the optimal development of the human being in all its amazing capacities, and child development is a process of spiraling outward through concentric circles of integrated understanding and experience, constantly reinterpreting one's current understanding of past experiences in light of new perspectives on one's horizon of development. We help the children keep the world of ideas firmly tethered to the ground of experience.

I believe this perspective is consistent with Dr. Montessori's views on the development of the human being and human culture. Indeed, signs of it are embedded in our curriculum and practice, and we can take these examples as paradigmatic of the things we need to be doing in many other areas that are not as well explored.

For example, young children are introduced to the Binomial and Trinomial Cubes as sensorial puzzles—take them apart, put them back together. In the Second Plane these materials are re-introduced, and the children discover a deeper meaning—that they are physical representations of an important algebraic reality that would otherwise remain sterile and abstract.

In the Third Plane and beyond, children can take a further step back and begin to see the use of the cubes in Montessori as a pedagogical strategy or principle from which they can abstract insights into the mind and human learning in general (that is, human beings learn best from an integrated experience of hands-on manipulation and mental abstraction).

So, as aids to the life of the developing human being, we need not only to bring new experiences and information to the children but also to help them revisit and rethink territory they have visited before—each time bringing more of the experience into conscious awareness as the *content* of the study.

It is in this spirit and with this purpose that I, as a guide, want to inspire the children to deeper and broader explorations of the world through Cosmic Education.

A Case Study

Some years ago, Donna Bryant Goertz, founder of Austin Montessori School and author of *Children Who Are Not Yet Peaceful*, realized that we needed to do a better job of helping our older children (our ten- to twelve-year-olds) bring to conscious awareness and understanding the years of Montessori experience they had had in our school. All through the Children's House and Early Elementary, the Montessori prepared environment had been the water in which they had swum. Now it was time for them to step back and see with fresh eyes the "how" and "why" of their experience.

To this end, Donna prepared a four-session short course called *The Study of the Child*. The specific purpose was to reconnect these Upper Elementary children with their Children's House experience and the development of the young child. Children were invited to request a seat in the course, with the understanding that it would also open up two future possibilities for them: participation in a Reading Buddies program we have with a neighborhood public school kindergarten and Mother's Helper training as adolescents (itself a preparation for babysitting certification).

Registrants were given their own folder containing all of the handouts for the sessions and a copy of the NAMTA booklet *What is Montessori Preschool?*, edited by David Kahn. Groups of three to five children were formed, and these groups were maintained throughout the course. Before the first session, each group was asked to read the NAMTA booklet as part of their classroom work in preparation for a discussion at the first session.

Each session was facilitated by someone on staff who had experience in the Children's House as well as some experience working with or parenting elementary children. Because the sessions are held in a conference room on campus and not in the children's classrooms, we consider them a sort of "on-campus Going Out," and the children are expected to prepare themselves physically, mentally, and emotionally for a Going Out.

In the first session we discussed the NAMTA booklet. We talked about many basic principles and concepts underlying the Montessori way of working with young children: the absorbent mind, the prepared environment and its freedoms, practical life, the sensorial materials, the cultural subjects, the three-period lesson, grace and courtesy, the giving of lessons with few words, the modeling of controlled movement, and much more. At each point, the children were invited to remember themselves in the Children's House environment and relate those memories to our discussion of the principles.

For the second session, appointments were made with our Children's House guides to host one or more groups for an after-school visit. Children and facilitator met to review a handout called "Areas of Purposeful Activity" that listed materials and work, grouped by subject and area of the classroom. Armed with clipboards and lists, each group was then given a tour of their host's prepared environment and observed as the guide and assistant prepared the environment for the following day.

Many points of interest were brought to the children's attention: the immaculate shelves and materials, the careful thought and planning behind placement of furnishings and the arrangement of materials in each area, the attention to beauty and sensorial richness in the display of the materials, the daily care and diligent work of the guide and assistant in maintaining the order, cleanliness, and beauty of the space in support of the absorbent minds of its young inhabitants.

Memories came flooding back to the children as they reencountered favorite materials, memorable rituals and customs, and even specific lessons that had made strong impressions. But now they were beginning to understand what had been hidden from them before: the *preparation* of the prepared environment and all that it entails.

The third session was devoted to a more focused discussion about the very special roles of the guide and assistant, as outlined in two handouts, "The Children's House Guide and Assistant" and "The Montessori Children's House." With a solid foundation of understanding of the physical environment in the Children's House and of the role of guide and assistant in supporting the children's development in all areas, the older children were now almost ready for the grand finale: observation during the morning work period.

The morning of each group's observation, we met to review the "Guidelines for Upper Elementary Child Observers." We role-played how to respond to children who approach you and attempt to engage with you while you are observing. (Say in a kindly voice "I am doing my work observing" and then turn away or look intently at your notes.) We reminded ourselves how the adults move in the classroom and determined to move that way ourselves getting to and from our observer's chairs. We thought how it would feel to a child to be stared at and then practiced looking at things obliquely or in a "scanning" way, not making eye contact.

The children observed for twenty-five minutes, three at a time, and then met to debrief and share notes with the facilitator who had been waiting for them elsewhere on campus. They each had a checklist of about twenty things one sometimes sees in a Children's House, and a number of children had the opportunity to observe everything on the list. The joy and excitement was palpable as the children eagerly shared their observations. Things they had taken for granted in their own Children's House experience just four or five years before now stood out to them as remarkable and fascinating, and they wanted to recount them in detail.

A new understanding of their own experience and that of the young children they had observed dawned brightly in the light of second-plane intelligence. ❖

Situations Calling for Grace and Courtesy around People in Power Wheelchairs

||||||||||||||||||||||||||||||||||||||||||||||||||||||||||||||||||||||||||||||||||||||||||||||||||||||||||||||||||||||||||||||||||||||||||||

I t is our responsibility, our privilege, and our joy to help the children in our care become more and more sophisticated in their ability to navigate with grace and courtesy the many social situations in which they find themselves. In some cases, we ourselves may not know with confidence what is the proper etiquette.

There came a day in the progression of my ALS when I could no longer walk around campus and began to get around in a power wheelchair. For the first time, I realized that most people, even with the best of intent, do not understand how to be around people in power wheelchairs. The children, while fascinated by my chair, clearly needed some help understanding how to keep themselves and me safe when we were together.

Here are a few suggestions I compiled for the guides to use in their grace and courtesy lessons with the children of all ages.

1. You meet a person in a wheelchair on the sidewalk or path. Step off the path and allow the wheelchair to proceed, because the wheelchair may not be able to drive off the sidewalk or path. Don't be offended if the person does not say thank you; perhaps they are not able to speak.

2. You step off the path to allow the wheelchair to pass, but other people with you on the path do not know or do not remember to step off. You might say to them, "Wheelchair coming! Please step off the path."

3. You are walking on a sidewalk or path behind a person in a wheelchair. Be patient and pace yourself, staying behind the wheelchair. Do not attempt to squeeze past the wheelchair or run ahead of it.

4. You are standing near a person in a stationary wheelchair. Try to position yourself away from the sides of the chair and so that the person in the chair can see you. Otherwise, the person may turn the chair and accidentally bump into you or run over your foot.

5. You see a person in a wheelchair waiting outside a manually-opened door. Open the door and stand aside while the wheelchair passes through; then close the door. Don't be offended if the person does not say thank you; perhaps they are not able to speak.

6. You see a person in a wheelchair approaching a door with an automatic door opener. Stand back and let the person in the wheelchair activate the door for themselves. Do not run ahead to activate the door for them. Do not attempt to close the door behind them; the door will close automatically by itself after a preset time.

7. You see someone in a wheelchair and wonder how you could help. Do not attempt to otherwise help a person in a wheelchair, unless they ask for your help. If it seems to you that they might need help, you may ask, "May I be of assistance?" or "Would you like some help?" If they do not respond, it may be because they are unable. ❖

A Boy's View of Taggart Lake

The Montessori guides I most admire and have tried to emulate have developed a keen sense of how a child's mind works at each stage of development. They have the ability to understand how children will see things and are able to bracket out their own adult understanding when empathizing with children.

In 2009 the AMI Elementary Alumni Association held its Summer Conference near Jackson, Wyoming, in the shadow of the Grand Tetons. Many of the participants, including me, went for a day hike around Taggart Lake, a beautiful, pristine glacial lake in the national park. I found myself wondering how the children in my class would experience the hike, and, having led them on many hikes in the Austin area, I thought I might have a sense of it. Here is the poem I wrote attempting to put into words how it might go.

Taggart Lake. Cool.

I don't know who Taggart is

but he sure has a great lake.

Smart of him to put it

right up against the Tetons like that.

He must get more tourists that way.

I wonder if he got the idea

from watching the Nature Channel.

Oh, they're talking about how old everything is again—
something happened a thousand years ago and
something else happened for a million years
then all these glaciers the size of the Empire State Building
made all these boulders.
How do they know all this stuff? Maybe it wasn't like that.
Maybe there were a whole lot of boulders and then
something came and piled them all up into
big mountains and these are the ones that were left
because they were afraid of heights.

Anyway, a thousand years is as good as a million
to me. Just really, really old.
I guess compared to these mountains
I hardly even exist. I'm already ten, though,
and that's pretty old for a kid.
I can do a lot of things. I can take those mountains
into my head and do stuff with them.
A mountain can't do that.
Neither can little kids. I mean, little kids are like
"Oh, there's a caterpillar! Oh, there's a squirrel!"
and they don't really stop to think about anything—
and I don't think they even know that.

I wish Mom wouldn't worry about me so much.
I really can take care of myself out here. I mean,
if a grizzly came out right now, we would just respect it
and leave it alone and never, ever mess with its babies.
I hope Mom never even finds out
about the Tetons having grizzlies!

OK, now we're supposed to be looking for birds?
I don't see any. How are we supposed to spot birds
when there are all these rocks in the trail
to trip over? Anyway I know they're out there,
birds and maybe some moose and wolves.
And grizzlies. *Secret Animals of Taggart Lake*—
I could write that and be famous.

I wish Colin and Zachary would just shut up
about skateboards already. We're supposed to be
learning nature, aren't we? I mean, there could be this bird
that lived its whole life just so that it would
be sitting in that tree just as I walked by
and it would make its special sound that it makes
and then it would die, and I would never hear it
with all this yakking!

Taggart Lake, I think you might be my best lake.
Maybe I could be the guy who drives the ski trams in town
and when I wasn't working I could come out here alone
and *really look* at stuff and write about it.

I don't think Mom would ever let me grow up
to be one of those parasail guys
who were jumping off the mountain! ❖

Part Three
To Share with Parents

An Open Letter to New Elementary Parents

||||||||||||||||||||||||||||||||||||||||||||||||||||||||||||||||||||||||||||||||||||||||||||||||||||||||||||||||||||||||||||

This 2013 article draws heavily on a parent orientation presentation that I inherited from Donna Bryant Goertz when I became our school's Elementary Coordinator. As a Montessori parent myself, I well remembered the many questions and anxieties I had as my son entered the Montessori elementary, and I speak to as many of these as possible in the article.

S oon enough our early elementary classrooms will be filling once again with children excited to begin the new school year. Among the happy faces will be those of the youngest children, those who are making the leap into the Second Plane of Development and experiencing for the first time the elementary environment that we will have so carefully prepared for them. In all the excitement of welcoming the new children, let us not forget their parents—for their parents, too, may be new to the elementary and just as much in transition as their children.

I would like to share with you a sort of "open letter" to these new parents—a letter that says what I would like to say to help them through their first months of parenting a new elementary child. Perhaps you will find some things in it that you would like to share with your own transitioning parents.

Dear Parents,

Welcome to our elementary community and to your new role as the parent of an elementary-age child. You did it! You successfully nurtured your child through the crucial first six years of life, giving them a solid Montessori foundation on which they will now begin to build a healthy childhood as the preparation for a healthy adolescence. It wasn't easy at times, and there was so much to learn about your child and yourself as a parent, so many surprises, so much to think about.

Much of what you now know about parenting will continue to stand you in good stead, but it is also important to acknowledge that you are now the parent of a *new child*. Those sweet, transparent, cuddly little ones that you have so loved and enjoyed will quickly be leaving their infancy behind, stretching and strengthening themselves to begin to venture out into the larger world. The environments and the relationships we and you so carefully prepared at school and at home to support the developmental needs of the young child no longer fit this new child. New preparations are in order! Not to recognize this and change our ways of working with the child would be like forcing a frog to continue living underwater as though it were still a tadpole.

Your child will very likely find their new elementary classroom to have much that is familiar to them from their previous school experience. They will see some of the same materials on the shelf. They will see children working by choice and with the grace and courtesy characteristic of the Montessori community. They will find that their new guide has the same respect for and commitment to children that their old guide had.

All the same, your new elementary child will need some time to grow into the new classroom environment. The elementary environment is full of freedom, friends, group work, and unstructured blocks of time, for these are some of the elements that elementary children need to reach their full intellectual and social-emotional potential. To a newcomer, however, it may seem like a never-ending party! Don't be too surprised if your little Primary worker bee is initially a bit disoriented and drunk on freedom. The guide and the community of older children will bring them around in due time and show them what it means to work productively in the collaborative environment of the Montessori elementary. The elementary is largely about learning to balance freedom and responsibility, and this is the work of years, not days or weeks.

Don't worry if your child is not yet reading or doing arithmetic. The elementary guide will know how to meet them wherever they are and keep them moving forward. From the first day of school, there will be work for them to do as they pick up the thread from last year. The beauty of Montessori education, and the reason it is still flourishing around the world in scores of countries, cultures, and conditions, is that it is organized to support the natural development of each child according to their individual developmental timetable. Save yourself and your child the anxiety created by comparing them to other children and to students in traditional curriculum-driven lockstep programs.

As a new member of the elementary community, you can expect the guide to provide extra support for you as well as your child. The guide will be working diligently to create a solid partnership with you on behalf of your child. They will also be working to help you and your child find your respective places in the community of parents and children. They will be getting to know your child and connecting them to meaningful work. They, with the help of the older children, will be acquainting your child with the culture and customs of their new community. Later, sometimes as late as the second year, they will be introducing your child to Work Journals or other tools that will allow your child to gradually take more and more responsibility for their own education.

It goes without saying that your child's guide is there to help them develop academically and intellectually. The bigger and even more important work they will be undertaking is the creation of a classroom culture that supports the development of character, positive habits of mind, and the social skills needed to be a happy contributing member of our work culture based on collaboration, mutual help, and mutual care. This greater focus on the social nature of work parallels the elementary child's psychological needs and natural interests. While the guide will continue to work with each child as they have need, they will work more often with the whole community. In a very real sense, the elementary child has two guides—the adult and the community of their peers—and a skilled guide will understand that they always have that other partner in the room to consider and support.

The stimulation and intensity of the well-functioning Montessori elementary classroom can be physically and emotionally exhausting for the new children who are still in transition. There is so much to take in, so much to think about, so much to learn! Plan now to offer them extra support at home by seeing that they have the very best nutrition and nine to eleven hours of sleep each night. Renew your commitment to protecting them from daily exposure to television, computer games, and video games. Give them lots of "down time" and time outdoors in nature. This is not the time to load up their schedules with private lessons and extracurricular activities! Read aloud to them daily from books recommended by your school or your child's guide. Have a family meal at least several times a week to practice the art of conversation about topics your child will be encountering in school. Practice giving your elementary child room to talk, to speculate, to question, to imagine aloud. Speak less and listen more.

Ask your guide to recommend good parenting resources for parents with elementary-age children. Be sure one of the books you read soon is *How to Talk So Kids Will Listen, How to Listen So Kids Will Talk* by Faber and Mazlish. Check out Sandy Blackard's book and online course at languageoflistening.com. And stay in touch with your guide as you have questions and concerns.

Above all, enjoy getting to know this new child of yours, as they come to know themselves. The elementary years will be rich, challenging, and full of new experiences and vivid memories. Grow joyfully along with your Montessori elementary child these next six years! Never again will you have such an opportunity for self-improvement and personal growth. This is the gift of your new child to you, if you will only accept it.

Sincerely,
John ❖

Updating Our Parenting Manuals

||

One of the challenges of parenting is that just as we learn how to parent our children effectively, we find that they have moved on, requiring us to "go back to the drawing board."

One of the big challenges of being human is that we do not come with an owner's manual. When we find ourselves responsible for care and maintenance of a new human being, not only can we not look up the answers to life's problems in the index, we cannot even find the instructions for reprogramming ourselves into Parent Mode. Instead, we are reduced to looking for advice in third-party manuals and relying on direct experimentation (otherwise known as flying by the seat of one's pants).

Human beings come preprogrammed to do quite a number of things, and with basic care and careful handling, they do get along. The trouble is that unlike even the most complicated machines, young humans are always changing into something they have never been before. What we think we know about them is always out of date and in need of updating. When we fail to see that, we end up doing the parenting equivalent of trying to use a Mac SE manual (circa 1987) for today's MacBook Pro. And, in any case, there will always be undocumented features.

Maria Montessori made some very helpful observations about the rate of change we can expect in our children. She called them the "Planes of Development." To press our metaphor a bit further, we can say that she noticed that although our parenting manuals will need constant small updates to stay abreast of changes in our children, every three years or so there will need to be a major update. Every six years there will be a paradigm shift comparable to the move from

DOS to Windows or from Mac OS 9 to Mac OS X; that is, the old manuals become little more than historical relics. These paradigm shifts occur at the boundaries between the planes, around ages five to seven and again around eleven to thirteen.

As the child nears one of these transformational boundaries, it is important to prepare to support the next stage of the child's life. Ask your Montessori professionals and Montessori parents of older Montessori children to recommend parenting books for that new age group. Review the child's role in the family—are they showing you that they are ready to take on more responsibility, to make more of their own choices? Are you speaking to them as though they are younger than they are? In the meantime, rest in the knowledge that at every stage of life, we humans need a continuous supply of love, respect, understanding, and forgiveness. ❖

Who Is the Elementary Child?

||||||||||||||||||||||||||||||||||||||||||||||||||||||||||||||||||||||||||||||||||||||||||||||||||||||||||||||||||||||||||||||||||||||||||||||||||||||||

Elementary children are on a journey toward adolescence; keeping that in mind demystifies many otherwise confusing things about childhood. At the same time, we must provide for them all the time they need to complete the work of childhood.

These astonishing, inspiring, infuriating, delightful, intellectual, affectionate, willful, imaginative, perplexing, energetic, shape-shifting, social, inconsistent, big-hearted, enigmatic, demanding, reflective, dramatic, complicated elementary children of ours: Who are they? They are like arrows shot from our bow, and if we would understand them, we must look far into the distance where they are aimed: adolescence. What complicates it is that while looking ahead we must also ensure that our child can live fully in the extended moment of childhood. An adolescent who has not lived out a long, slow childhood is an adolescent who has a shaky foundation.

The elementary years are years of vigorous, continual growth stretched between the two poles of the First and Third Planes of Development. Building on the foundation—whether solid or shaky—of the first six years, they aim for the heights of adolescence. Everything that we have a hope of understanding about these elementary children can be understood as a function of three things: the raw materials of personhood that they bring with them from early childhood; the developmental trajectory toward adolescence; and the quality of the support they have from us along the way.

Adolescence is a supremely social time of life dominated by the work of self-understanding, of orienting oneself in society and history, and of beginning to experience oneself as a power in the world. Our elementary children are on the way to this and are therefore increasingly social, increasingly independent and competent, and possessed of an increasingly penetrating intelligence. They are increasingly keen observers of adults' behavior and quickly (even eagerly) note the differences between what we say and what we do.

As Donna Bryant Goertz likes to say, if first-plane children are like tadpoles, elementary children are like the frogs into which they were transformed, and to keep a frog in the underwater environment that was right for the tadpole will kill it. Both guides and parents must dramatically alter their way of working to match the very different needs of the new elementary child before them.

This does not mean that we begin to treat our elementary children as though they were adolescent, in a misguided attempt to "help them grow into it." The needs of the child are just as different from the needs of the adolescent as are the needs of the child under six from the child over six. We help the tadpole become a frog by making sure his underwater environment contains all that a tadpole needs. When he begins to absorb his tail and sprout legs, we make sure a rock that extends above the water is available and easily accessible. We don't take the tadpole out of the water and place him on the rock. We let him do that himself. We don't allow the water to evaporate while he is still in need of it. We keep it there for him even after he has pulled himself up onto the rock.

Much of what we can do for our children comes in the form of protection. Powerful media, marketing, and peer pressures constantly send our elementary children the message that to be a child is to be something inferior, that childhood is something to leave behind as soon as possible, and that the whole world is watching to see how quickly they can divorce themselves from their true needs and put on the masks of pseudo-adolescence. To abandon our elementary children to bear these pressures alone in the name of "freedom" is the recipe for an unhappy childhood and a difficult adolescence.

On the contrary, children need for us to be fierce protectors of their extended, six-year-long childhood, by which I mean protectors of that safe space and time in which they can run the many social and intellectual experiments, experience the many little and not-so-little failures and successes, and learn the many ins and outs of their maturing bodies and brains that necessarily constitute "growing into" adolescence. ❖

A Community's Work Is Never Done

||||||||||||||||||||||||||||||||||||||||||||||||||||||||||||||||||||||||||||||||||||||||||||||||||||||||||||||||||||||||||||||||||||||||||||||||||||||||||||||||||||||||

Much of the power and success of the Montessori elementary can be attributed to the cohorts of children being not age-segregated classes but multi-age learning communities. The hard work of creating and living in community more than anything else prepares the children for a healthy adolescence and the demands of adulthood.

It's hard to live in community. Communities make demands of us. Communities have ways of life, rules, customs, beliefs, and traditions with which one may feel out of sorts. Communities are always in process, always changing, often inconsistent and ambiguous—and that can occasionally be disconcerting for anyone and perhaps always disconcerting for those who long for permanence, certainty and clarity.

Yet we are social creatures, and as elementary children and adolescents, we feel the full weight of the biological imperative to associate, to find a community. Few of us, even as adults, are fit for the life of the recluse.

Those who guide youth from ages six to eighteen must be engaged in community building, for that is the work of the age, and these young people will link everything one undertakes with them to their ongoing work of social development in the context of community. When we know and acknowledge this truth, we come to see that all of our interactions—even those traditionally thought of as "academic"—are part of their social and emotional development.

Allyn Travis, AMI elementary trainer, has written about the work of the guide:

> As Montessori teachers we know that "work" will normalize the child, and so we are often focused on getting the children back to work with the materials or lessons. We, therefore, intervene much too soon, thinking that getting back to material or research or whatever will take care of the problem. *Working out emotional or social issues needs to be just as much a respected part of the classroom and the activities that go on there.* (emphasis added)

Montessori educators are committed to this work of aiding the social-emotional life of the child and the community. But what are the components of that work? Here is a very incomplete list of the sorts of thing that guides and their communities are always working on—the elements of emotional intelligence.

- Learning how to name what one is feeling,
- learning to handle strong feelings (joy, grief, anger, fear) without losing oneself,
- employing strategies for soothing one's own anxiety, fear, and insecurities,
- regaining balance when something pulls one off-center,
- learning to handle change and transitions,
- developing empathy and the ability to take another's perspective,
- allowing others to change,
- giving and receiving compliments,
- looking inside, and accepting what you see (especially the nine-to-twelve's and twelve-to-eighteen's),
- avoiding cliques,
- learning to appreciate people unlike oneself,
- dealing with competition or rivalry over friends,

- being oneself in the face of pressure to conform to others' idea of how or who one should be,

- being able to set appropriate boundaries,

- knowing how to "back down" or "lose" gracefully,

- knowing how to create win/win solutions,

- setting realistic goals,

- being able to accurately assess one's abilities,

- being "friendly" with failure (as Dr. Montessori put it),

- being able to admit mistakes and make amends,

- and risk-taking (for the timid) and thinking about possible consequences (for the daredevils).

If we are honest with ourselves, how many of us adults could say that we have completed our own work on many of these issues? Our children are fortunate to have the opportunity to do this work now, and, since living with our children gives us the opportunity to revisit whatever is left unfinished in our own maturation, we are fortunate, too. Truly, this is preparation for the "real world." ❖

When a Loved One Dies

||||||||||||||||||||||||||||||||||||||||||||||||||||||||||||||||||||||||||||||||||||||||||||||||||||||||||||||||||||||||||||

As adults, we understand that death is a part of life, but when our children encounter death, whether it be the death of a beloved pet, family member, or friend of the family, it can be difficult to know how to talk about it with the child. Children of different ages will need different kinds of support. This article focuses on how to talk to elementary children about death.

I t is often during the elementary years that a child first experiences the death of a loved one—frequently a grandparent or great-grandparent, but sometimes an aunt, uncle, parent, or sibling. These times can be very difficult and confusing for us as adults caring for elementary children. Younger children also suffer loss, but they may have an easier time accepting that this is just the way things are. It may be only much later that they revisit and truly comprehend the loss through a process of reflection.

As someone fully engaged with the great work of understanding how the world works, the elementary child is keenly interested in all aspects of death: how it happens, why it happens, what happens after death, in what way the family will commemorate the death, how the various family members will be affected, and much more. The reasoning mind of the Second Plane wants to understand all this, even as the child may be also suffering emotionally. For the grieving adult, the barrage of questions may be hard to take, and it may even seem that the child cares more about the factual details than about honoring the deceased or appreciating the emotional stress of the adults.

Maria Montessori wrote of a Montessori school in which first- and second-plane children were together in the same classroom. (She and her collaborators tried many different arrangements before settling on the one that is now our standard practice.) One morning the children arrived at school to find that all the fish in the classroom's aquarium had mysteriously died. All of the children were interested in what had happened, but the younger children would run to tell each new child that arrived at school, "The fish have died!" and then return to their work. The second-plane children stood around in hushed groups asking each other, "What happened? Why did the fish die?" and debating the possible causes.

The point is that for the second-plane child, understanding how to think about the death is an important part of beginning the emotional process of acceptance, grief, and recovery.

The elementary guides lay a foundation in the classroom for the second-plane children's conversations about death with each other and their parents. In the children's study of living things, death is presented as a natural process, an inevitable part of each individual organism's life, without which the larger world of life could not go on. The children become aware of life cycles appropriate to each kind of living thing. Dead insects and small animals found on the school grounds are marked off and left to return to nature, so that the children can both show respect for and observe nature's ways. Religious beliefs and customs around the world are a part of the children's study of society, including beliefs and customs related to death.

Books read together with the child or read alone by the child and discussed with the parent can be very helpful when one is at a loss for words. Three of my favorites are Leo Buscaglia's *The Fall of Freddie the Leaf,* Bryan Mellonie's *Lifetimes,* and Chuck Thurman's *A Time for Remembering.* Buscaglia and Mellonie's books beautifully depict the lifecycle and the great wheel of life and death. Thurman's book is particularly suitable for discussing the death of a grandparent. In it, a boy finds a beautiful, symbolic way of remembering his grandfather. ❖

A Letter about Talking to Children about Death

||||||||||||||||||||||||||||||||||||||||||||||||||||||||||||||||||||||||||||||||||||||||||||||||||||||||||||||||||||||||||||||||

This letter was distributed to all families at our school upon the sudden death of a prominent and much loved parent just before the winter break.

Dear Parents,

We are a small, close-knit community of families, and a tragedy such as the death of [John Doe], a long-time and active parent in the school, will be deeply felt by many. The children of the Upper Elementary have entered upon a long process of healing, and the death of a parent has become real in a way that it perhaps was not just a few days ago. The Upper Elementary guides and our elementary coordinator have been discussing with the children how they can best support each other, their young friend [Jane Doe] and the Doe family. They have discussed that healing from such a loss is a long process with sometimes unpredictable twists and turns along the way. They have agreed that feelings have their own rhythm, that each individual may have different feelings at different times, and that we can all be there for each other whatever we're feeling in a way that is appropriate to the specific feeling and time. Already, at last night's Candlelight Poetry Night, children could be overheard practicing very skillfully what they had talked about together—being there for each other in a very sensitive and conscious way.

Our Montessori-educated children have a solid foundation on which to progressively construct an understanding of death and its place in the great scheme of things. In Montessori education, death is treated reverently as a part of life; something that belongs to the richness of human experience;

something that everyone naturally wonders about; something around which there can be mutually respectful, open discussion, not secrecy, shame or undue fear. This message is consistent across developmental Planes, and only the language used and the extent and sophistication of information given is changed to match the cognitive and emotional development of the children and adolescents at each age.

The next weeks are a time to carefully observe your children at home—to listen to what they say and to be alert to changes in mood or behavior that might be traced to an unexpressed concern or wondering about death. There is a danger that in all the jollity and whirlwind activity of the season, feelings that would otherwise be expressed and noticed may be suppressed or unnoticed.

Some of you who are especially close to the Doe family or for whom such a loss brings back painful memories of your own young life will be on your own journey of grief and healing. We encourage you to recognize that and to get whatever support you need, even as you are compassionately supporting others in the community. Your children will be sensitive to your feelings, and seeing you taking care of your own feelings in an authentic and healthy way is a lesson they will carry with them into their own future trials.

We are attaching an article, "Talking to Children About Death," that presents the psychology profession's best mainstream understanding of how to support children during experiences of death.[1] We hope it will be of help to you in thinking about how your own family will welcome discussion of this most important topic.

In solidarity,
The Administrative Team ❖

---

[1]You can access "Talking to Children About Death" at cc.nih.gov/ccc/patient_education/pepubs/childeath.pdf.

Boys and Gun Play

||||||||||||||||||||||||||||||||||||||||||||||||||||||||||||||||||||||||||||||||||||||||||||||||

Sometimes parenting is made more difficult because it touches on some subject of controversy in the adult world. Our adult feelings, beliefs, commitments, and experiences naturally rush in to color our perspective as parents. In those cases, it is important that we step back and look at the issue from the perspective of child development, bracketing out for the moment our adult interpretations. Since Montessori education specifically bills itself as "education for peace," we are often asked by parents how we think about children's attraction to weapons and playing at war. Here is one answer.

Elementary children need to experience themselves as increasingly powerful agents in the world. As their personal power increases with age and maturity, they begin to encounter all of the classical questions about power with which humanity has struggled and continues to struggle. At the root of these questions is the fact that power and its uses define relationships.

There is something in the male psyche, in particular, that is fascinated with the projection of personal power at a distance. The emperor sits in his throne room ruling his far-flung empire. The generals gather in the war room to talk about "force projection." CEO's earn their bonuses by expanding the "global reach" of their corporations. The eminent professor sits in his study writing books and papers calculated to demolish the theories of his colleagues on the other side of the world and change the direction of his academic discipline for all time.

Boys, on the other hand, just like to throw things. Rocks, snowballs, mud balls, dirt clods, sticks, spears, Frisbees, boomerangs, baseballs, footballs, basketballs—all involve projecting power at a distance—and if accuracy is involved, so much the better. Standing right here, I can have an effect way over there. I can get that wooly mammoth, bear, or dog before it gets me. I can get you before you get me. And I can do it even if I'm not as big, strong, fast, ferocious, agile, or smart as you.

Guns are technology's answer to this fascination with the projection of power at a distance. This attraction, this fascination is, in itself, neither good nor bad. It just is. Yet it is clear that in the context of a life and a culture, how a boy learns to relate to his capacity to project personal power can lead to good or bad habits of mind and good or bad outcomes for the boy, his family, and his society.

As with all of the raw-but-wonderful psychic energies of childhood, the key is not to squelch the energy but to channel it in positive directions. To my mind, guns are far too ambivalent a force in our world to be offered as toys to children experimenting with personal power. During my son's childhood, there were no toy guns in our house, but there was always a clear message: "In our family we don't pretend to shoot people; shooting people is a very serious thing and not something anyone should do for fun." Instead, there were many choices of what Sandy Blackard has called a "Can Do": "Maybe you could set up this bunch of tin cans in the backyard and see how far away you can stand to hit them with these tennis balls." "Maybe we could all go to the lake to skip rocks." "Maybe you could play catch." "Let's go shoot some hoops. I could use some practice with my free throws." If the child rejects all of the "can do's," the bottom line is "There must be something you could do that's exciting and fun. Pretending to shoot people is not an option."

Many parents and teachers are reluctant to redirect gun play because they fear that forbidding a child something they want will drive the need underground or cause the child to fixate on it. I disagree for two reasons. First, in raising my own son and in working with many hundreds of children over the years, I have never found that to be the case. This is especially true if alternative "can do's" are offered, instead of a stark, shaming, or angry "no!" Very often when children push back it's because they feel misunderstood and disrespected, not because of what we are asking them to do or not do. Setting a firm but respectful boundary about gun play is no different than setting one about anything else.

Second, I notice that this rationale is offered time and time again for gun play, but rarely for the many other things that we forbid our children to do when they do them, such as lying, stealing, cheating, hitting, being cruel to animals, bullying, or using vulgar language. "It really upsets me when Johnny leaves his dirty clothes all over the house, but I dare not say anything to him about it lest he become obsessed with it or just do it when I'm not around." No, we rarely hear that. This suggests to me that our adult perspective on the controversy surrounding guns may be clouding our otherwise clear parenting vision.

Ultimately, it comes down to a matter of values. If our notion of masculinity involves being casual and comfortable with the use of lethal force, if we believe that Montessori's "education for peace" has a place for happily role-playing activities that in the adult world are seen as crimes punishable by life imprisonment, if we think it is helpful to children to practice psychologically contradictory traits such as empathy or compassion and objectification of other human beings as no more than "hits" in a game of laser tag, then we will continue to offer our children guns and other toys of violence. If we have a different vision of the future for our children and our world, we will find ways to support their need for intensity and challenge that are not confounded with current culturally acceptable violence. ❖

The Gift of the Family Meal

‖‖

This article was written at the request of Virginia McHugh Goodwin, former Executive Director of AMI/USA, for publication in the May 2007 edition of AMI/USA's Parenting for a New World series. There is, if anything, an even more pressing need to recover the family mealtime now than there was in 2007.

We parents are rightly skeptical of the many unproven nostrums that come our way from the parenting-advice industry. We like to remind ourselves that there are no silver bullets when it comes to parenting. True enough, but there actually is something that has emerged from recent research studies looking very silvery indeed: the intentional practice of regular family meals as part of the family's identity and shared ritual.

For example, for over a decade, the National Center for Addiction and Substance Abuse (NCASA), a privately funded research and social advocacy organization, has gathered data on teens, looking for the factors that make certain teens more vulnerable to substance abuse and others virtually immune. In the report of a 2005 national phone survey of 1,000 teens and 829 parents, the Center reported, "one factor that does more to reduce teens' substance abuse risk than almost any other is parental engagement, and one of the simplest and most effective ways for parents to be engaged in their teens' lives is by having frequent family dinners."

William J. Doherty, Professor of Family Social Science and Director of the Marriage and Family Program at the University of Minnesota, is passionate about family mealtimes. According to Doherty, "One of the core predictors of children's well-being and academic success is how much time they spend eating with adults." Doherty and the

NCASA researchers both believe that it is daily parental engagement, not eating together per se, that is the key factor, but they pragmatically point out that for most families, family mealtimes are the easiest and most practical time to get together every day. We all need to eat, and tying family time to meeting this universal need can ensure that it actually happens on a daily basis.

Anthropologists, such as the eminent Robin Fox of Rutgers University, might argue more specifically for eating together as a special ritual of family bonding. Fox recalls that our very first and most powerful bonds to family are related to eating: "Food is the most important thing a mother gives a child; it is the substance of her own body, and in most parts of the world, mother's milk is still the only safe food for infants. Thus food becomes not just a symbol of, but the reality of, love and security." In cultures around the world, eating together is the quintessential act of acceptance, joining, and positive association. As Fox says, "Every meal is a message, and where we eat is as important as what we eat in getting the message across." From this perspective, we could say that a family intentionally eating together at home is saying to itself and to the world, *We belong together. We want to be together. We know where we stand as a family; we act on our values. We take care of each other here.* This is the message that children must regularly hear if they are to have the confidence required to meet the challenges of life.

Nutritionists and pediatricians recommend family meals for yet another reason: Studies at Harvard Medical School, the University of Minnesota School of Public Health, and elsewhere show that children and adolescents eat better when the family eats together. For example, one Harvard study concluded that eating family dinner "was associated with healthful dietary intake patterns, including more fruits and vegetables, less fried food and soda, less saturated and trans fat, lower glycemic load [less sugar], more fiber and micronutrients from food, and no material differences in red meat or snack foods" (Gillman, et al.).

The Power of Intent

Doherty and other researchers into family dynamics and child development stress the importance of family rituals in creating safety and solidity for children and spouses alike. Doherty helpfully distinguishes between *ritual* and *routine*. Both occur regularly, if not daily, but the difference is the shared meaning that ritual creates and keeps alive in those who practice it. A family ritual, then, is a repeating, planned activity of significance to the family; it helps define the family as a group and holds it together. In short, rituals do not happen by accident; rituals are necessarily intentional acts.

In today's world, families that have the best of intentions about spending quality time together every day can find that it also requires a great deal of focus, collective will, and even some sacrifice to make those intentions a reality. Formidable cultural forces have arrayed themselves against the integrity of the modern family. Among these are fiercely competitive workplaces that expect parents to be employees first and parents a distant second; the prevalence of single-parent families and the added time pressure that can create for parents; fears that children who are not over-scheduled with a broad range of sports, private lessons, and other activities may fall behind their peers; and the ubiquitous distractions of the entertainment and communication industries that make it easy for us to escape the hard work of developing authentic relationships with ourselves and our family members. As Doherty argues, in today's busy, individualistic world, if the family drifts with the culture, it is very likely to drift apart.

The Importance of Starting Young

Although studies such as that of the NCASA focus on teens, the message for parents of younger children is clear: Start now to build your family rituals. As children grow in ability and sophistication, family rituals will need to grow and develop along with them, but such refinement works best on a firm foundation of family tradition that can begin as soon as the first child is born, or even before. Early, consistent efforts pay enormous dividends during adolescence, when well-established, clear, nurturing communication channels between parents and teens can (sometimes quite literally) mean the difference between life and death.

The NCASA study also found that among the teens surveyed, those "who confide in one parent or both parents have a much lower substance abuse risk score than the 26 percent of teens who would turn to another adult to talk about a serious problem or the 7 percent of teens who have no adult to confide in." Interesting; but how can we encourage our teens to talk to us? Start young. It is much easier for parents to keep communication open with adolescents with whom they have a long history of open communication than it is to "start from scratch" to build such levels of trust with them. Moreover, it is a mistake for parents to think it sufficient to merely invite teens to come to them "if you need to talk." Teens who are not in the habit of regularly discussing all the joys and small sorrows of life with their parents are not likely to feel comfortable broaching the big issues.

Do It for Them, Do It for Yourself

Although some of the best arguments for creating a family dinner tradition have to do with the positive effects on the children, there is another side: the positive effects on the parents. In this regard, we should allow ourselves to be selfish and not let our children grow up without enjoying them. There is a reason that parents of teens and young adults are often heard lamenting how fast their children grew up. Childhood is over before you know it, and neither you nor your child can turn back the clock. To parents who are willing to put parenting first, children can be both life's greatest joy and a most powerful avenue of personal and spiritual growth. Although it is somewhat against the grain of modern American culture to say so, there is probably nothing you can experience in your vocation or avocations that can stretch you and enlighten you as much as whole-hearted engagement with your children over the span of childhood and adolescence. We adults give our children life and knowledge; in return, the children give us wisdom.

The Nuts and Bolts of a Successful Family Meal Ritual

To build a successful tradition of family mealtimes, remember Doherty's distinction between *ritual* and *routine*. The difference is the significance and shared meaning that comes with intentionality; success begins with a clear decision on the part of the parents that such daily family time is a top priority. If such a notion is new to the family, there will need to be a conscious re-visioning of mealtimes as family times, not pit stops for refueling. In the pit-stop model, individuals opportunistically eat whatever is at hand whenever they are hungry. By contrast, a family meal requires a modicum of planning, scheduling, and self-discipline so that everyone in the family can participate.

The busier family members are, the more important it is that family mealtimes be appointments for the family to keep with itself—and these appointments must be scheduled-around and consistently kept. Doherty suggests that parents agree with each other ahead of time how many nights a week the family will eat together and then keep that agreement sacred.

The NCASA study found that thirty-seven percent of teens surveyed reported that even when they do eat with their parents, the TV is on in the dining area. Whatever the pros and cons of TV watching may be, it is clear that for a family to watch TV during the family mealtime defeats the whole purpose of their time together: talking to, listening to, and being fully present to and for each other. So, for the duration of the family meal, banish TV, radio, computers, videogames, and similar distractions. Turn off all the cell phones and let the answering machine take messages from the landlines. Such intentional guarding of sacred family time will send a clear message to children that this time is truly *their* time to receive their parents' full attention and truly something of great importance to the family. If parents are not willing to make family time uninterruptible, how can they expect their older children and teens to do so?

To create a greater sense of ownership among all family members, involve the children in as much of the planning, shopping, and meal preparation as possible. Montessori parents may have an advantage here, since many Montessori schools include food preparation in the practical life activities of the classroom.

At the table, the focus should be on conversation, taking care to insure that everyone has an opportunity to be heard. In families with older children, it may be useful to create a rotating "facilitator" role so that all family members have practice helping the conversation to flow in a balanced way. Conversation at the table should have a positive, peaceful tone. It is probably not a good place to process a bad day at the office or to discuss difficult or emotional topics.

Table manners are important life skills, and family meals are a perfect training ground for such social graces. Nevertheless, it is important not to let an overemphasis on manners steal the focus from the deeper purposes of family time. Parents can help children understand that practicing polite table manners is one way that the members of the family show their love and care for one another. Pragmatically speaking, if children cannot and do not practice polite table manners at home, they will very likely not know or remember how to do so when they are away from home and thrust into situations where others may judge them by their manners. Parents who personally disdain what may seem like restrictive or elitist social conventions at the table should consider that the child who does not know how to navigate with confidence the full range of social protocol cannot truly be said to be free; they are limited by their own ignorance to a much smaller set of social possibilities.

Older children are ready to learn and openly discuss different levels of formality—from picnics on the beach to black-tie formal dinners—and to practice the various social protocols that go along with each. To this end, some families enjoy occasionally scheduling a formal dinner at home just for the fun of it. This would be a time to go "all out"—setting a formal table, lighting candles, dressing up, perhaps serving a multi-course meal.

Family meal rituals should have a clear beginning. Traditionally, the family meal began with the blessing of the food with a prayer. For religious families, this will still be the preferred practice. Even if your family does not participate in a religious tradition, your Montessori children will no doubt be familiar with the idea of gratitude for one's food and for all the many hands along the way that helped produce it, distribute it, and prepare it. Many Montessori classrooms and families have gained inspiration from Elizabeth Roberts's *Earth Prayers from Around the World*, a popular collection of prayers and sayings from a wide range of traditions. Many of these prayers can be easily amended to align with the family's particular values while still retaining the prayers' freshness and creativity. Children may enjoy selecting the blessing from this book or writing their own blessing.

Doherty suggests that a clear finish is equally important to the success of family meals. Parents can set the expectation that everyone will stay at the table until the meal has been declared finished. If family members are allowed to eat quickly and drift off to other activities, the meal ceases to be a family ritual and becomes a mere routine—hardly worth the trouble it may be to gather the whole family in the first place. Good rituals have a sense of closure, and your family may want to establish a customary way of ending the meal—perhaps thanking the cooks or observing a certain way of clearing the table and washing the dishes together.

Look to Your Community

It is not easy to swim upstream against the societal pressure to over-schedule ourselves and our children, letting family time take a backseat to our other ambitions. Having the support of a community can really help. Your Montessori school community may be your ace in the hole. Parents who choose Montessori education for their children have already shown that they are willing to take special measures to give their children the best—they, as well as your children's Montessori teachers, are natural allies in the difficult business of raising strong, healthy children. Make family meals a topic of conversation in your parent community. Share with each other what has worked and not worked for your family. Allow your Montessori "village" to help with this aspect of raising your child. You, your children, and their peers at school all deserve the gift of the family meal. ❖

We Are What We Eat

This piece appeared in a weekly series of parenting articles written for parents at Austin Montessori School. If we are serious about serving "the whole child," we must also seek out the best information about childhood nutrition.

In May 2010, researchers at Harvard and the University of Montreal reported the results of a study that finds a strong correlation between levels of organophosphate pesticide exposure and symptoms of ADHD in children. The researchers analyzed urine samples of 1,100 children, ages 8–15, and found a 35 percent increase in the chances of developing ADHD for every 10-fold increase in pesticide residues in the urine. Most pesticide exposure comes from ingesting the residues left on industrially farmed produce. According to *Time,* "Increasingly, research suggests that chemical influences, perhaps in combination with other environmental factors—like video games, hyperkinetically edited TV shows and flashing images in educational DVDs aimed at infants—may be contributing to the increase in attention problems" (Park "Study").

We talk a lot at our school (although maybe not enough) about the negative effects of TV, video games, and invasive advertising to children, but diet is an equally important aspect of an optimal home and school environment

Perhaps because guides are trained to carefully observe the effects of physical environment on the behavior and development of each individual child and perhaps because we have historically worked with so many children who have learning differences, it has been clear to us for a very long time just how right the old truism is: You are what you eat.

Our school has high standards for our children's nutrition precisely because we see it as a *developmental* issue. We know that what our children eat not only affects them today and tomorrow in the classroom, but that it is in childhood that we establish the eating habits that could last a lifetime—habits that will be very hard to change in later life. For this reason, the work that we do today to create optimal relationships with food will bless not only our children but their children and future generations in our families.

Our elementary children undertake studies of the human body, its various systems, its cycles, and what it needs for optimal health. The children learn about the "Dirty Dozen," the twelve kinds of fruits and vegetables that are most likely to have significant levels of pesticide residue: peaches, apples, strawberries, pears, cherries, imported grapes, nectarines, lettuce, kale, carrots, bell peppers, and celery. These are all wonderful foods that we want to have in our diets, but when we cook with those foods at school or buy them for school events such as camping trips, we buy organic or look for another food to substitute. When possible, we eat those things right out of our own school's organic gardens.

If I could only recommend one book to read to support better nutrition for our families, it would be Michael Pollan's *In Defense of Food: An Eater's Manifesto.* This amazing book goes far beyond the usual discussions of nutrition to look very deeply at our industrialized food system and how we as individuals and families can work around it to our betterment. Once you have digested Pollan, you may be ready for Jack Norris and Virginia Messina's *Vegan for Life: Everything You Need to Know to Be Healthy and Fit on a Plant-Based Diet.* ❖

Supporting the Elementary Child's Work at Home

||||||||||||||||||||||||||||||||||||||||||||||||||||||||||||||||||||||||||||||||||||||||||||||||||||||||||||||||

In a previous article, "An Open Letter To New Elementary Parents," I gave advice intended to help parents of children entering the Montessori elementary begin to understand the changes they would need to make in order to fully support their child in this new environment. A very conscientious parent who had received a copy of the article from their child's new teacher, wrote to me with some questions. I would like to share with you her questions and my response.

The parent wrote:

"I understand that homework is frowned upon in the Montessori method—that's one reason why we decided to pursue the method for our children. (We have found that much of the homework that comes home in a traditional school setting is busy work and not much value added.) However, I have come across more than a few parents in the Montessori setting that find themselves lost with regard to what their children are learning in the elementary environment. *They don't know what questions to ask, how to help reinforce concepts as they are taught in the classroom, or how to connect with their children on an intellectual level* (since many of them were traditionally educated).... I'm not looking to quiz my children at home (again, that's one of the reasons we pursued Montessori), but to understand what they are learning and how and when they are learning it. We ask plenty of questions, but often hear an answer something like "I don't remember" or "nothing, really." I hope you can help us get past this by pointing me in the right direction for some additional resources.

Montessori Homework

The concept of Montessori homework is very important, and, sadly, is not well understood by many Montessori guides or schools. Basically, there needs to be a shift in thinking of the Montessori school as the place where the child is being educated to thinking of it as just one of the places in the world where the child pursues self-development. (Development is much bigger than education.) The elementary classroom, in particular, equips the children to educate themselves and inspires them to do it—largely outside the classroom.

Your child will learn many things in the Montessori classroom, but the most important thing a well- and fully-implemented Montessori education can give is not a list of things learned, but a deeply ingrained orientation toward life as a journey of learning and service. John Seely Brown speaks of this as being an "entrepreneurial learner," someone who "constantly looks around, all the time, for new ways, new resources, to learn new things."

This is an excellent description of Montessori homework. It's not worksheets. It's not assignments. It's practicing being an entrepreneurial learner in the context of the family. It's self-chosen, interest-driven activity and active engagement with the day-to-day life of the family. This means that the life of the family must be one configured to support the development of children, not an exclusively adult-centered one in which children are an afterthought.

Here are some thoughts on your specific questions.

They don't know what questions to ask. Don't ask many questions of the child. It doesn't work and it's not good for the child. You will either get stonewalling, or content-free answers like the ones you are getting, or answers that make sense in the child's mind but which will lead anyone with an adult brain in the wrong direction.

For example, I'm thinking of a mom I know who almost pulled her eight-year-old out of a Montessori school because she asked him in January how many lessons he had gotten that week and he replied in all sincerity that he had not received any lessons all year, not a single one! Further questioning only produced more vigorous expressions of the same assertion. The now very concerned parent called other parents and prompted them to ask their children the same question. Sure enough, most of the children claimed that they had never received any lessons.

Perplexed adults at the school knew the children in that class were flourishing intellectually and working up a storm, but it was their word against that of the children. Anyway, it turned out that the guide in that classroom never used the word "lesson" with the children. Instead, the guide would just say, "Come over here—I have something I'd like to show you!" The children didn't see this as "getting a lesson" and responded accordingly. I could tell you dozens of anecdotes like this. Read *How to Talk So Kids Will Listen, How to Listen So Kids Will Talk* by Adele Faber and Elaine Mazlish for more on the important topic of questioning. Save the questions for the child's teachers. It's their job to answer the questions.

Instead, begin to relate to the child a little more like you would relate to one of your adult friends. In other words, create open social space for natural conversations to happen. Begin to share little bits of your own life and thinking with the child. Have books around about things you know the child is or might be interested in. Read them yourself and make comments about what you're reading. "Wow, you know this book says that great horned owls can grow to be over two feet tall!?"

If the child is not used to having peer to peer conversations with you, it may take them a while to kick in, but eventually they will begin to come back with their own thoughts about the subject or to offer things that they have been learning about. In other words, model the information sharing you want to see from the child, and then give them as much time and space as they need to reciprocate. If you establish this pattern in Early Elementary, it can grow and expand all through the elementary years and—most critically!—into adolescence, when it is of utmost importance to keep communication channels open.

If you absolutely must ask the child a question, I suggest the one that physicist and world-class entrepreneurial learner Richard Feynman said his parents regularly asked him: "What questions did you ask today?" But, really, even that is best modeled, not asked.

How to help reinforce concepts as they are taught in the classroom.
As a parent myself, I understand where this is coming from, but give
it up. Completely, permanently, and joyfully resign your role as the
Reinforcer. Instead, cultivate the art of conversation; as discussed
above, take note of what the child is interested in and try to take an
interest in that as well.

If it is something that you are truly not interested in, that's great! Then
you have an opportunity to demonstrate for your child how someone
cultivates an interest in something they are not immediately drawn to.
Show that you care about what they're interested in, but let it continue
to be *their* interest. Show them how you can come at a subject from
different angles until you find a personal connection. Show them how
you seek out other people who are interested in the subject and talk to
them about why they are attracted to it. Show them how you look for
connections between it and things you are already interested in. Later,
when your child is having difficulty relating to some subject at school,
they will have the resources to develop a personal interest.

When you are taking an interest in something the child is
interested in, you can lightly offer ideas—"What you were telling
me about crystals the other day is really interesting. I heard there is
a museum at the University that has lots of crystals. It might be fun
to go visit some time." There is an art to this. Young children are
just developing the notion and having the experience of "owning"
and actively exploring their interests, and it is easy for an adult to
unwittingly co-opt the child's interest in an attempt to support them.
(Guides can do this too!)

Also, just because the guide has introduced the child to something
at school, doesn't necessarily mean that it will turn out to be the right
time for the child to work on that. A skilled guide will present a
lesson and then watch what happens. It may be that the child was not
really ready or even that the lesson came too late. If the lesson came
at just the right time, it will likely inspire the child to a good deal of
spontaneous activity in that area, and the child may *want* to continue
that at home. So, it is important that you have prepared a place at
home for the child to continue work or to work on projects that they
invent for themselves at home. Talk to your guide about what specific
tools and preparation they recommend for a home workspace. If you

can provide at home basically the same kind of paper, pencils, pens, et cetera, that the child uses at school, they will more naturally and easily work spontaneously at home. (Children up to about age eight or nine are still very concrete and literal, and if they've learned to do a kind of work on one kind of paper, it may boggle their minds to do it on a different kind of paper.)

Offer the child a wide range of Montessori homework options. Let them shadow you as you take care of various things around the house. Let them do little bits and pieces of it with you, as they have interest. Gradually turn more and more over to the child, until they are ready to be the person who does that particular thing for the family.

Take very seriously the child's developmental need for outdoor free play, daydreaming time, and rest. Avoid over scheduling with extracurricular activities, lessons, et cetera. Their elementary school (unlike my traditional elementary school back in the 60s) is going to be intellectually very stimulating, and there's no need to push the child academically at home. Find the child's rhythm and follow that. Also, let downtime really be downtime. We adults these days tend to think of downtime as sitting in front of the TV or distracting ourselves in some other way with electronic gadgets. It's exactly the kind of overstimulation that children don't need. (And neither do we, to tell the truth.)

How to connect with children on an intellectual level. I hope I've addressed this in my previous comments. I would add that the trick is to understand that the child of six to twelve is really working on maturing as an intellectual being—a multi-year project. Their reasoning minds are constantly exploring, testing, and trying to order their experience and the tsunami of new information that is offered to them. They want nothing more than to experience themselves as powerful actors in their world, and a very big part of that is coming to understand the adult world and how to navigate in it. The Montessori elementary classroom is based on that, and if you can begin to think of your child in that way and include them gradually in your own cultural and intellectual life, there will be a very special synergy (and a lot more fun).

The child of three to six wants adults to "help me do it myself," and the child of six to twelve wants us to "help me think my own thoughts." It's not easy at times to remember to reframe one's intellectual relationship with the child more along the lines of peer-to-peer, because, frankly, they are still children, with a child's limited experience of the world and with a child's limited logic. But that's what they need from us. They need respect and a safe space in which to try out and gradually master the new powers of intellect and will that are coming online for them. Above all, we need to keep them in the role of Project Manager of their own self-construction project and to not try to do that for them.

Form a support team with the guide. Finally, build a strong relationship with your child's guide based on an understanding of you and the guide being partners on your child's "support team." I suggest using that metaphor very explicitly. If the guide has not already communicated something similar to you, I would meet with them and let them know that's how you would like to work with them. Then you could talk about how to work together as a team and what the different roles of the team members are. I've sketched out above what I have found works best, and the only other thing I would say is that it is the guide's job to ask for any specific help that they feel your child needs at home.

There are situations in which it is appropriate for parents and children to work together in a more specific and directed way to address an academic difficulty, but the guide must take the lead on that. As I said in my open letter, when adults attempt to drive the pace of the child's education according to their own schooling experience or the opinions of the dominant culture, it makes the magic of Montessori impossible. Let the guide know that you are able and willing to support the child at home in whatever way they request and that you trust and expect that they will not hesitate to ask for that help, should it be necessary. Then give the child and the guide time and space to work. It's sometimes scary, and rarely easy, but as someone who has parented a Montessori child all the way to adulthood, it is totally worth the effort! ❖

Montessori Homework for the Upper Elementary

||||||||||||||||||||||||||||||||||||||||||||||||||||||||||||||||||||||||||||||||||||||||

Why Homework?

Both a century of Montessori experience and the last thirty years of educational research agree that people learn best when they are learning something that personally interests them and that having some sense of control over one's learning is a prerequisite of personal interest. This means that coercing someone to "learn" something in which they have no personal interest is often worse than never introducing them to it at all. The negative emotion that accompanies being coerced to "learn" is likely to remain permanently attached to the subject of the "learning" and may obstruct all future attempts to learn that subject. Moreover, repeated experiences of this sort typically lead to passivity in the learner and frequently to the development of a negative self-image with regard to one's ability and fitness to learn a broad range of subjects and skills. These are among the main reasons Montessori teachers do not give assignments and, in particular, do not assign traditional homework.

On the other hand, the freedom to choose one's work and to go as deeply as possible into a few subjects means that the learner must spend more time learning in order to get a well-rounded education. The school day is short, and there is simply not time for most children to accomplish enough during the school day. For this reason, elementary guides depend on their parent partners to provide at home a rich learning environment where the child can build on the work they began at school. Without this, the child's development will seem delayed, and the education may seem spotty or shallow.

In the absence of traditional homework assignments, it may seem that the parents of Montessori students are not as directly involved in their children's homework as parents of traditionally educated children. On the contrary, Montessori children have more work to do at home than anyone, and their parents must be highly involved and highly resourceful—but not in a traditional sense of helping children complete worksheets and assigned projects. It is hard work, but good work—just like guiding an elementary class.

In summary:

- Homework is *not optional* for Montessori students.

- The school day is *too short* for learning to end there.

- The absence of screens and social phone calling on school nights creates the *time* for homework.

- *Assignments* are not effective and may be harmful in the long run.

- The list of homework ideas in the appendix, to which the child and parent may propose additions, offers the important element of *choice*.

What Homework?

If homework is not assigned reading, worksheets, and projects with deadlines, what is it? What we are looking for is to give the child the experience that meaningful work is always available and that learning is something that happens all the time and everywhere, not just at school. Ideally, children will have many opportunities at home to both consolidate and expand the knowledge they are working with in the classroom. Inevitably, these real world experiences will also spark new questions and other interests which the child will bring back to the classroom, enriching both their own classroom work and that of the other children. We want to foster this sort of "virtuous feedback loop" between school and home to the benefit of both and to the great benefit of the child.

We are looking not for worksheets and assignments but for *learning as a way of life*, both at home and at school. And, of the two, the home will ultimately have a far greater influence on the child's future way of life than will the school.

In the Upper Elementary, homework should consist mostly of the child's active involvement with the practical, intellectual, and artistic life of the family and of the child's own projects in areas they are drawn to pursue.

In summary:

- Homework consists both of the child's *active involvement in the life of the family* and in *personal projects* they undertake on their own.

- The list of homework ideas in Appendix B, to which the child and parent may propose additions, offers the important element of *choice*.

- Montessori homework seeks to inculcate *learning as a way of life*.

Guidelines for Home Work

In order to better support learning as a way of life, we are providing the following guidelines for the child's work at home.

1. The child should spend at least *three hours per day* on Montessori homework. Three hours a day of homework allows the child to spend time each day on a *wide variety of activities*, including physical exercise, service, intellectual activity, household responsibilities, and the arts.

2. At least thirty minutes of that time should be spent *reading* from books on the Upper Elementary Reading List. ❖

Computers in the
Montessori Home:
Guidelines for Decision-Making

||||||||||||||||||||||||||||||||||||||||||||||||||||||||||||||||||||||||||||||||||||||||||||||||||||||||||||||||||||||||||||||||||||||||||

This is the first Montessori article I wrote and the first that was published. Knowing of my background as a computer scientist and software engineer, Donna Bryant Goertz encouraged me to write on the fraught topic of children's use of computers at home. The first version of the article was published in the 1999 volume of AMI/USA's Parenting for a New World *series. I rewrote the article in 2010 and found that I needed to make only minor edits in 2014 for the version included here. Although current digital technology such as smart phones and tablets is revolutionary in many ways, the developmental needs of children remain the same, as do the arguments for keeping children's use to a minimum.*

Forty years ago, digital computers were large, complex machines expensive enough to be owned only by businesses, universities, and governmental agencies. Today computers are small, complex machines cheap enough to be owned by children. It is almost taken for granted in America that children who do not have ready access to computers at home are at a terrible educational disadvantage. Hardware and software manufacturers have found, to their delight, that parents who would never buy computers and software for themselves can be persuaded to buy them for their children. In many households, the family computer monitor has become (along with video games and network television) the third in the unholy trinity of screens that dominate the family's recreational life. As the adults in the family become more and more attached to their computers, disappearing into individual screens can become what the family typically does "together."

There is no doubt that the personal computer, when used wisely and with attention to the child's true developmental needs, can be a powerful adjunct to classroom learning. However, it is often difficult to sort out what "wise use" means in concrete situations—all the more so because of the confusing messages circulating in the culture and its media.

Perhaps the most important thing that Montessori educators can say to today's parents is "Relax. Your child will not be intellectually stunted because they do not have access to a home computer. Virtually nothing a well-rounded child needs to know requires the use of a computer to learn it." In truth, with the possible exception of certain mathematical and engineering ideas related directly to the design and programming of computers themselves (hardly the focus of most software marketed to children), the introduction of the digital computer has changed almost nothing in the fundamental intellectual landscape of childhood. This is largely because the child's most important intellectual tasks are determined not by fads or the advent of new technologies, but by the unfolding of the human organism according to a genetically coded plan conditioned by the entire span of human evolution. It was the genius of Maria Montessori that she was able to map out much of this process of human development and begin to understand how educators might support it in a systematic and universal way. When we understand the true needs of the developing child, much of the hype about how indispensable computers are to children quickly evaporates.

Many of us already have computers at home, and we will have noticed that our children seem to be fascinated by them. How can we use the computer in the best interest of our child's learning and development? Here are four questions that may help.

1. Is my child at least seven years old, reading fluently, and writing effortlessly in cursive? If not, the child is simply not ready to use the computer—or, more accurately, the computer is not designed to support your child's development. Children below age seven learn in ways very different from those of adults and older children. Young children learn primarily through physical movement and by using all of their senses to explore the physical environment. Computers restrict both of these modes of learning. Young children also tend to uncritically absorb whatever is presented to them—a disturbing thought, considering many of the sounds and images that flow through the multimedia screens of our home computers.

2. Does this software support my (older) child's current developmental needs? Are there better ways to meet those needs? Most software marketed to children can be divided into two categories: games and "educational software." Some educational software is packaged in a game-like format, ostensibly to make it more interesting to the child.

The question to ask about games (computerized and non-computerized) without educational content is "Could my child be having the same kind of relaxation and fun doing an activity that is not a developmental waste of time?" With a little thought and creativity, we can almost always answer "yes." Educational games and other educational software need to be carefully reviewed, case-by-case. The educational benefits of the software need to be balanced against the potential side effects, such as:

- social isolation;
- missed opportunities for collaborative learning;
- missed opportunities for neurological development that comes from activities based on intensive use of the hands, body, and creative thinking;
- development of sedentary habits (contributing to the current epidemic of obesity in children);
- presentation of material in ways that conflict with the Montessori child's classroom experiences;
- and substitution of extrinsic rewards for the intrinsic joy of learning.

This last side-effect deserves more comment. Much software for children is based on the tacit assumption that children are not intrinsically interested in learning and must therefore be tricked or manipulated into learning by hiding the educational content under layers of multimedia gimmickry. Nothing could be farther removed from the Montessori philosophy and experience. On the contrary, it is precisely the joy of learning and increasing self-mastery that drive the child to overcome the challenges of the material. If a child finds certain material uninteresting, the Montessori educator would usually take this to mean that it was not yet the right time for this child to learn that material. From this perspective, it can be a real harm to seduce a child into "going through the motions" just to be rewarded with a funny noise or a favorite cartoon character cartwheeling across the screen. What is the child really learning? That learning is boring, but cartoons are fun? To expect whiz-bang showbiz responses at school for each little increment of effort? That they cannot learn without an authority figure to validate and praise their efforts? All this is really just a high-tech way of once again imposing an adult educational agenda on the child, instead of supporting the child in the exciting task of constructing a self according to the blueprint that is uniquely theirs.

Proponents of video-gaming and other computer software for children are now citing research that shows that children who play video games out-perform their peers in certain aspects of cognitive development. This is hardly a surprise: People do tend to get much better at things they extensively practice, and the brain adapts to whatever training it receives. Closer examination of these claims reveals that unless one wants to be an air traffic controller or a fighter pilot, these enhanced cognitive-spatial skills are good for little more than playing more video games. All that time and effort is better spent developing cognitive skills that can only be developed the "old-fashioned" way: by many years of creative use of hands, body, and mind in a sensorially and socially rich environment. It is these higher "executive function" thinking skills that research profoundly links to success and happiness throughout life. And if it is extra cognitive development you seek, the research supporting the cognitive enhancement gained by learning to play a musical instrument is much more robust than that cited by the pro–video game crowd.

3. Does this software support my family's values? The values of the school community of which my child is a member? Many computer games, and even some "educational games," have shocking amounts of violence. Unfortunately, this will continue to be the case since violent games sell like hotcakes in our country. Nevertheless, protests from parents have made software developers a little more sensitive to the needs of the children's software market. Sometimes the violence is softened by presenting it as "good guys versus bad guys" or "monsters fighting monsters." Even non-violent software can have questionable content. For example, at the end of one popular game, a bikini-clad girl runs in from the side of the screen and gives the winning character (always male) an adoring kiss. What messages is this game sending about gender equality and human dignity? Suffice it to say, parents need to review software before giving it to children and make conscious choices about what is acceptable in their family and in the larger school community.

Whether you know it or not, you are in competition for your young person's heart and mind with some very savvy, well-funded, and ruthless competitors. Dave Arnold, one of the lead developers and writers for the violent videogame *Call of Duty,* recently spoke openly about the videogame industry's approach, which he proudly described as "brainwashing" (Eidelson "Call of Duty"). He states, "When we have a new product that has elements that we're not sure how people will respond to, what do we do as a corporation? We market it, and we market it as much as we can—so that whether people like it or not, we do all the things we can to essentially brainwash people into liking it before it actually comes out."

If adult members of the family choose to play violent or sexually suggestive computer games, it is very important to do it when the children are asleep or not in the house. Earphones will keep children in their beds or playrooms from hearing the gunfire, explosions, screams, profanity, war cries, and other disturbing sounds that go along with most violent games.

4. Does this software ultimately increase or decrease my child's creativity and natural self-expression? Most adult computer users have found that they can do things well on the computer that they could not do by hand—at least not in the available time. It is easy to assume that what is wonderful for us will also be wonderful for our children. Not necessarily. For example, desktop publishing tools are a boon to the writer or the small business owner; they even appear to have played a part in the democratization of Eastern Europe. However, in the hands of a child struggling to master cursive handwriting or conventional spelling, they may become a way of avoiding the difficulties of mastery. Computer graphics tools have opened up a whole new range of possibilities for modern visual artists. Yet, will the child who makes complex, fantastic digital collages from images captured from the Internet be more motivated or less motivated to master the classic art of drawing a human face with paper and pencil? The general principle here is an important one: Walk before you run. Our children will have plenty of time as adults to use sophisticated software to do all sorts of amazing things. Childhood is for laying the groundwork of creativity by training the eye, the hand, the ear—using simple, time-tested tools specifically designed for each. Although they are not the first generation to have tried, our children are the first generation to actually have the option of leaving the basics of craft to automation; so far, the aesthetic results are not promising.

Some computer software can be viewed as a surrogate for adult expertise. For example, a good chess program can teach a child far more about chess strategy and tactics than most of us personally can. There are musical ear training and music theory programs that can tutor a child (or an adult) almost as well as the average music teacher. For adolescents, access to the Internet can open up the world in a very effective and exciting way. In the right social context, and with ongoing parental observation and monitoring, these sorts of application can be a positive addition to the home learning environment.

Most importantly, the computer should be used as a tool to accomplish some purpose greater than the use itself. For example, older children who are fluent readers and writers of cursive, can use the word processing capabilities of the computer to explore different ways of composing a story; or they can use music software to learn how to write a fugue or harmonize a melody. The computer is ideally suited to powerfully present information that is naturally organized into a hierarchy with many layers, for example, biological taxonomy at the Tree of Life Project (tolweb.org).

What must be avoided at all costs is the use of the computer as an open-ended entertainment device. The child should sit down at the computer with a clear purpose and plan, not with the question, "I wonder what I can find to do on the computer to amuse myself?" As an open-ended entertainment device, the computer has a remarkable ability to become an addiction; as a purposeful tool, it does not. Children who use the computer as a tool may become "addicted" to writing stories or composing music or exploring fractal geometry, but they will not become addicted to "using the computer." Nevertheless, even goal-directed computer use should be restricted to one twenty to thirty minute session per day, at most. Longer sessions can strain on young eyes, necks, and hands.

Finally, if you have read this far and are still feeling that such a conservative approach to children's use of computers and related devices is just very out of touch with the mainstream—after all, aren't today's children "digital natives," different from previous generations?—you can take some comfort in knowing that Steve Jobs raised his children this way. When asked by a New York Times journalist, "So, your kids must love the iPad?" he replied, "They haven't used it. We limit how much technology our kids use at home."

If you would like to read more extensively on the effects of computer use on children and families, an excellent place to start is the report "Fools Gold: A Critical Look at Computers in Childhood," available online from the Alliance for Childhood (allianceforchildhood.org). ❖

If You Want Your Children to Love Reading and Writing...

1. Demonstrate your own love of reading and writing by...

- reading and writing with or in the presence of the children;
- creating "sacred" times for reading, writing, talking, and listening;
- owning and prominently displaying books, magazines, and newspapers at and above the children's reading level;
- taking regular trips to the library to load up on books for yourself and your children;
- talking about what you are reading;
- giving and receiving books as gifts;
- reading aloud and listening to the children read aloud;
- listening to books-on-tape.

2. Have regular, leisurely, sit-down, family meals during which...

- the TV, radio, cell phones, computers, and other electronic gadgets are *off*;
- the conversation is broad-ranging, including discussion of what you and they are reading, current events, et cetera;

- a great percentage of the time you are listening to them, not the other way around;

- their questions are welcomed, answered if possible, and the others looked up together after the meal.

After the meal, the dishes can be cleared and washed together (more time for talking!), then the board games can come out.

3. Play with language whenever you have a spare moment.

- Puns, tongue twisters, songs, et cetera.

- Try out funny accents.

- Play word games, both informal and organized—charades, Apples to Apples Jr., Scrabble, Boggle, Dictionary, UpWords, et cetera.

- Turn off the car radio and talk or play word games instead.

- Keep magnetic letters on the refrigerator.

4. Keep language materials on hand.

- Paper, journals, et cetera.

- A variety of writing instruments.

- Stationery (that the children find attractive).

- And provide quiet places to read or write.

5. During the school year, limit combined computer and TV time to ninety minutes per week (and only on the weekends) so that you and your children will have time to do all of these wonderful things! ❖

Reading Aloud:
The Most Important Thing
You Can Do for
Your Child's Reading

||||||||||||||||||||||||||||||||||||||||||||||||||||||||||||||||||||||||||||||||||||||||||||||||||||||

O ver the past twenty years, reading experts have agreed about relatively little. At times the debates between the various camps—especially between phonics advocates and "whole language" advocates—has become downright vicious. Nevertheless, there has been at least one thing that has always been strongly recommended by all sides as vital to the development of children's reading skills: reading aloud to them. Indeed, a landmark 1985 review of research on reading conducted by the U.S. Department of Education concluded, "The single most important activity for building the knowledge required for eventual success in reading is *reading aloud* to children" (in Jim Trelease).

Regular read-aloud sessions help children in a number of ways. They allow children to see the adults they admire and want to emulate enjoying books. They model for the child the many subtle skills associated with good reading. Good read-aloud sessions are interactive times, leading to interesting conversations that would never have happened otherwise. Parents who establish a read-aloud relationship with their children and keep it going through late childhood and into adolescence find that they have a ready-made forum for communication with their children about otherwise difficult topics.

Choosing What to Read

Sometimes families who have established a healthy read-aloud culture with their young children stop reading aloud when their children start reading for themselves. Don't make this mistake! By carefully choosing what you read aloud, your read-allow times will actually stimulate your children to read more for themselves. The basic rule of thumb is to choose material that is both age-appropriate in content and about two years ahead of your child's silent reading level.

But how does one know the reading level of a given text? There is no universally accepted definition of "reading level." Children's books sometimes come labeled with a reading level such as "4.2," meaning that it is at the level of most children just starting fourth grade. This is known as the Flesch-Kincaid Grade Level system, and it is calculated by a formula that takes into consideration the average length of a sentence and the average number of syllables per word in a text sample. There are online Flesch-Kincaid calculators that one can use.

However, online calculators are of little use when you're at the bookstore or a library trying to decide about a particular book that has no Flesch-Kincaid rating. I recommend that parents spend some time reading through a series of Flesch-Kincaid-rated books to get a general sense for what each grade level involves. Then make an educated guess about unrated books.

How can you know what your child's silent reading level is? One simple method is to listen while they read aloud a page of a book, counting each word that trips them up. If they get to the end of the page with no more than five miscues, that's a book that's about right for their silent reading level. (If they read it with no errors, it's too easy for them.)

Try to choose topics that interest both you and your child. When you are genuinely interested in what you're reading, you read it more effectively. Over time, explore all the different genres available: general fiction, historical fiction, fantasy, biography, poetry, plays, religious literature, non-fiction, magazine articles, newspaper articles, and essays. Choose books set in a wide range of times and places. Take this opportunity to explore with your child other cultures and other belief systems. What rich discussions you can have with your older children!

Reading That's Fun and Effective

Reading aloud well to children does not come naturally to everyone. It takes time and practice to develop read-aloud skills, especially if we were not read aloud to ourselves. How we deal with the challenges of book selection, timing, pace, emotional tone, inflection, diction, and interactive inquiry determines just how effective our reading aloud will be and how eager our children will be to engage in it with us. The payoffs for both sides, however, are well worth the effort. Here are a few things to consider.

First of all, any reading aloud is more effective than no reading aloud! So don't let your lack of skill or confidence stop you from reading to your children. If you feel you have a lot to learn, work on one thing at a time.

It helps to have a special place and time for read-aloud, and to make it a regular part of your routine, something that you and your children can look forward to each day, knowing that it will happen. Have young children sit next to you so that they can see the pictures and maybe help turn the pages. Experiment with having your child sit on one side of you and then the other, and notice if their response is different. Just as your child has a dominant hand, he or she has a dominant ear and may prefer to have that ear closest to the reader.

If possible, know something about the author and try to have the author's voice—or what you imagine to be the author's voice—in your head as you read. In fiction, imagine a voice for each character and read that character in their unique voice. (Think about it: Would Frodo and Gollum have the same voice?)

Pacing is one of the most important considerations. On the level of the sentence, pacing is modulated by punctuation. The comma is a "yield sign" at which one slows down as if to look both ways; the period is a "stop sign." Listening requires thinking, and the effective reader reads at a pace that allows the child to process and comprehend what has been heard. At a higher level, pacing follows the emotional tone of what is being read. A faster pace naturally goes with action and excitement, a slower pace with reflection, sadness, fatigue, and so forth. The register and tone of voice and the pace determine the emotional tone that comes across to the listener.

Preview the book ahead of time to find words that may be new to you or to the child. Make sure you know ahead of time how to pronounce difficult words, foreign names, phrases from foreign languages, et cetera. It's good to keep a dictionary close at hand when reading to children of elementary age and above. If you encounter a word that's new to one or both of you, you and the child can look it up together.

During your preview, look for content that may be age-inappropriate or likely to disturb your child, and be ready to skip or edit those parts as you read. As the child grows older, you may decide to read these passages as they were written, but be ready to discuss them with your child.

In a good read-aloud session, the children are not passive. It's good to stop to clarify or highlight something that just happened in the story, savor a particularly luscious sentence or description, notice features of the author's style and unique voice, share points of view, and anticipate what is to come in the story.

Poetry can be particularly challenging. If the poem has meter and end rhyme, try to strike a balance between enjoying the rhythm and allowing the poem to become "sing-songy." The music of the poem shouldn't drown out the words and meaning! If the poem is in free verse or unrhymed, don't pause at the end of lines with no end punctuation or comma.

Resources

I recommend three books that will help you both with choosing what to read and reading it effectively: *The Read-Aloud Handbook* by Jim Trelease; *Best Books for Kids Who (Think They) Hate to Read* by Laura Backes; *Classics to Read Aloud to Your Children* by William Russell. Finally, I highly recommend storyteller Roger Jenkins's videos on reading aloud, which can be found on YouTube and at his website rogerjenkins.com.sg. Jenkins illustrates many of the reading techniques mentioned above, as well as others. ❖

Appendix:
Montessori Homework Ideas
for the Upper Elementary

|||||||||||||||||||||||||||||||||||||||||||||||||||||||||||||||||||||||||||||||||||||||||||||||||||||||||||||||||||||||||||||||||

The Most Important Things You Can Do to
Get Smarter and Stronger

- Whenever you feel like turning on the TV or playing computer games, first come get this list of ideas and pick something from it to do *before you spend any time in front of a screen.* Then, if you still want to sit in front of a screen, set a timer for thirty minutes and make yourself turn off the electronics when the timer goes off. Be sure to limit yourself to no more than one hour of combined screen time per day.

- If you really want to get smarter and stronger, turn off the TV and computer for a month. Yes, you can do it. You won't die. I promise. After the initial shock, most people find they even like it.

- If you do use the computer, use it as a tool for making yourself smarter and stronger: Write with it, do math with it, do art with it, or explore enchantedlearning. com with your mom or dad. So far nobody has ever gotten smarter and stronger playing computer or video games, and you're probably not going to be the first.

Creative Arts / Construction

- Knit, crochet, spin, weave, sew, quilt, hook rugs, embroider, tie-dye, bead, paint, sculpt.

- Make pottery at a local pottery studio.

- Learn new art projects by reading in books or taking an art class. Prepare an art project to teach to the class.

- Get a copy of *Curve Stitching* by Jon Millington and work your way from front to back. You'll be ready to invent your own curve stitching designs before you know it!

- Take weaving classes or painting classes.

- Work with a knowledgeable adult to build a fence, a doghouse, a bike ramp, a bookcase, a bench, et cetera.

- Find an adult who has a lot of tools and likes to build or repair things. Learn the names of all the tools the adult has. Learn to write the names as well as say them. Learn what each tool is used for.

- Learn photography—how to take a really good picture.

- Learn how to operate a video camera. Make your own movies. Document a week in the life of your family using a camcorder or camera. Write a paragraph about each family member and what they will be doing for the summer. Mail the package to your grandparents or some other relative or friend who would like to receive the update.

- Practice your musical instrument or learn new songs to sing. If possible, take private music lessons on your musical instrument.

- Learn a new song to teach the class in the fall. Bring a copy of the words when you teach it to us.

- Learn to dance.

- Visit one of the art museums in town. Visit the gift shop after you've toured the museum. Buy postcards of your favorite works and try to copy them at home with colored pencils or watercolors.

Language / Words / Literature

- Schedule a weekly trip to the public library. Plan to spend at least an hour looking through books, looking up things in the catalog, reading magazines, etc.

- Take regular trips to bookstores. Make a list of all the good bookstores in town and try to visit each one at least once so you can learn what sorts of book each store offers.

- Read books from the Upper Elementary Reading List. Keep a list of the books and the number of pages you read in each.

- Join a children's reading program at the public library.

- Write a description of a friend, a friend's house, a pet, a favorite place, a vacation spot, et cetera.

- Interview your family and relatives. Start a family newsletter.

- Enter an essay, story, or poetry contest. Submit your work to magazines that publish student work.

- Practice telling stories. At the library, look for books of folktales from around the world. Pick a few to learn by heart. Plan to tell them to us on the fall camping trip.

- Find a newspaper article you want to read and discuss with your family. Set aside a specific time and place for the discussion.

- Have a family reading time. Everybody reads whatever they want in the same room. Start small: perhaps for fifteen minutes after dinner. Gradually increase the time.

- Have a read-aloud time. One person could read while the others clean up from dinner or do some other simple task. Family members take turns being the reader.

- At the bookstore, look for books of crossword puzzles, anagrams, and other word games. Keep a book of word puzzles in the car to work on whenever you are riding around.

- Play great board games such as Scrabble, UpWords, Boggle, or Word Thief.

- Write with your family. Start a family journal. In the journal, keep lists of things to do around the house, descriptions of special events such as hosting houseguests, notes about phone calls to family friends and relatives, anything you want to record from your everyday life. See Peter Stillman's book *Families Writing* for more ideas and inspiration.

- Listen to books on tape while driving around on errands or on vacation.

- Read and write poetry. Memorize a poem a week.

- Choose a story to practice reading aloud. Practice the pronunciations of all the words. Try giving each character a different voice when you read. Try to use your voice to make the story more interesting to your audience.

- Put on some calming music (Bach, Mozart, Satie, and Gregorian chant are nice) and practice making the most beautiful cursive or italic letters you can.

- Instead of phoning, write letters to your friends and relatives. Try starting a round robin letter to your friends or relatives. First, make up a list of three to five people and their addresses; put your name and address last on the list. Write a letter to the first person on the list, and enclose a copy of the list of addresses. The person you wrote to writes a letter and sends it, your original letter, and the list of addresses to the next person on the list, and so forth. Eventually, all the letters will come back to you!

- Write a review of a book you read or a movie you saw. Tell the basic idea of the book or movie and what you liked and didn't like about it. What did the author do well? What did they not do so well?

- Learn to touch type (that is, type without looking at the keys or your fingers). You might want to use a software package such as Master Key or Mavis Beacon Teaches Typing.

Math / Numbers / Geometry

- Comparison shopping: figuring price per pound, calling various stores, et cetera. When you shop at the grocery store, take along a pad and pencil; keep a running total of the cost of items you buy. Check your answer against the cash register receipt you get when you pay for your items.

- Read *The Number Devil* by H. M. Enzensberger. This is an especially good book for people who have not yet learned to love math, but those who have will enjoy the book, too. Every Upper Elementary student should read this book.

- Keep statistics. Graph when you go to bed, how many pages you read each day, how far you walk each day, how many ounces of water you drink per day, how often you have friends over, how long it takes you to eat breakfast, how many meters per day you swim, how fast you can jog around the block, how many multiplication facts you can do in a minute, and so forth.

- Measure things around the house and calculate their surface area and volume. Take trips to the park, et cetera to measure things there.

- Help with the family budget. Record the family expenditures for a week. Help your parents write the checks when they pay the bills (they'll have to sign the checks).

- Play good "thinking" games such as chess and Go. Learn how to notate chess games. Learn to play chess by mail with your friends (that's where you mail your moves back and forth on post cards or in letters).

- Make up math problems for yourself to work. Consider making a "Math Workout" for yourself once a week.

- Work on memorizing all of your multiplication, division, addition, and subtraction facts, if you haven't already done so. Once you've mastered your math facts, work on speed.

Nature / Plants / Animals

- Whenever you travel to a new city, visit the local zoo, aquarium, or natural history museum.

- Check out the camps and activities sponsored by the nearest zoo.

- Before you travel to another part of the country or to a different country, read about the biomes there. Read about their climate, animals, and plants. While you're there, look for things you read about.

- Go camping with your family or friends.

- Learn more about nutrition. Visit hsph.harvard.edu/nutritionsource/pyramid-full-story/ to learn about the Harvard Food Pyramid. For a week, keep a journal of what you eat. See if you are in balance with the Harvard Food Pyramid. Pick one or two things you can do to start moving your diet closer to the recommendations of the pyramid.

- Make a botany map of your backyard. Place each plant in its place on the map and label each plant with its common name and scientific name. (You might need some help from a library book or a knowledgeable adult gardener.)

- Go berry picking on a local farm.

Science

- Visit the nearest science museum.

- See if there is an amateur astronomy club in your area. Find out when they are sponsoring star parties, and attend one.

- At the library, look through the children's books on science. Choose one that has experiments you can do at home, such as the books by Janice Van Cleave. Try some experiments at home with your parents.

- Consider the books available from Terrific Science (terrificscience.org).

- Try some of the activities from the San Francisco Exploratorium website: exploratorium.edu/explore/activities. The Exploratorium is one of the country's premier science museums; they are especially good at devising hands-on activities.

- Explore the *Life on Earth* site at the University of California, Berkeley. ucmp.berkeley.edu/alllife/threedomains.html. This is pretty advanced stuff, but, boy, is it cool!

- Build electronics projects from kits or books. Good books to start with: *Electronics Projects for Dummies* and *Circuitbuilding Do-It-Yourself for Dummies*.

History / Geography

- Help plan the family vacation. Research the landmarks, geography, culture, and special attractions of the area you'll be visiting. Map out the route you'll take.

- Make a map of your house and garden. Make a detailed map of your room.

- Study world religions. Pick a religion you don't know much about. Read about it in books you check out from the public library. See if you can find a local group that practices that religion. Plan with your parents to visit their church, temple, synagogue, mosque, or other place of worship. Good religions to start with: Baha'i, Buddhism, Christianity (Catholic, Orthodox, Protestant), Hinduism, Islam, Judaism, Sikhism, Unitarianism.

- Visit local history museums or ethnic cultural centers.

- The website at besthistorysites.net/index.php links to hundreds of other sites on ancient civilizations.

- Pick a continent you'd like to know more about. (If you can't decide, work on Europe first.) Using an atlas, make flash cards of all the countries in that continent. On one side of the card have the country's name, on the other side, the country's capitol city. Memorize all the countries and capitols in that continent, then do the same for another continent.

- Interview someone from another country. Ask them about their country's history, landmarks, cities, agriculture, industries, religions, festivals, form of government, famous scientists, famous artists and writers, et cetera. Ask them for permission to tape the interview. From the tape, makes notes. From the notes, write a summary of what you learned about the person's country.

Sports / Exercise

- Play on a team. Practice a sport or physical skill.

- Hike, bike, skate, swim, walk, cave, climb, canoe, snorkel, run, do gymnastics, play basketball.

- Spend as much time outdoors as possible. If your body gets used to staying indoors in the air conditioning all the time, you will be at risk for heat stroke if you do need to do something physical outdoors.

- Download a free book of cooperative games at freechild. org/gamesguide.pdf. Try these with your friends.

- Find out if there are beginning rock climbing lessons in your area.

- Go canoeing on a nearby lake.

- Find out if there are skating lessons in your area.

Community Service / Activism

- Keep a scrapbook of newspaper articles on issues you care about in the community or world. Write letters to elected officials (congresspersons, senators, the president, city councilors, et cetera.) expressing your opinions about issues you've read about.

- Participate in an environmental cleanup. This might be as simple as going to the park with your family or friends and filling up a big trash bag with all the trash you can pick up. Save recyclable bottles and plastic in a separate bag to recycle later.

- Help younger children learn to do something they want to do.

- Visit an elder. Look for opportunities to assist the elderly. Some children call out bingo at a retirement home every other week.

- Volunteer at a local animal shelter or zoo.

- Volunteer at Meals on Wheels.

- Offer to help neighbors with pet sitting, picking up their newspaper when they're out of town, et cetera.

Household Service

- Help out more with the household tasks. Learn to do some new things such as washing clothes, ironing, folding laundry, polishing furniture, vacuuming, mowing the lawn (if your parents agree). Work alongside another family member whenever possible.

- Cook together with your family. It can be more fun than cooking by yourself.

- Be responsible for one or two meals per week. Plan the menu with your parent(s). Make a shopping list. Do the shopping. Cook the meal with your parent(s). Try not to use a microwave oven when you cook! ❖

Bibliography

||||||||||||||||||||||||||||||||||||||||||||||||||||||||||||||||||

The Writings of Maria Montessori

Montessori, Maria. "1948 Course Inaugural Lecture." *Association Montessori Internationale,* 5 Dec. 2014. <ami-global.org/training/maria-montessori-1948-course-inaugural-lecture>.

---. *The Absorbent Mind.* New York: Henry Holt and Company, 1995.

---. *The Advanced Montessori Method.* Vol. 1 and vol. 2. Oxford, England: Clio Press, 1991.

---. *Education and Peace. Oxford, England: ABC-CLIO Ltd., 1992.*

---. *From Childhood to Adolescence.* Oxford, England: Clio Press, 1994.

---. *To Educate the Human Potential.* Oxford, England: ABC-CLIO Ltd., 1989.

---. *The Montessori Method.* Trans. Anne Everett George. New York: Frederick A. Stokes Company, 1912. *Celebration of Women Writers.* Ed. Mary Mark Ockerbloom. Web. 5 Dec. 2014. <digital.library.upenn.edu/women/montessori/method/method.html>.

---. *What You Should Know About Your Child: Based on Lectures Delivered by Maria Montessori.* Trans. Gnana Prakasam. Oxford, England: ABC-CLIO Ltd, 1989.

Others

"Albert Einstein: Image and Impact." American Institute for Physics Center for History of Physics. Web. 1 Dec. 2014. <aip.org/history/einstein/early2.htm>.

Backes, Laura. *Best Books for Kids Who (Think They) Hate to Read*. New York: Random House, 2001.

Brown, John Seely. "Entrepreneurial Learning." *Educate the Young*. 4 Jan. 2013. Web. 30 Nov. 2014. <educatetheyoung.wordpress.com/2013/01/14/entrepreneurial-learning>.

Buscaglia, Leo. *The Fall of Freddie the Leaf: A Story of Life for All Ages*. Thorofare, New Jersey: Slack Incorporated, 1982.

Carey, Benedict. "Research Finds Firstborns Gain the Higher I.Q." New York *Times*. 22 June 2007. Web. 8 Dec. 2014. <http://www.nytimes.com/2007/06/22/science/22sibling.html?pagewanted=all&_r=0>.

Carson, Rachel. *The Sense Of Wonder*. 1956. New York: HarperCollins, 1998.

Cordes, Colleen and Edward Miller, eds. *Fools Gold: A Look at Computers in Childhood*. Alliance for Childhood. Web. 8 Dec. 2014. <allianceforchildhood.org/fools_gold>.

Doherty, William J. *The Intentional Family*. New York: Addison-Wesley, 1997.

---. *Take Back Your Kids: Confident Parenting in Turbulent Times*. South Bend, Indiana: Sorin Books, 2000.

Eidelson, Josh. "Call of Duty Director Says U.S. Should Station Soldiers in Schools." *Bloomberg Businessweek*. 2 Oct. 2014. Web. 1 Dec. 2014. <businessweek.com/articles/2014-10-02/call-of-duty-director-says-u-dot-s-dot-should-station-soldiers-in-schools>.

Enzenberger, H. M. *The Number Devil*. Trans. Michael Henry Heim. 1998. New York: Holt Paperbacks, 2010.

Faber, Adele and Elaine Mazlish. *How to Talk So Kids Will Listen, How to Listen So Kids Will Talk.* 1980. New York: Scribner, 2012.

"Formative Years" The Center for History of Physics. Web. 5 Dec. 2014. <aip.org/history/einstein/early2.htm>.

Fox, Robin. "Food and Eating: an Anthropological Perspective." Social Issues Research Center. Web. 8 Dec. 2014. <http://www.sirc.org/publik/food_and_eating_0.html >.

Gillman, Matthew W., et al. "Family Dinner and Diet Quality Among Older Children and Adolescents." *Archives of Family Medicine.* 9 (2000): 235-240. Web. 8 Dec. 2014. <triggered.edina.clockss.org/ServeContent?rft_id=info:doi/10.1001/archfami.9.3.235>.

Goertz, Donna Bryant. *Children Who Are Not Yet Peaceful.* Berkeley: North Atlantic Books, 2001.

The Importance of Family Dinners II. National Center for Substance and Alcohol Abuse at Columbia University, Sept. 2005. Web. 8 Dec. 2014. <casacolumbia.org/addiction-research/reports/importance-of-family-dinners-2005>.

The Inclusive Bible. Lanham, Maryland: Rowan & Littlefield, 2006.

Jenkins, Richard, ed. *Questions of Competence: Culture, Classification and Intellectual Disability.* Cambridge: Cambridge University Press, 1998.

Mellonie, Bryan. *Lifetimes: A Beautiful Way to Explain Death to Children.* New York: Bantam, 1983.

Montessori, Renilde. "Greeting to Students." Association Montessori Internationale. Web. 8 Dec. 2014. <ami-global.org/training/renilde-montessori-greeting-students>.

Norris, Jack and Virginia Messina. *Vegan for Life: Everything You Need to Know to Be Healthy and Fit on a Plant-Based Diet.* New York: Da Capo, 2011.

Neumark-Sztainer, D., P. Hannan, M. Story, et al. "Family meal patterns: Associations with sociodemographic characteristics and improved dietary intake among adolescents." *J Am Diet Assoc.* 103.3 (2003): 317-322 (March, 2003).

Park, Alice. "Study: A Link Between Pesticides and ADHD." *Time.* 17 May 2010. Web. 1 Dec. 2014. <content.time.com/time/health/article/0,8599,1989564,00.html>.

Pink, Daniel. *Drive: The Surprising Truth About What Motivates Us.* New York: Teachers College Press, 1998.

Pollan, Michael. *In Defense of Food: An Eater's Manifesto.* New York: Penguin, 2003.

Popol Vuh. Trans. Ealph Nelson. Web. 27 Nov. 2014. <archive.org/stream/popolvuh00nelsrich/popolvuh00nelsrich_djvu.txt>.

"Profile: Albert Einstein." *Seminars on Science: Frontiers of Physical Science.* American Museum of Natural History. 2003. Web. 1 Dec. 2014. <amnh.org/learn/pd/physical_science/profiles/aeinstein.html>.

Rig Veda. In *Sacred Scriptures of the World Religions: An Introduction.* By Joan Price. London: Bloomsbury Academic, 2010.

Roberts, Elizabeth. *Earth Prayers from Around the World.* San Francisco: Harper, 1991.

Robinson, Sir Ken. "Bring on the learning revolution!" *TED.* May 2010. Web. 8 Dec. 2014. <ted.com/talks/sir_ken_robinson_bring_on_the_revolution/transcript?language=en>.

Russell, William. *Classics to Read Aloud to Your Children.* 1984. New York: Crown, 2011.

Smith, Frank. *The Book of Learning and Forgetting.* New York: Teachers College Press, 1998.

Srinivasan, Meena. *Teach, Breathe, Learn: Mindfulness in and out of the Classroom.* Berkeley: Parallax Press, 2014.

Stillman, Peter. *Families Writing.* New York: Houghton Mifflin Harcourt, 1998.

Thich Nhat Hanh. *Teachings On Love*. Berkeley: Parallax Press, 2006.

"Talking to Children About Death." Clinical Center, National Institutes of Health. 2006. Web. 8 Dec. 2014. <cc.nih.gov/ccc/ patient_education/pepubs/childeath.pdf>.

Thurman, Chuck. *A Time for Remembering*. New York: Simon & Schuster Children's Publishing, 1989.

Travis, Allyn. "The Development of Morality in the First and Second Planes of Development" AMI/USA. Web. 8 Dec. 2014. <kentplace.org/ftpimages/509/download/Moral%20 Development%20-%20Association%20Montessori%20 Internationale.pdf>.

Trelease, Jim. *The Read-Aloud Handbook*. New York: Penguin Books, 2006.

Trent, James W. *Inventing the Feeble Mind: A History of Mental Retardation in the United States*. Berkeley: University Of California Press, 1994.

Vygotsky, L.S. *Mind in Society: The Development of Higher Psychological Processes*. Cambridge, Massachusetts: Harvard University Press, 1978.

Willingham, Dan. "A Cognitive View of the Learner: The Three-Period Lesson as a Knowledge Model." NAMTA. Atlanta, Georgia. 11–14 Nov. 2010.

"Young Einstein." *Albert Einstein Site Online*. Web. 1 Dec. 2014. <alberteinsteinsite.com/einsteinyoung.html>. ❖

About the Author

John R. Snyder is an essayist, speaker, and poet. He taught and served as an administrator at Austin Montessori School in Austin, Texas, and is former Chair of the AMI Elementary Alumni Association, a member of the Montessori Administrators Association, and a charter member of the Montessori Leadership Collaborative. He has also been a regular columnist for the quarterly *Public School Montessorian.* He holds degrees in music, philosophy, and computer science and the AMI elementary diploma from the Washington Montessori Institute. His website is ordinarypersonslife.com.